NEWCASTLE-UNDER-LYME
COLLEGE LIBRARY

Investigating Political Sociology

D0480767

Other titles in this series:

Investigating Families and Households, Nik Jorgensen
Investigating Education and Training, Paul Trowler
Investigating Work, Unemployment and Leisure, Nick Madry & Mark Kirby
Investigating the Media, Paul Trowler
Investigating Deviance, Stephen Moore
Investigating Health, Welfare and Poverty, Paul Trowler
How To Do Social Research, Audrey Dunsmuir & Lynn Williams

Investigating Political Sociology

Mark Kirby

306-2-KIR
NEWCASTLE-UNDER-LYME
COLLEGE LIBRARY
DC024760

Collins Educational

An imprint of HarperCollins*Publishers*

Published by Collins Educational
An imprint of HarperCollins*Publishers*
77–85 Fulham Palace Road
Hammersmith, London W6 8JB

The HarperCollins website address is
www.**fire**and**water**.com

First published in 1995
Reprinted 1999

© Mark Kirby and HarperCollins*Publishers* Ltd 1995

This book is copyright under the Berne Convention
No reproduction without permission. All rights reserved.

ISBN 0-00-322405-8

Mark Kirby asserts the moral right to be identified as the author of this work.
A catalogue record for this book is available from the British Library.

This book may contain references to fictitious characters in fictitious case studies. For educational purposes only, photographs have been used to accompany these case studies. The juxtaposition of photographs and case studies is not intended to identify the individual in the photograph with the character in the case study. The publishers cannot accept any responsibility for any consequences resulting from this use of photographs and case studies, except as expressly provided by law.

Commissioned by Emma Dunlop
Edited by Kay Wright
Cover artwork and design by Derek Lee
Illustrations by Julia Osorno
Typeset by Harper Phototypesetters Ltd, Northampton
Printed and bound by Scotprint Ltd, Musselburgh

Contents

Acknowledgements

Sociology teaches us that society is an interrelated whole in which our actions are both dependent on and have an effect on others. Writing a book such as this provides a microcosm of this truth. It seems rather unfair that only one person's name appears on the cover since many others have contributed with their help, support and encouragement in this venture. I would like to thank all those people and in particular: John Clossick, Jan Derry, Richard Dunn, Alison Kirton, Francine Koubel, Chris LeBlond, Maria Lenn, Nick Madry, Sarah Marks, Eddie Sanderson, Helen Tucker, Mary Waterhouse and The Computer Unit at Amersham & Wycombe College.

The library staff at Amersham & Wycombe College dealt with a whole series of unreasonable requests in a way which shows how invaluable and talented they are.

Tony Lawson has given me invaluable advice and Pat McNeill always remained positive and encouraging. Emma Dunlop, Jim Ryan, Louise Wilson and Kay Wright had the unenviable task of turning my rambled scribblings into something which could be published and the final appearance of this book owes everything to their skills and forbearance in the face of my stupidities!

Finally, I would like to thank my A-level sociology students at Amersham & Wycombe College for putting up with me, and for making teaching such an enjoyable and rewarding experience. At the end of the day, there is a good reason why only one name appears on the cover, as that person alone bears sole responsibility for any errors that may have slipped through the net provided by the others named here.

Mark Kirby 1995

The author and publisher are indebted to the following:

For permission to reproduce text extracts:

Basil Blackwell; Bookmarks; Channel 4/*New Statesman and Society;* Clarendon Press; George Allen Unwin; Grant McIntyre; Harvard University Press; The Labour Party; Lawrence Wishart; Macmillan Press Ltd; Methuen; Nelson; *Open House;* Oxford University Press; Paladin; Penguin; Phillip Allen Publishers Ltd; Pluto Publications; *Politics Review;* Polity Press; Routledge; *Sociological Review;* The No M11 Link Campaign; Verso Books; Virago; Yale University Press.

For permission to reproduce photographs, cartoons and illustrations:

Batsford (Fig 8.3, p155); Freedom Press (Fig 8.1, p152); Greenpeace (Fig 4.1, p83); Icon Books (Fig 3.4, p53); Macmillan Press Ltd (Fig 7.4, p145); Phil Evans Cartoons (Figs 1.1, 3.1; pp4, 47); Polity Press (Fig 5.6, p109); Routledge (Fig 10.1, p194); Steve Bell (cartoon, p12); The Hulton Deutsch Collection (Fig 6.1, p117); The Labour Party (Fig 7.3, p172).

While every effort has been made to contact copyright-holders, this has not proved possible in every case. The Publishers would be pleased to hear from any copyright-holders not acknowledged.

Preface

The Sociology in Action series aims to provide readers with an interesting up-to-date account of the main themes in the areas covered. The series has been written primarily for students following the sociology 'A' and 'AS' level syllabuses. However, it is also designed to be helpful to those entering for GCSE examinations in sociology as well as related disciplines. The series will also prove valuable for those preparing for the certificate qualifications in social work and General National Vocational Qualifications, and for undergraduates following sociology subsidiary courses. To this end, each book relates the issues specific to its subject area to the broader concerns of social science and the humanities. The philosophy underlying the series has been to encourage students to deepen their understanding of the subject by engaging in short exercises and larger-scale projects as they progress through the books. The authors have followed the student-centred approach which provided the impetus for the establishment of the GCSE syllabus and such innovative courses as the AEB's 'A' level syllabus and the new A-level syllabus developed by the InterBoard consortium.

Investigating Political Sociology provides a picture of the social analysis of political behaviour in the world we now live in. For many years, political sociology has been confined to a study of voting behaviour and theories of the state. It is the belief of this author that these topics can be supplemented by a large range of new areas such as the rise of the new social movements, the political impact of globalization, sociological theories of citizenship, theories of nationalism and new approaches to the study of power in society.

This book therefore attempts to provide an up-date on more familiar areas and to provide some brief coverage of new areas of investigation within the broad field of political sociology.

The book includes exercises and suggestions for coursework which it is hoped will be used and developed according to the aims and needs of the students and the facilities available. The book was written primarily from a sociological perspective, though with a belief that the distinction between politics and sociology in this area is somewhat arbitrary, and it is therefore hoped that the book may be of some interest to those following an 'A' level course in politics.

I hope you find the book useful and interesting and beg your indulgence for my many and varied foibles and shortcomings.

Mark Kirby 1995

For Costas, Julian, Lesley and Rachel who have taught me so much.

' . . . all the essential questions of sociology are nothing
other than the questions of political science . . .'

Antonio Gramsci, *Prison Notebooks*

'Governments crack and systems fall
Cause unity is powerful
Lights go out – walls come tumbling down'

The Style Council, *Walls Come Tumbling Down*

Political action

People may not generally seem to attach much importance to politics, or at least not enough for them to do anything about it. A Gallup poll published in 1983 showed that 2 per cent of respondents claimed to have canvassed for their party during the General Election of that year, and 4 per cent said they had heard a candidate speaking at an indoor meeting (quoted in Butler and Kavanagh 1984, p. 249). For comparison, in the mid-1980s there were eleven sporting activities in which at least 3 per cent of the population took part (General Household Survey 1987, quoted in *Social Trends* 1992, p. 183).

1) Before you read this chapter, draw up a list of examples of what you consider to be 'political actions'. Do this individually or in groups. Try to rank them in terms of their importance. You will need to decide on what you mean by 'important'.
2) Go to the library and read a selection of current newspapers and see if you can locate any reports relating to the types of action you have identified.

In a MORI survey conducted in April 1991 only 3 per cent of people included 'Go into politics' on their list of aspirations. This placed it twenty-fifth out of a total of twenty-seven aspirations (Jacobs and Worcester 1991, p. 56).

1) Devise a method to test the relative importance of 'politics' and other activities in the lives of other students in your school/college or alternatively your friends. You may wish to consider some of the findings reported in this chapter as a spur to devising your questions.
2) Compare the findings to those outlined in this chapter and/or more up-to-date sources of information in the library. Make a note of any differences and try to explain these.

An official government survey, *Young People in the 80s,* appeared to endorse this picture of a low priority attached to politics, as Table 1.1 shows.

1) How far do you agree that this table endorses the view that people attach a low priority to politics?
2) Write a summary outlining the main explanations for the lack of interest this table points to.
3) Use these questions to survey students in your own institution and consider any differences that emerge.

Table 1.1 Young people's attitudes to politics

All respondents = 100%	Total 635 %	C 442 %	WI 97 %	A 96 %
Apathy/disenchantement Agree that...				
Young people like me don't normally take much interest in politics	73	74	70	73
Older people don't normally understand the needs of young people	72	71	79	73
Nobody listens much to what young people have to say about anything	60	55	77	64
Politicians generally seem to be aware of young people's needs	14	12	21	19

Notes: C = Caucasian; WI = West Indian; A = Asian

Source: DES (1983), p. 71

Political concern

Despite this picture of apparent apathy, there are indications of an alternative interpretation that does give political and social issues some importance in people's lives. For example, 61 per cent of the sample just quoted argued that it is important for young people to vote as soon as they are 18 in order to influence the government. The survey also indicated that young people were not indifferent to the fate of society and its citizens, as shown in Table 1.2.

Table 1.2 Some views and concerns of young people

Percentage agreeing with the following views:	
For equality of races	86
Trade unions are necessary	58
For women's liberation	56
Against the persecution of homosexuals	62
Against abolishing royalty	78
Against abortion on demand	58
For the reinstatement of hanging	59
Percentage seeing the following as important concerns:	
Looking after the handicapped	66
Making towns/cities better places to live	70
Campaigning for employment	61
Collecting money for Third World	49
CND movement	40

Source: Adapted from DES (1983), pp. 70–1

Thus there is evidence to support a picture in which there is greater concern and a positive involvement with issues that most of us would agree are 'political' in some sense.

It is therefore not possible to dismiss political inactivity as a result of a lack of concern for issues. Neither does it seem that young people are passive because they are happy with the present state of affairs. In the same survey only 14 per cent agreed with the proposition that 'Politicians generally seem to be aware of young people's needs.' (See Table 1.10)

1) *Conduct a survey to draw up a list of issues that concern young people today. Use the methods section of your textbook to consider whether you should prompt issues or not. How might you test whether this would make a difference?*

2) *To what extent does your survey reveal a change in attitudes since the 1980s? Write a short report summarizing your findings.*

Reasons for inactivity

One possible explanation for people's relative inactivity is a feeling of powerlessness. This interpretation is suggested by the very low percentage of young people in the DES study who felt that politicians listen to them.

The idea that politics is for the politicians is enhanced by the concentration of media comment and even academic sociologists and political scientists on the actions of professional politicians.

1) *Who might be included in the category 'professional politicians'?*

2) *Watch TV news programmes to test whether they concentrate on professional politicians. Are there any variations between TV stations?*

Another linked explanation is the idea that politicians are untrustworthy and politics is a dirty business. This comes across in Table 1.3, which summarizes a survey on the respect that people accord certain professions and institutions.

Table 1.3   Who do young people respect?

Which of the following groups do you think live up to higher moral standards than ordinary people?		By their actions, which of these do you think have helped lower moral standards?		Which of the following institutions do you feel has helped raise or maintain moral standards?	
Clergymen	43%	The Monarchy	36%	The Monarchy	11%
Royalty	16%	The Church	13%	The Church	45%
MPs	5%	The Government	49%	The Government	10%
Ministers	9%	The Law	14%	The Law	27%
Teachers	13%	The Police	14%	The Police	20%
The Police	13%	Parliament/MPs	52%	Parliament/MPs	4%
Social workers	13%	Teachers	9%	Teachers	33%
Judges	16%	Journalists	49%	Journalists	4%
Don't Know	24%	Don't Know	4%	Don't Know	13%

Source: ICM survey for the *Daily Express*, 7 March 1994

The MORI survey quoted earlier also includes the following comment:

MORI's recent State of the Nation survey for the Rowntree Reform Trust updated a survey for the Crowther-Hunt Commission in 1973. Nearly two decades ago almost half the British said they were satisfied with the system governing Britain. By 1991, only a third said they were satisfied, a drop of 15 percentage points in only 15 years.

What possible explanations for this finding can you think of?

Political inactivity is itself highly political. If politics is concerned with the distribution of power in society, and people are inactive because they feel powerless, this tells us quite a lot about the reality of political structures and decision making in this country.

One basic notion of democracy is that it means rule by the people, but if the vast majority of people feel powerless, this calls into question the extent to which the political system of this country can be described as democratic.

Therefore if we simply measure the extent of political activity, 'politics' seems to be a marginal activity. If, however, we go on to investigate why people are so little involved, we run straight into a central debate in political sociology, namely the question of the distribution of power in society and the meaning of democracy. This has been a question of central concern for the leading social thinkers of all ages, and it is still clearly an issue.

An ICM survey commissioned by Channel 4 for a series of programmes on democracy shown in May 1994 found that only 61 per cent of respondents regarded Britain as a 'democratic country', and 30 per cent said that it was not democratic (Smyth, Jones and Platt 1994). While this country can be classified as democratic on the basis that there is universal adult suffrage (since 1928) it is clear that most do not regard this as giving them enough control to describe government as democratic. Sixty per cent of people questioned in the same survey said that voting in a General Election does not give them enough control over government, as against 33 per cent who said it did.

Figure 1.1 Is having a vote the same as democracy?

1) *Explain the meaning of the cartoon. How far do you think this is a valid comment on democracy in Britain?*
2) *Which sociological perspectives do you think would agree with the message of the cartoon and which would not?*

If people were unconcerned and totally apathetic about political issues, their inactivity would perhaps be easy to explain, but since they are not indifferent to such issues their inaction seems to fit oddly with their attitudes. Perhaps, however, people are not in fact as inactive as the statistics suggest.

Forms of political activity

Many academic studies concentrate on voting behaviour. Perhaps as a result, the camera of sociological observation has missed a host of activities that those involved might themselves not categorize as political but that are nonetheless concerned with using power to achieve social ends.

The narrowing down of consideration of political action to voting behaviour has certainly been predominant in sociology, but it has been criticized, most notably by radical and Marxist sociologists (see Chapter 7). Martin Shaw, for example, makes the following point:

> All too often the overall framework of the political process is submerged in the detail of party organization, pressure groups, or – that highest peak of quantitative sociology – voting behaviour. The ideological assumptions, implicit or explicit, are generally of a 'liberal pluralist' society with 'democratic processes'.
>
> (Shaw 1977, Section 12)

Lester Milbraith identifies four levels of political participation. His work is reported in Haralambos and Holborn (1991, p.163). To what extent does his categorization of political participation rely on the view of political sociology criticized by Shaw?

1) Consider whether you agree with Shaw about the following points:

2) There is an overemphasis on voting behaviour in political sociology. This is linked to the ideological bias of prominent sociologists.

3) Political sociology should concern itself with political action other than voting behaviour.

Try to think up some examples of your own that might fit the category of political action other than voting.

If we consider the evidence relating to involvement in other forms of political behaviour, our picture of the extent of political activism begins to change. For example, David Nicolson Lord recently pointed out:

> Membership of green groups in Britain is estimated at around five million, an increase of two-thirds since the late 1980s. This is probably about eight to ten times the combined membership of the three main political parties. More than a quarter of Britons were last year classed by MORI as environmentalists and over 40 per cent as green consumers.
>
> (quoted in Ward 1994, p. 25)

Political participation: changes over time

In their book *The Civic Culture*, Almond and Verba (1963) reported that 47 per cent of the population belonged to some organization, but only 19 per cent belonged to an organization they considered political. It is open to question whether certain organizations categorized as non-political are better considered as political – for instance, trade unions and business organizations, to which respectively 22 per cent and 4 per cent of this sample belonged. However, accepting the proportions given by Almond and Verba, one of their findings was that the reason for low levels of political participation was a feeling of powerlessness.

1) *Discuss whether you think organizations such as trade unions and business organizations are 'political'. Make a list of points for and against their 'political' status.*
2) *Can you think of any organizations that are (a) obviously political, (b) obviously non-political?*

One reason for studying political participation is to consider whether changes have taken place since Almond and Verba's study was conducted in 1959. In a study of the radicalization of attitudes and action during the Thatcher period, Edgell and Duke (1991) asked people about political participation. They also argue that a focus on voting behaviour is limiting: 'It is to be regretted that political participation was almost invariably measured in earlier surveys by voting behaviour' (p. 192). Voting was excluded from their study, and instead they focused on other actions, both orthodox and unorthodox.

Their list of the most important actions and the percentages engaging in such an action in their two surveys conducted in 1981 and 1984 are given in Table 1.4. They argue there are two possible explanations for these changes, and in particular the greater involvement in demonstrations:

Table 1.4   Types of action taken against spending cuts

Percentage taking action	*1981*	*1984*
Signing a petition	2.2	5.5
Attending a meeting	4.3	1.2
Marching in a demonstration	1.8	2.8
Total (all actions)	11.2	12.3

Source: Adapted from Edgell and Duke (1991), p. 193

... it could be interpreted as indicating the relative ineffectiveness of other forms of more 'orthodox' protest under Thatcherism. The urban riots in Britain during 1981–2 and the miners strike of 1984–5 may also be seen in this light. Alternatively, it could be interpreted in terms of the debate about the increased preparedness of citizens to participate in direct political action in 'mature' democracies.

(Edgell and Duke 1991, p. 193)

1) *Do you agree with Edgell and Duke's emphasis on greater participation on the basis of their figures?*

2) *Which of the possible interpretations offered by the authors seems more plausible to you?*

3) *Does it matter which interpretation you take? What are the implications of the two different interpretations?*

The British Social Attitudes survey undertaken in 1991 suggested that there had been an increase in the willingness to engage in political action since the time of Almond and Verba's study (Jowell *et al.* 1992). The authors argue that 'Britain is becoming a more active and assertive society' (p. 189). In their survey they asked people to consider what action they would be willing to take against a proposed unjust or harmful action on the part of the government. They point out that compared to Almond and Verba's study (from which their question was drawn), which found that 32 per cent of the population would do nothing in 1959, their own study found that by 1991 this figure had gone down to a handful. Their findings are presented in Table 1.5.

Table 1.5 Changes in willingness to take action

Percentage taking action	1983	1986	1991
Personal action:			
Contact MP	46	52	48
Speak to influential person	10	15	17
Contact government department	7	12	11
Contact radio, TV or newspaper	14	15	14
Collective action:			
Sign petition	54	65	78
Raise issue in an organization I belong to	9	10	9
Go on a protest or demonstration	8	11	14
Form a group of like-minded people	6	8	7
None of these	12	10	6

Source: Jowell *et al.* (1992), p. 189

Which (if any) of the actions referred to in Table 1.5 have you taken part in during the previous twelve months? Why did you do so?

1) *Identify the type of action in which there has been the greatest change in terms of people taking such action between 1983 and 1991.*

2) *Do you agree with the conclusions concerning the number of people willing to do nothing made by the British Social Attitudes team in 1991?*

3) *Summarize the main changes that have taken place during the course of the 1980s.*

4) *What explanations can you give for this situation?*

5) *How important do you think the outcome of elections in this period was in affecting these statistics?*

Obtain a copy of the British Social Attitudes survey. If your school/college library does not possess a copy you could try the local reference library. Look at the section on political action and write a short report of about 1,000 words on this piece of research and present it to your class.

A comprehensive study of political participation in Britain, based on a survey of 1,578 respondents in 1985, was undertaken by Parry, Moyser and Day (1991). They concluded that only 4 per cent of their respondents were totally inactive. However, these researchers found that the only activity (not including voting in a General Election) in which a majority of the population was involved was signing petitions, which 63.3 per cent of the population had done in the previous five years. As for actually organizing a petition, only 8 per cent had done that, and not more than 10 per cent had been involved in a group to raise a particular issue.

It seems from this study that the degree of activity is greater than normally supposed, but activism as such is still a minority pursuit. Parry, Moyser and Day concluded that substantial activity beyond voting was confined to 25 per cent of the population. Out of a total of 23 possible activities, these active citizens engaged in between 6.5 and 15.75 activities. The characteristics of the more and less active are summarized in Table 1.6.

Table 1.6 Profiles of more active and less active citizens

Type *Percentage*	*Class[1]* *Salariat[0]*	*Gender* *Male*	*Party[2]* *Labour*	*Outlook[3]* *Left*
Less active 75%	20.5	43.3	30.9	25.2
More active 25%	37.8	46.3	29.7	29.4
Whole population[a]	24.9	44.0	30.6	26.2

Notes: [1] class was measured by occupation; [2] party self-identification; [3] outlook was determined by questions about attitudes towards police power over demonstrators, equality of wealth, privatization of industry, and government spending on job creation; [0] professional and managerial occupations; [a] based on the survey in which the total number of respondents was 1,578.

Source: Parry and Moyser (1993), p. 21

1) *Construct an ideal type of a more active citizen and a less active citizen. Are there any other social characteristics that you think might have been included?*

2) *To what extent does the fact that only 25 per cent of people are 'active' constitute a weakness or a strength for democracy in this country?*

As well as the social characteristics of their sample, Parry, Moyser and Day also considered their respondents' political and social attitudes. Their findings on this issue are presented in Table 1.7.

Table 1.7 Political and social attitudes of Parry, Moyser and Day's sample

Issue[a]	*Rank order of issues mentioned*			*Rank order of issues on which action was taken*
	Whole population	*Less active 75% of sample*	*More active 25% of sample*	
Environment and planning	1	2	1	2
Economic matters	2	1	2	8
Unemployment	3	3	6	10
Transport	4	4	3	3
Education	5	8	4	4
Housing	6	5	9	1
Defence/foreign affairs	7	6	5	9
Law and order	8	7	7	6

Health	9	9	8	5
Youth	10	10	10	7

Note: ª respondents were asked to name issues which most affected themselves, their families, the nation or the locality; the size of the sample in the survey was 1,578.

Source: Parry and Moyser (1993), p. 22

Compare and contrast the findings of Parry, Moyser and Day with the work of Lester Milbraith reported in Haralambos and Holborn (1991, p. 163). What problems are there in making such a comparison?

Consideration of these studies shows that while it is clear that voting is the only regular activity that the majority of the population are engaged in, there are other form of political action that take place and have an effect in changing the political and social environment. Often the two are linked. The 'Diary of an activist' reprinted here is an example.

The diary of an activist

Saturday

The BNP is having a press conference with Derek Beackon outside its HQ, which we are campaigning to close down. We organise a counter-protest which attracts about 50 local people.

We wonder about the state of the BNPs morale. The last week has seen their national organiser and deputy leader jailed, their councillor pictured Sieg Heiling in every national newspaper and the suspension of one of their members from his job as a caretaker for Greenwich Council. The cherry on their cake must be the ANL welcoming parties that we arrange every time they try to organise.

Sunday

Up at 6am for a Radio 4 interview before heading off for Brick Lane for the protest against the BNP paper sale.

We want to repeat the success of last Sunday when we prevented them selling. The demonstration is bigger today. Cheers greet the news that the fascists have been stopped by the police. People march off down Brick lane chanting "Brick Lane – Nazi free" and "We are black. We are white. Together we are dynamite."

Some have argued that we are as bad as the fascists for daring to demonstrate against them. Yet if we hadn't mounted opposition they would be free to sell their racist literature and to practise their race hatred. Now what better way is there to spend your Sunday morning?

Monday

Can't believe the early morning call from my sister when I'm desperate for some sleep. I don't know who's winning the phone war – the press or my relatives and friends. Ever since the British National Party won a council seat on the Isle of Dogs the Anti Nazi League has been inundated with people joining or volunteering their energies to the fight against fascism.

The office is like Piccadilly Circus. The phones and the mail never stop (and no one ever wants to wash the coffee cups). Everyone is busy building the October 16 Unity march on the BNP HQ: community centres, union branches, pensioners and school students have been ordering transport, posters and leaflets.

I go and meet the press (to the chagrin of the others trapped in the office). Today it's Capital Radio and the Evening Standard in Brick Lane, the heart of the Bengali community in east London. It's here where Nazis rampaged in the 1970s, terrorising Asians and smashing shops. Who would believe that we'd be back fighting in the 1990s? Horrific. Only a mile away in the London Hospital lies 17-year-old Quddus Ali, fighting for his life after a racist attack by a white gang. Finish the day off eating a satisfying curry with local community leaders, discussing how we can best unite our forces. Everyone happy that the demonstration yesterday stopped the BNP selling their racist filth at the top of Brick Lane.

Source: Adapted from the *Guardian*, 2 October 1993

 Make a list of all the political actions engaged in by this person over the period reported.

Here voting leads to other activities in protests surrounding the outcome of the election. Even if people are happy with the result of an election, it is fairly likely that there will be protests and action other than voting before the next election comes along. The poll conducted for Channel 4 by ICM pointed to one of the key reasons for this, shown in Table 1.8.

Table 1.8 Ordinary voter's control over government policies between elections

| | Between elections, how much power: | |
	should voters have? (percentage)	do voters have? (percentage)
A great deal	31	2
A fair amount	47	14
A little	12	53
None at all	4	26
Don't know	6	6

Source: Weir (1994), p. 12

The mismatch between the amount of power people think they should have and the amount of power they actually have suggests that between elections governments are not much constrained by the wishes of voters. This provides the basis for conflict when government policies are seen not to be supported by the views of the electorate. In this sense the government might be said to have lost an element of legitimacy (though not power).

This issue is central to considerations of power in a social context. It is legitimacy that distinguishes authority from power in the famous ideal types of power drawn up by Max Weber. The notion of legitimacy is also central to political action and participation. If people do not regard the actions of government as legitimate they may be more likely to engage in political action beyond voting. It is certain that between elections you cannot vote, so if you wish to protest you will have to take action other than voting.

Case studies of political action

The following case studies examine four events from the last ten to fifteen years that have helped shape the UK and the world we live in today and have also led to intense political debate.

Case Study — The Poll Tax protest

The 1987 Conservative Party Manifesto pledged to abolish the then existing system of local taxation, domestic rates. The government proposed to replace it with a community charge, which became commonly known as the Poll Tax. This tax caused widespread anger as it was seen as unfair and unjust since it was a flat-rate tax payable by all adults (though some were eligible for rebates). The tax was defended as being equal precisely because all adults in an area paid the same, but a report by the Child Poverty Action Group argued that 'a flat-rate charge clearly falls more heavily on those with low incomes than on those with high incomes' (Oppenheim, 1987). The government's table is reproduced here as Table 1.9.

Table 1.9 Relationship of rates and the Poll Tax to net income

Weekly net equivalent income £s	Net rates £s per week	as a % of net income	Net poll tax £s per week	as a % net income
Under 50	1.12	2.1	1.02	1.9
50–75	2.65	3.3	2.68	3.3
75–100	5.03	3.7	5.32	3.9
100–150	5.82	3.2	6.08	3.3
150–200	6.37	2.8	6.33	2.8
200–250	6.74	2.6	6.16	2.4
250–300	7.59	2.6	6.06	2.1
300–350	8.32	2.5	6.12	1.9
350–400	9.50	2.5	6.08	1.6
400–500	10.16	2.3	6.00	1.4
Over 500	12.48	1.8	6.64	1.0
All households	4.81	3.0	4.77	3.0

* income adjusted for family size (GB, 1984/5 prices)

Source: Green Paper, *Paying for Local Democracy*, quoted in Oppenheim (1987), p. 27

It was also felt that some might try to avoid paying the tax by failing to register to vote, thus losing their democratic rights. A third concern was that the new system would curb the rights of elected local councillors to determine spending in their area. An opinion poll in the *Daily Telegraph* found that 54 per cent thought it a bad idea and only 28 per cent a good idea.

1) *It has been argued that the protests against the Poll Tax affected the validity of the 1991 Census. Use newspaper reports from July 1991 (look them up on a CD-ROM if available) when the initial returns from the Census were published to explain why this might be the case.*

2) *The 1992 Electoral Register contained 43,252,965 names, up 0.2 per cent from 1987, while the overall population of the UK in the same period rose by 1.2 per cent. How might this be linked to the Poll Tax? What implications does this have for democracy in the UK?*

Despite the opposition, the government introduced the Poll Tax in Scotland from April 1989 and in England and Wales from April 1990.

Almost immediately local anti-Poll Tax groups sprang up. They argued that people should refuse to pay the tax. There were massive demonstrations outside council chambers. Such demonstrations even occurred in areas where a majority of voters supported the Conservative Party.

Explain the meaning of the cartoon.

By February 1990 it was estimated that one in three adults in Scotland had not paid the Poll Tax, and 145,000 people in Glasgow had not paid a single penny.

At the same time large demonstrations were taking place in England and Wales. In February 1990, 2,000 people marched against the Poll Tax in Maidenhead in Berkshire. In March 1990, 5,000 people demonstrated against the tax in Hackney and in Bristol, 2,000 demonstrated in Lambeth and 1,000-strong marches took place in Barrow, Crewe, Norwich, Telford and Lancaster.

Despite opposition to the idea of non-payment, the marches and the non-payment campaign in Scotland continued to grow. Simultaneous marches against the tax were organized for 31 March 1990 in London and Glasgow. The Glasgow march was estimated to be 40,000 strong, and in London over 200,000 marched. It was on the London march that riots broke out in Whitehall and Trafalgar Square. In response the police arrested over 500 people in relation to alleged offences on the demonstration.

By June 1990 it was estimated that one-third of people had not paid their Poll Tax, and in parts of London the figure rose to 80 per cent. This campaign of non-payment became one of the biggest campaigns of civil disobedience in UK history.

The evident unpopularity of the Poll Tax added to unease among Conservative MPs and was a contributory factor in the decision to ditch Margaret Thatcher as leader. Soon afterwards Michael Heseltine announced that the Poll Tax would be abandoned, and a new form of local taxation, the Council Tax, was introduced with effect from April 1993. The Poll Tax, which Margaret Thatcher had once described as her flagship, had lasted four years.

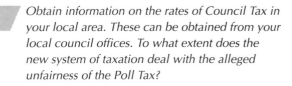

Obtain information on the rates of Council Tax in your local area. These can be obtained from your local council offices. To what extent does the new system of taxation deal with the alleged unfairness of the Poll Tax?

1) *Explain and evaluate the basis for legitimacy of the actions of both the Conservative government and the All-Britain Anti-Poll Tax Federation.*

2) *Under what circumstances do you think it is legitimate, if ever, to engage in civil disobedience?*

Case Study   The urban riots of the 1980s

In the summer of 1981 there was a large wave of urban riots throughout the UK. The first occurred in Brixton in April 1981. By July there were riots in Southall in West London, Toxteth in Liverpool and Moss Side, Manchester. Further riots broke out in Handsworth (Birmingham), Leeds, Bolton, Luton, Leicester, Nottingham, Hull, High Wycombe, Southampton, Halifax, Gloucester, Sheffield, Coventry, Portsmouth, Bristol, Edinburgh and Reading. There were also riots in various parts of London, notably Wood Green, Woolwich, Hackney, Walthamstow and Dalston. The weekend of 10–12 July saw the largest concentration of riots.

It was argued that a major cause of these riots was the policing of inner-city areas, particularly those with a large ethnic minority population, exacerbated by the economic crisis of the period that had led to a massive rise in youth unemployment. Both black and white youths felt marginalized from society, and blacks youth in particular felt that they were facing increased police harassment.

The Scarman Report, commissioned after the Brixton riots, noted the underachievement of black children but focused on failure at school rather than more overt forms of discrimination. Police evidence to the Scarman commission seemed to show that they regarded areas with large ethnic minorities as potentially troublesome.

The tense atmosphere this created continued, and further riots broke out in 1985, in Handsworth in Birmingham and in Brixton and Broadwater Farm (Tottenham) in London. In Brixton police had shot Cherry Groce while searching for her son, and in Tottenham Cynthia Jarrett died during a house search by the police.

The situation leading up to the riots had been analysed by sociologists such as Stuart Hall, who made the following comments about the riots:

> In 1978 I and a number of colleagues . . . published a book entitled *Policing the Crisis*. This book traced the rising curve of racism in Britain, charted the deteriorating situation between young black people and the police in the inner cities, predicted the growth of the political 'New Right' in the country and prophesied, as a consequence, greater social unrest in the 1980s. It's not a subject I feel especially proud to have been right about – but it does suggest the events of recent weeks are in no way so surprising, unexpected or 'unpredictable' as they have been said to be in the British media.
>
> (Hall 1985)

The Broadwater Farm riot became notorious due to the death of a police officer and the consequent legal trial which led to the prosecution of Winston Silcott for his murder. The case had further repercussions since the convictions for murder passed against the Tottenham Three (Silcott and two others) were quashed on appeal (Rose, 1992). This case, and the successful appeals of the Birmingham Six and the Guildford Four, led to a widespread questioning of the effectiveness of the judicial system and the methods employed by the police.

1) How valid is Stuart Hall's explanation of the roots of the 1980s urban riots?

2) To what extent is rioting a form of political action?

3) To what extent is it seen as legitimate?

A more detailed explanation of 'policing the crisis' can be found in *Investigating Deviance* by Stephen Moore (1991).

Case Study   # The Greenham Common women's peace camp

The rise to prominence of the Campaign for Nuclear Disarmament (CND) as a mass movement in the 1980s arose from the decision to base American Cruise missiles at air bases in Britain. By this time some of the dangers involved in nuclear power and nuclear arms were well known, and anti-nuclear sentiment was buoyed up by the explosions at the Three Mile Island nuclear plant in America in 1979 and Chernobyl in the USSR in 1986. By 1984 membership of CND had reached 100,000, and it organized some of the largest demonstrations ever seen in London.

However, perhaps the most famous symbol of the peace movement in the 1980s was the Greenham Common women's peace camp in Berkshire.

1) *CND was the organization studied by Frank Parkin as the basis for his book* Middle-Class Radicalism *(1968). Use your textbook to examine the reasons he gave for the rise of CND. You can find accounts of this in your sociology textbook. Consider the validity of this work as an explanation of the re-emergence of CND in the 1980s and the Greenham Common women's peace camp.*

2) *An alternative feminist interpretation of Greenham Common is provided by Roseneil (1995). An alternative explanation of CND as a whole is provided in Mattausch (1989). You might be able to locate copies of these in a local higher education library. If you cannot find the books themselves, you should be able to find reviews of them in sociological journals such as* Sociology *or the* British Journal of Sociology. *Examine the*

*differences between the three accounts of
the peace movement.*

Nawal el Saadawi (1985) describes the time she spent at the Greenham Common women's peace camp:

> She leaned over a hole in the ground. It contained a number of huge iron scissors. She pulled one of them out, put it in my hand, and gave me a piece of steel wire.
> 'Try and cut it,' she said.
> I put the wire between the two edges of the scissors and pressed down with all my might. Immediately it broke into two pieces.
> I heard her chuckle again: 'That's what we do at night. Yesterday they saw four of us cutting the wire and put them in jail. But next Saturday we will assemble five thousand men and women to cut the whole fence. Do you know,' she added, ' that in England now there are 102 military bases? We have become an occupied land. If we want to be free these must be closed down.'
>
> (el Saadawi 1985, pp. 242–3)

The camp, alongside the Miners' Wives Support Groups that sprang up in the 1984–5 miners' strike, is often cited as one of the major examples of women's political activity in the 1980s. The camp did indeed draw together a number of different strands to be found in the new social movements. As well as being part of the peace movement, which in the form of CND also grew massively in the mid–1980s, the camp was inspired by a feminist view that saw war as a result of the nature of male-controlled society. This was emphasized in the slogan 'Take the toys from the boys', the 'toys' being nuclear weapons.

1) *Use your library to investigate the strategy pursued by the Greenham Common peace camp in further detail. What were the main forms of action taken there?*

2) *Explain why the camp became a women's camp. How adequate do you find the feminist explanation of the causes of militarism?*

3) *To what extent do you feel the actions described above were legitimate?*

The use of military force in Russia

In 1991 an attempted military coup in the Soviet Union against Mikhail Gorbachev failed due to a lack of public support for its leaders. However, it did expose the weakness of the Soviet government under Gorbachev. One of the key leaders of the opposition against the coup was the President of the Russian Republic, Boris Yeltsin, who was himself a political opponent of Gorbachev.

Search recent newspapers and magazines in the library to find out if there are any more examples of military coups and the use of force in political struggle. Make a list of any that you find.

Following the coup the Soviet Union began to disintegrate, and power became fragmented in the hands of the republics. The pace of economic reforms towards a more market-based economy increased. Yeltsin was convinced of the need for a market economy after visiting the USA in 1987. However, this policy caused friction between him and his supporters in Parliament, who were equally concerned that the pace of change would lead to social unrest and poverty.

Within four months prices rose between five and ten times. By 1993 price rises amounted to 2,600 per cent, industrial output was 60 per cent of its 1990 level and 60 million pensioners were facing starvation.

Facing continuing criticism, Yeltsin suspended the Constitution and Parliament. His former allies argued that this was illegal and invoked a clause in the Constitution to remove him from the Presidency and install the suspended Vice-President, Alexander Rutskoi, in his place. For a couple of weeks Russia had two governments, until Yeltsin sent in tanks to disperse the Parliament and arrest its leaders.

Yeltsin then declared that there would be elections for a new parliament in December and a referendum on a new draft constitution on the same day. Because this draft constitution would give greater powers to the President and less to Parliament, some declared that there was a dictatorship in the making.

Yeltsin hoped the elections would provide him with a parliament more favourable to reform. In this respect his wishes were not entirely met. However, the new constitution was approved, so the parliament had less power than before.

> The crux of the problem is a contradiction between legitimacy and legality . . . The decisions of the Parliament are not legitimate because they no longer represent the wishes of the people.
>
> Gregory Yavlinsky, supporter of Boris Yeltsin, quoted in the O*bserver*, 26 September 1993

> In Russia today practically all democratic institutions have stopped working. A military-police dictatorship is in place.
>
> Roy Medvedev, writing in the *Guardian*, 9 October 1993

Consider which of these two contrasting opinions of events in Russia has greater validity.

Arguments in favour of Yeltsin

- Yeltsin was the elected President of Russia.
- The Parliament was an old one, having been elected in 1990, and no longer represented the wishes of the people.
- Yeltsin was supported by the major Western leaders, including John Major.
- A referendum on Boris Yeltsin's economic policies in April 1993 led to their endorsement by the Russian population.
- The referendum held in December 1993 on the new constitution drafted by Yeltsin approved it.
- Yeltsin's victory over the Russian parliament was welcomed by the world's stock markets. Thus it could be expected to lead to more foreign investment, which might help the economy.

Arguments against Yeltsin

- Yeltsin suspended the Constitutional Court and the elected Parliament of Russia.
- Yeltsin's actions were intended to allow him free rein to act, even against democratic institutions. This is tantamount to totalitarianism.
- The lifetime of the parliament elected in December 1993 has been reduced to two years.
- Alexander Rutskoi was elected as acting President by the Russian Parliament in conformity with the Russian Constitution.
- Yeltsin used tanks against the Russian Parliament.
- In the period leading up to the elections in December 1993, several opposition parties and newspapers were banned. Altogether about a third of election candidates were banned.

1) *This case study shows that questions about the legitimacy of the exercise of power can be very complex. We have listed some of the arguments for and against Boris Yeltsin's claim to legitimacy. Add to the list based on your own reading and from reports of subsequent developments. The case study has purposely stopped in December 1993 to allow you to do this.*

2) *To what extent do you think Boris Yeltsin's actions were legitimate? What is the basis, if any, of his legitimacy?*

3) *Use any standard sociology textbook to look up Max Weber's distinction between power and authority and the different bases of legitimacy for authority. Write a short report of about 200 words applying these concepts to the situation described in this case study. Are Weber's concepts useful in explaining events such as these?*

Essay Questions

To what extent does sociological evidence support the idea that there has there been a change in the nature and extent of political participation in Britain in recent years?

Coursework suggestions

Construct a questionnaire to test what a representative sample of people consider to be legitimate and illegitimate forms of political action. You should consult the British Social Attitudes Surveys for help in this venture and also the study by Parry, Moser and Day (1992) listed in the bibliography.

Compare your findings with those reported in these studies and consider any major differences that arise.

Analyse the responses in terms of the various social categories you have used to build up a representative sample.

Bibliography

Almond, G.A. and Verba, S. (1963) *The Civic Culture,* Princeton, NJ: Princeton University Press

Butler, D. and Kavanagh, D. (1984) *The British General Election of 1983,* London: Macmillan

Department of Education and Science (1983) *Young People in the 80s: A Survey,* London: HMSO

Edgell, S. and Duke, V. (1991) *A Measure of Thatcherism,* London: Routledge

el Saadawi, Nawal (1985) 'Politics – United Kingdom', in *Women: A World Report,* London: Methuen

Foot, P. (1977) *Why You Should Be a Socialist,* London: Socialist Workers Party

Hall, S. (1985) 'Riots not as "surprising" as media suggests', *Open House,* 5 November

Haralambos, M. and Holborn, M. (1991) *Sociology: Themes and Perspectives,* 3rd edn, London: Collins Educational

Jacobs, E. and Worcester, R. (1991) *Typically British?,* London: Bloomsbury

Jowell, R., Brook, L., Prior, G. and Taylor, B. (eds) (1992) *British Social Attitudes: The 9th Report,* Aldershot: Dartmouth

Light, M. (1993) 'Russia's demon democrat', *Guardian,* 23 September

Mattausch, J. (1989) *A Commitment to Campaign: A Sociological Study of CND,* Manchester: Manchester University Press

Moore, S. (1991) *Investigating Deviance,* London: Collins Educational

Oppenheim, C. (1987) *A Tax on All the People: The Poll Tax,* London: Child Poverty Action Group

Parkin, F. (1968) *Middle Class Radicalism,* Manchester: Manchester University Press

Parry, G. and Moyser, G. (1993) 'Political participation in Britain', *Politics Review,* November

Parry, G., Moyser, G. and Day, N. (1991) *Political Participation and Democracy in Britain,* Cambridge: Cambridge University Press

Pilger, J. (1993) 'The war against democracy', *New Statesman and Society,* 8 October

Rose, D. (1992) *A Climate of Fear: The Murder of PC Blakelock and the Case of the Tottenham Three,* London: Bloomsbury

Roseneil, S. (1995) *Disarming Patriarchy: Feminism and Political Action at Greenham,* Buckingham: Open University Press

Shaw, M. (1977) *Marxism against Sociology,* London: Pluto

Smyth, G., Jones, D. and Platt, S. (eds) (1994) *Bite the Ballot: 2,500 Years of Democracy,* London: Channel 4/New Statesman and Society

Ward, C. (1994) 'DIY democracy', in Smyth, Jones and Platt (1994)

Weir, S. (1994) 'Crisis of confidence', in Smyth, Jones and Platt (1994)

2 Recent trends in voting behaviour

In 1992 the Conservative Party won its fourth General Election in a row. The result is summarized in Table 2.1.

Table 2.1 Results of the 1992 General Election

Party	% of vote	% change on 1987	MPs elected	Change on 1987
Conservative	42.8	-0.4	336	-39
Labour	35.2	+3.7	271	+42
Liberal Democrat	18.3	-4.8	20	-2
Nationalist	2.4	+0.7	7	+1
Others	1.3	+0.8	0	-1

Source: Adapted from Crewe (1992)

Find out which party won each General Election in the UK since 1945. Which party has spent most time in government since 1945?

We can also look at the shares of the vote gained by the parties in the four elections since 1979. These are shown in Table 2.2.

Table 2.2 Shares of the vote, 1979–92

Party	1979	1983	1987	1992
		% share of the vote		
Conservative	43.9	42.4	42.3	42.8
Labour	37.0	27.6	30.8	35.2
Liberal Democrat/Alliance	13.8	25.4	22.6	18.3
SNP & PC	2.0	1.5	1.7	N/A
Others (Mainly N.I.)	3.2	3.1	2.6	N/A

Three points can be made about these figures:

- The Conservative vote remained fairly consistent throughout this period (the greatest divergence being a change of only 1.6 percentage points from 43.9 per cent in 1979 to 42.3 per cent in 1987).

- The Labour vote fell fairly dramatically and then rose again but did not quite reach the level of 1979 in 1992. Over the whole period Labour's share of the vote declined by 1.8 percentage points (from 37.0 per cent to 35.2 per cent).

- There was a large increase in the centre vote during the period of the existence of the Liberal/SDP Alliance (1983 and 1987), but then the Liberal Democrat vote fell. Nonetheless over the whole period the centre vote rose by 4.5 percentage points.

Sociologists are interested to know whether these trends are permanent or otherwise, and what determines them.

Will the Conservatives always win General Elections?

What is your prediction about the result of the next General Election? Outline the evidence on which you base this prediction.

When discussing trends of this kind, it matters greatly which starting and finishing points we choose. If we were only to compare 1979 and 1983 rather than 1979 and 1992, the trends would appear very different, in particular in relation to the Labour Party and the then existing Lib/SDP Alliance.

This point is important in relation to any set of figures, and something to bear in mind when considering all election figures. There is sometimes a tendency to project into the future on the basis of the most recent trends, and this involves the assumption that these trends will continue. This is particularly important in relation to recent electoral history since arguments that contemporary trends will continue would suggest that the Conservative Party will be in government for ever. This notion has led some thinkers to see Thatcherism as an all-powerful monolith, and this in turn has influenced the policy changes inside the Labour Party. If, on the other hand, one believes these trends to be fairly short run and temporary, then a very different picture emerges.

Martin Jacques defines 'Thatcherism' in the following way:

> The precise character of Thatcherism is complex. Two clear elements, however, can be pinpointed. Firstly there is a strong emphasis on a more traditional, arguably petty-bourgeois ideology – the virtues of the market, competition, elitism, individual initiative, the inequities of state intervention and bureaucracy ... secondly, Thatcherism has successfully attempted to organize the diverse forces of the 'backlash' – reacting against trade union militancy, national aspirations, permissiveness, women's liberation – in favour of an essentially regressive and conservative solution embracing such themes as authority, law and order, patriotism, national unity, the family and individual freedom.
>
> (Hall and Jacques 1983, p. 53)

To what extent do you think the removal of Margaret Thatcher as leader of the Conservative Party meant the end of 'Thatcherism'?

Arguments for continuing Conservative dominance

Arguments that may be given in support of the proposition that the Conservative Party will continue to dominate elections include the following:

- They have won four General Election victories in succession, even during the economic recessions of the early 1980s (1983 election) and the early 1990s (1992 election).

- The traditional class basis of voting is declining. Between 1979 and 1992 the percentage of the electorate voting on class lines, i.e. working-class people voting Labour and middle-class people voting Conservative, declined from 51 per cent to 47 per cent.

- The working class is divided electorally. In 1992, 41 per cent of C2s (skilled manual workers) voted Conservative compared to 40 per cent for Labour.

- People today are voting on the basis of new divisions, crucially housing ownership, geographical region and union membership. All of these are subject to social trends that favour the Conservative Party.

Use your textbooks/notes to find out what is used to measure class in traditional models of voting. To what extent do you feel these are adequate as measures of class?

Why are these trends supposed to help the Conservative Party? How has this notion been affected by the slump in the housing market since the late 1980s?

What other sectoral divisions might be considered important as bases of voting behaviour?

Ivor Crewe has produced many articles underlining the strength of recent electoral performances by the Conservative Party. The following quotes from his work give a flavour of the debate:

> Despite similarities between the results of the 1979 and 1992 General Elections, the underlying basis of the vote changed in three important ways. First, long-term party loyalties have shifted in the Conservatives' favour; secondly, the geographical axis of the Conservative vote has tilted further from North to South and West to East; and thirdly, the traditional class basis of the vote has further weakened.

> (Crewe 1993, p. 32)

Ivor Crewe talks about three ways the underlying basis of voting has changed. Identify ways in which each of these indicators could be measured. Obtain up-to-date figures for each. Is Crewe's point still valid?

> [In the 1992 General Election] Labour's performance, whether measured by its share of the vote (34.4 per cent) or its distance behind the Conservatives (7.4 percentage points) was its third worst since 1945 – an improvement only on the immediately preceding elections of 1983 and 1987. For the sixth consecutive election Labour failed to reach 40 per cent of the vote. The 1992 election confirmed its status as a long-term opposition party.

> (Crewe 1992, pp. 2–3)

Research the performance of the three main parties (or four if you live in a region with a nationalist party) in your region in 1992. Write a short report of about 100 words on each party. Compare their performance in your region with their national performance. Make a list of any major differences.

The perceived strength of the Conservative Party during the 1980s has influenced debate inside the Labour Party about how to respond to these election defeats.

1) Obtain information from newspapers and magazines about the arguments between traditionalists and modernizers inside the Labour Party. Which view appears to be stronger inside the party?

2) If you were a Labour supporter, which view would appeal to you?

3) If you were considering voting Labour, which view would be the more likely to make you do so?

Arguments against continuing Conservative dominance

Arguments that may be given against the proposition that the Conservative Party will continue to dominate elections include the following:

- The 1992 margin of victory was relatively narrow. If 1,247 people had voted differently in 1992 the Conservatives would have lost their overall majority in the House of Commons.

- In each election since 1983 the Conservative lead over Labour has been declining. It was 14.8 percentage points in 1983 and then fell to 11.5 in 1987 and 7.6 in 1992.

- The combined non-Conservative vote (meaning the votes for Labour and the Liberal Democrats/Lib-SDP Alliance) has been increasing. It was 50.8 percentage points in 1979 and then rose to 53 in 1983, 53.4 in 1987 and 53.5 in 1992.

1) In which constituencies would the 1,247 voters mentioned in the first point above have had to be registered to produce such a different result?

2) Who would these 1,247 people have had to be, and in what ways would they have had to change their voting behaviour?

3) If 1,247 people can influence the outcome of an election, are all votes equal?

4) How is the crucial status of these 1,247 dependent on the actions of others?

Does this mean the Conservative Party has no real legitimacy as a government since a majority voted against it in the last three General Elections?
Use a politics textbook to examine the concepts of 'representative democracy' and the 'first past the post voting system' to help you answer this question.

The following quotes from Marshall and Heath give the flavour of this debate:

> Class identification is particularly important for the Labour vote since, even among those presently in the relatively privileged service-class position, Labour has a majority at the polls – providing those individuals identify themselves as working class.

> (Marshall 1987, p. 39)

What is meant by the term 'class identification'? Is this the best way to define class? What alternative measures of class might be used?

. . . we can begin by asking whether these divisions within the classes were new in the 1980s or whether they already existed in 1964, when the first British election survey was conducted. Our answer to this question is that they were not new.

What we find is that the classes were divided back in the 1960s (and they were probably divided in the 1950s as well).

(Heath 1992, p. 22)

This overall point of view has also influenced politicians in their actions. Divisions inside the Tory Party over the Treaty of Maastricht were to some extent weakened by the threat of John Major to dissolve Parliament if he lost the vote. Conservative backbench MPs decided not to vote the government down in this instance, since polls indicated they would probably heavily lose a General Election.

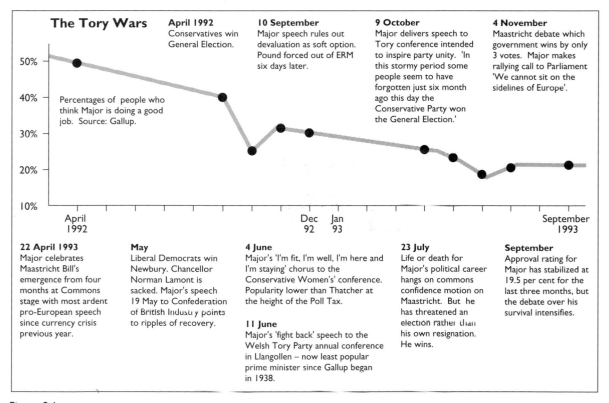

Figure 2.1

John Major's popularity slips

Source: *Observer*, 10 October 1993

Using newspaper reports (use a CD-ROM if one is available in your library), identify which section of the Conservative Party was most prominent in the rebellion over the Maastricht treaty. Why were they rebelling?

A Gallup Poll in the *Daily Telegraph* of 9 July 1993 showed the government's approval rating down to 12 per cent, the lowest since regular polling began after the Second World War. This is lower than the 18 per cent rating achieved by Mrs Thatcher's government in 1981. In terms of voting intention the Conservatives (with 24.5 per cent) were in third place behind the Liberal Democrats (26.5 per cent) and Labour (43 per cent).

 Use back copies of newspapers or CD-ROM if available to seek out more recent opinion polls and write a short summary of about 250 words on their contents. In what ways may they be unreliable as indicators of voting intentions at a future election?

As noted earlier, talk of trends depends crucially on the starting point of one's analysis. Most recent commentators take 1979 as a starting point, for the obvious reason that this was the first General Election that Margaret Thatcher won. However, it is possible to take an earlier starting point. Table 2.3 shows the votes cast in all General Elections since the Second World War.

Table 2.3   UK General Election results since 1945

| | Percentage of votes | | | | Seats | | | | |
	Con	Lab	Lib Dem	Nat	Con	Lab	Lib Dem	Nat	Total
1992	41.9	34.4	17.8	5.8	336	271	20	24	651
1987	42.3	30.6	22.5	2.0	376	229	22	6	650
1983	42.4	27.6	25.4	1.7	397	209	23	4	650
1979	43.8	36.8	13.8	2.2	339	269	11	4	635
1974 Oct.	35.8	39.2	18.3	3.5	277	319	13	14	635
1974 Feb.	37.9	37.2	19.3	2.8	297	301	14	9	635
1970	46.4	43.1	7.5	2.4	330	288	8	5	630
1968	41.9	48.0	8.6	1.1	253	364	12	1	630
1964	43.4	44.1	11.2	0.9	304	317	9	0	630
1959	49.4	43.8	5.8	0.6	365	258	6	0	630
1955	49.7	46.4	2.7	0.9	345	277	6	2	630
1951	48.0	48.8	2.6	0.4	321	295	8	3	625
1950	43.4	46.1	9.1	0.6	298	315	9	2	625
1945	39.6	48.0	9	1.4	210	383	12	6	640

Source: *Guardian*, 11 April 1994

 1) *Imagine you were asked to write a summary of recent voting trends in (a) 1945, (b) 1963, (c) 1978. Which factors would you highlight as important elements of the political context in those years?*

2) *Research the three time periods. Write a short summary of each and consider how the future looked in each of those three years.*

Try to use Table 2.3 to develop more detailed points both for and against the proposition that the Conservative Party will continue to be dominant into the future based on the rather longer-term trends outlined here.

You first need to consider what these trends are, and then you should attempt to explain each one. In relation to the 1960s the concept of embourgeoisement was one attempt to provide an explanation for the trend perceived. Use your sociology textbooks to research the debate over embourgeoisement and write a summary of its implications for theories of voting behaviour.

What causes trends in voting?

The present debate takes as its starting point an existing consensus about voting behaviour that was established by earlier studies. In many ways it is this consensus that is at the centre of recent debates.

The consensus or orthodoxy that sociologists developed in the 1950s held that the two-party system arose on the basis of the two main social classes in Britain. In short, it was argued that the middle class voted Conservative and the working class Labour. Social class was therefore central to explanations of voting behaviour.

This view was exemplified in the idea of partisan alignment developed by Butler and Stokes. They maintained: 'Class has long been pre-eminent among the factors used to explain party allegiance in Britain . . . There is, in fact, evidence that partisanship has followed class lines more strongly in Britain than anywhere else in the English-speaking world' (Butler and Stokes 1974, p. 67).

The central problem with this model is the numerical predominance of the working class in the population. The fact that the Conservative Party won the 1951, 1955 and 1959 General Elections meant that some working-class people must have voted for them. This led to the development of explanations based on deviant voting.

The debates in the 1980s developed these themes in a number of ways. The greater emphasis on considering how a political party might help meet individual aspirations as a key motivation for voting suggested a very much more individual calculation than the collective notion of social class background determining voting behaviour.

One important shift has been that in the 1960s all explanations of 'deviant' voting (notably working-class people who voted Conservative) operated against the norm of Butler and Stokes's social class model, whereas in the 1980s the debate turned on whether class was still central. It was pointed out by Rational Choice theorists (see below) that 'deviant' voters were only deviant if the norm was assumed to be voting according to social class. As we have noted, the percentage of voters voting on traditional class lines fell to 47 per cent in 1992. The deviants are now in the majority. This is precisely why notions of deviant voting have largely disappeared.

In considering the recent history of voting behaviour sociologists need to consider two issues:

- the relative importance of political and social factors; and

- the basis of the social structuring of voting.

By 'political' is meant factors such as the increase in the number of candidates put forward by the Liberal Party or the rise and fall of the Liberal/SDP Alliance. By 'social' is meant, for example, the changing social class structure.

 Should sociologists be concerned with the effect of political factors? Which political factors might be important?

Which social trends do you think sociologists need to consider when explaining voting behaviour? Justify your choices.

This is the overall context in which to consider the various models that have been developed in recent times to explain voting behaviour. Miller (1992) provides a diagram (see Figure 2.2) which, he argues, shows all the important factors determining voter choice and all the key links between them. Broadly social factors form the left-hand side and broadly political factors form the right-hand side.

Figure 2.2

Miller's diagrammatic representation of the factors affecting voting behaviour

The introduction of the Poll Tax can be seen as an example of government and party actions affecting attitudes and the way people declared they would vote. This influence can be traced from the top right-hand corner of the figure, down arrow E affecting attitudes, and then down arrow J affecting the way people vote. Another example might be the negative comment in the media over the Labour Party's tax plans in 1992. The factors involved here would again be party actions, passing down arrow D to media context, then arrow F, then arrow J.

Source: Miller (1992), p. 44

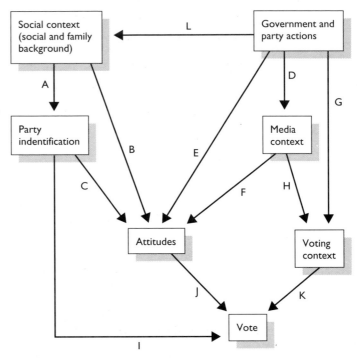

1) Explain the meaning of each of the arrows on the diagram.
2) Which categories in Figure 2.2 do the following fit into:
   Attending a meeting of a local Conservative Association
   Obtaining a degree in Sociology
   Having a father who is a factory worker
   A Sun editorial
   The General Election of 1992
   Believing tax cuts are a bad thing
   Supporting the NHS
   John Major's 'Back to Basics' Campaign
   Joining the Labour Party
   Supporting proportional representation
3) Working in groups, make up your own list of two examples for each of the categories in Miller's diagram. Present a report back to the rest of the class.
4) Make a note of all the examples cited. Try to explain the effect of each example on the way people vote. Write a short report (100–200 words) summarizing the effect of each category identified by Miller, incorporating reference to the examples you have compiled.

Models of voting

This section will outline some of the main theories that have been developed to explain voting behaviour, focusing on their relevance to the contemporary debate outlined above. The models to be discussed are as follows:

- The Rational Choice Model (Himmelweit *et al.* 1985)

- The Radical Voting Model (Dunleavy and Husbands 1985)

- The Class Dealignment Model (Crewe 1977, 1984)

- The Embourgeoisement Model (Saunders 1990)

- The Interactionist Model (Heath *et al.* 1985, 1991)

- The Social Class Model (Marshall *et al.* 1988)

- The Class Struggle Model (Callinicos and Harman 1987)

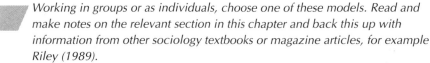

Working in groups or as individuals, choose one of these models. Read and make notes on the relevant section in this chapter and back this up with information from other sociology textbooks or magazine articles, for example Riley (1989).
Present a report back on the model you have chosen to the rest of the class.
Try to think which factor(s) on Miller's diagram would be emphasized by the model you have chosen.

The Rational Choice Model

David Downs (1957) argued that the way people vote is not determined by some social characteristic; rather they choose who to vote for on the basis of a rational calculation of the parties' policies. Parties and their policies are therefore seen as equivalent to supermarkets and products, and voters shop around with their currency, i.e. their vote.

Consider what is meant by 'rational' in this model. Do you agree with this definition?

Adam Smith wrote in The Wealth of Nations *(1776) that 'Every individual endeavours to employ his capital so that its produce may be of greatest value. He generally neither intends to promote the public interest, nor knows how much he is promoting it.'*

1) How can this theory be applied to voting behaviour? To what extent can it be the basis of an adequate explanation of how people vote?
2) How could this theory be tested?

The implication of this model is that social structuring of voting (expressive voting) is not important; what matters is voting based on attitudes to policies (instrumental voting). According to this argument, voters think about their own attitudes to various issues and then select the party whose policies most approximate their own attitudes. It follows that voters act more as individuals than as members of social groups.

Provide an example of expressive voting and an example of instrumental voting.

The Rational Choice Model became popular because it seemed to offer a better explanation than earlier models based on notions of class-based voting. One key problem with the latter, as we have seen, was so-called deviant voters. The Rational Choice Model has no such problem and indeed argues that these voters were only seen as deviant because it was assumed that social class ought to determine their behaviour. On this view, voters act more as individuals than as social groups.

 Why might the Conservative Party particularly emphasize and support the Rational Choice Model?

The key empirical study to support this view is that of Himmelweit *et al.* (1985). On the basis of a longitudinal study of the voting behaviour of a sample of voters between 1959 and October 1974, these authors claim to be able to explain 80 per cent of voting. Since this is a higher percentage than could be explained on the basis of a class voting model, this represents an advantage for the Rational Choice Model.

Table 2.4   The five issues chosen by respondents as the most important in the 1987 General Election

Issues	All voters (%)	Change since 1983	Conservative recruits	Conservative defectors	Labour recruits	Labour defectors	Lib/SCP recruits	Lib/SDP defectors	Party advantage [b] 1987	1983
Unemployment	49	-23	29	50	59	51	50	44	Lab+34	Lab+16
NHS/Hospitals	33	+22	18	33	45	44	43	36	Lab+49	Lab+46
Education	19	+13	14	26	23	22	26	25	Lab+15	N/A
Defence	35	-3	59	32	25	38	33	4	Con+63	Con+54
Pensions	10	+2	5	12	10	10	12	7	N/A	N/A

Notes: The five issues above were most frequently cited in an open-ended question on issues.
The party advantage shows the lead of the party chosen as the best on that issue over the next party, among respondents for whom the issue was important.
N/A means that the figure is not available.

Source: Crewe (1987), p. 7

 1) What evidence does this table provide in support of the notion of voters as rationally choosing actors?
2) What evidence against this notion does the table provide?
3) What further evidence might you need in order to evaluate the quality of evidence provided by this table?

However, Himmelweit's study has been subject to a number of criticisms, both methodological and substantive.

As concerns method, by October 1974 Himmelweit's sample was very small, numbering only 178. All of these were male, middle aged and middle class.

 Use the Methods chapter in your textbook or your notes on methodology to explain why this matters.

As for the substantive argument, the idea of voters choosing which way to vote on the basis of party policies seems to be undermined by the fact that in both 1987 and 1992 the top three issues voters were concerned about were unemployment, the

National Health Service and education. On all three issues voters saw Labour as the better party, yet Labour lost both elections.

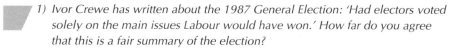

1) Ivor Crewe has written about the 1987 General Election: 'Had electors voted solely on the main issues Labour would have won.' How far do you agree that this is a fair summary of the election?
2) Crewe has also outlined his views on the 1992 General Election in an article in Politics Review, September 1992. Obtain a copy of this article and consider whether he held the same view of the 1992 and the 1987 General Elections.

Compare and contrast the evidence on voting behaviour in the 1987 General Election presented in Table 2.4 with the data on 1983 given in Figure 2.3. Are they consistent? Should they be consistent?

Figure 2.3

Preferences and policies in the 1983 General Election

Source: *Sunday Times*, 29 May 1983, quoted in Leeds (1986)

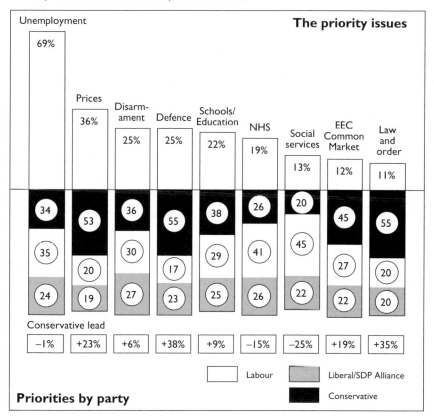

Table 2.5 provides similar figures for the 1992 General Election.

In the same vein, British Social Attitudes Surveys consistently showed certain policies to be unpopular, yet these were policies associated with the Conservative Party. On this basis Miller (1992, p. 53) has commented that 'the rational-choice model fails simple tests in spectacular fashion'.

Try to obtain up-to-date figures about political attitudes (either from more recent editions of the British Social Attitudes Survey or from back copies of newspapers

Table 2.5 The issues cited by survey respondents as most important in the 1992 General Election

Issues	All voters (%)	Change since 1983	Conservative recruits	Conservative defectors	Labour recruits	Labour defectors	Party advantage 1992	1987
NHS/Hospitals	41	+8	23	45	47	40	Lab+34	Lab+49
Unemployment	36	-13	35	31	42	51	Lab+26	Lab+34
Education	23	+4	15	30	27	23	Lab+23	Lab+15
Prices	11	+5	15	9	7	10	Con+59	N/A
Taxation	10	+3	26	11	5	7	Cons+72	Cons+68
Poll tax	8	+7	6	11	15	7	N/A	N/A
Pensions	6	-4	7	10	6	6	Lab+35	N/A
Defence	3	-32	6	1	1	1	Cons+86	Cons+63

Source: Gallup post-election survey, 10–11 April 1992, cited in Crewe (1992)

using a CD-ROM if available) and then analyse whether they are in tune with current government policy.

Finally, the model provides no explanation of the basis of people's attitudes. It has therefore been argued (for example, by Dearlove and Saunders 1991) that it is not a theory at all. Notions of rational choice usually start from the idea of the isolated individual trying to work out what is in his or her best interests, but the focus on individuals fails to provide an explanation for the origins of their political attitudes.

1) Does this matter? Why?
2) Can studies of attitudes be used to predict actual behaviour? What problems might arise in doing this?

We have noted Miller's comment that 'the rational-choice model fails simple tests in spectacular fashion'. How far do you agree with this assessment of the model? Write a short report of 100–200 words outlining your view.

The Radical Voting Model

This model was developed by Dunleavy and Husbands in their book *Democracy at the Crossroads* (1985). They made two main arguments: first, that models based on social class are inadequate since they fail to take into account important new sectoral divisions; and second, that these divisions are enhanced by ideologies that direct political consciousness away from more fundamental issues.

Sectoral divisions

What examples of sectoral divisions other than class can you think of?
Work in small groups and try to come up with as many as possible. Report back and note down any mentioned by other groups that do not appear in your list. As a group discuss which you think are the most important for voting behaviour.

One of the key debates in sociology has been the extent to which divisions based on production (occupation and therefore class) are being replaced with divisions based on consumption.
Lukes (1984) makes the following point: 'Labour, or work itself, and the sphere

of production seems to be becoming less central to the identity and consciousness of workers, while consumption, especially with regard to housing and transport, has become more central to their interests.'
Using evidence from this chapter, assess the extent to which this is a valid view of contemporary Britain.
Use the Theory section of your textbook to explain how this debate links into the debate between Marxist and Weberian sociologists.

Husbands and Dunleavy argue that the most important of the new sectoral divisions is that between the public and the private sector, with which are associated different views on taxation and public expenditure. The idea of sectional divisions within social classes has been utilized by a number of writers. Ivor Crewe's work on class dealignment, and Edgell and Duke represent two contrasting views which have been influenced by these ideas.

The idea that sectoral divisions are important in modifying class-based divisions receives some support from the work of Stephen Edgell and Vic Duke: 'we agree that class dealignment is a myth, but our data also suggest that sectoral factors are an important influence on the variation in voting behaviour from one election to the next' (Edgell and Duke 1991, p. 69).

There are various versions of this theory, offering the picture of a society divided between haves and have-nots. This is sometimes called the two-thirds/one-third society. Those dependent on the public sector either for employment or for state benefits want higher levels of public expenditure, which entails higher levels of taxation, whereas those dependent on the private sector want tax cuts.

In order to examine this picture, let us look at Tables 2.6 and 2.7, which provide figures for class voting divided into those who work in the public and the private sectors.

Table 2.6	Divisions in working-class voting behaviour, 1987 and 1992 General Elections			
	Public Sector		Private sector	
	1987	1992	1987	1992
Conservative	32	36	38	32
Labour	49	48	39	50
Liberal/SDP	19	16	23	18

Source: Adapted from Crewe (1987, 1992)

Table 2.7	Divisions in middle-class voting behaviour, 1987 General Election	
	Public Sector	Private sector
Conservative	44	65
Labour	24	13
Liberal/SDP	32	22

Source: Adapted from Crewe (1987)

Draw out three points from these tables that support the Radical Voting Model, and three that do not.

The role of ideology

The more interesting part of the Radical Voting Model lies in its use of the concept of an ideology affecting the way people, particularly working-class people, vote.

Use the chapter on Power and Ideology in this book and other sources such as any dictionary of sociology or Martin Slattery's Key Ideas in Sociology *to find out the various meanings attached to the term 'ideology'. Provide what you think is the most appropriate definition. Discuss this with your classmates and compare your definition with theirs.*

A key example of the use of ideology as an explanatory variable is the depiction of 'Thatcherism' as a set of ideas that won popular support and thus brought the Conservative Party election victories in the 1980s and 1990s.

 The concept of ideology can be traced back to the writings of the Italian Marxist Antonio Gramsci. You can find a summary of Gramsci's work in your textbook or in Hoffman (1988). Write a report of about 300 words to explain how Gramsci's ideas can be used to explain Thatcherism. Try to consider whether you think this interpretation of Thatcherism is supported by other evidence such as that provided by the British Social Attitudes Survey. Include a consideration of this in your report.

The notion of Thatcherism as a coherent ideology has been subject to some criticism since:

A) the policies themselves, for example the Poll Tax, the privatization of electricity and water, and the development of a two-tier NHS, were never particularly popular, and

B) the champions of Thatcherism often disagreed fundamentally about what it meant; some were neo-liberals who believed in individual liberty and the free market, while others were neo-conservatives who believed in the defence of what they termed 'traditional' values.

 Ralph Miliband (1985) has argued that the concept of 'Thatcherism' overstates the support for Conservative policies and therefore overstates the power of Thatcher.
Use newspaper and magazine articles (use a CD-ROM to locate these) to consider the validity of this point of view. Look up references to divisions within the Thatcher governments, for example during the Westland crisis. A short summary of the Thatcher period is included in Chapter 5 of this book. How far do you agree with Miliband?

On this subject Anthony Giddens has argued:

> It is easy to suppose that the policies associated with Mrs Thatcher's Governments (which came to power in 1979) were more unified and consistent than is in fact the case. Thatcherism has certain guiding threads, but is in most aspects a fairly loose collection of programmes and initiatives.

> (Giddens 1989, p. 317)

In relation to the concentration on ideology in the Dunleavy and Husbands model and elsewhere, criticisms made by Abercrombie, Hill and Turner (1980) are also pertinent. They argue that surveys of attitudes show widespread levels of disagreement, indicating that a large proportion of the population have failed to internalize the values attributed to the dominant ideology, which they do not believe has a powerful effect at all. The only real function of the dominant ideology is to help hold the bourgeoisie together. Workers are not kept in line by ideology but by more concrete economic factors such as poverty, unemployment and tax changes.

One possible economic factor is the changing regional patterns of public expenditure shown in Figure 2.4. It might be argued these can explain the North/South divide in voting patterns depicted in Figure 2.5 on page 32.

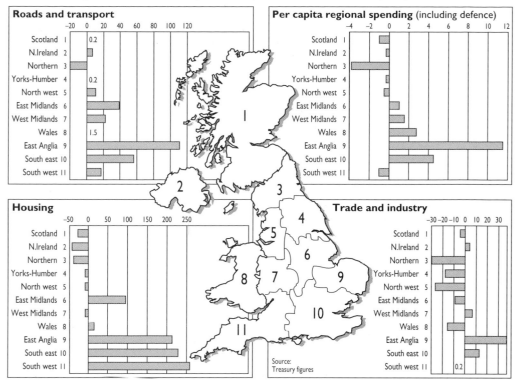

Who's losing out Percentage change in spending, 1987/88-1990/91 (1990/91 prices)

Figure 2.4

Regional changes in public expenditure, 1987–91

Source: *Guardian*, 9 February 1993

1) *How might the changes identified in Figure 2.4 explain the regional voting patterns shown in Figure 2.5? Assess the relative importance of ideological and economic factors in explaining the North/South divide.*

2) *To what extent do these figures justify arguments about the existence of a North/South divide? How might the following regions fit into such a picture: (a) Greater London, (b) the North, (c) Wales?*

Class and sectoral divisions

In their analysis of Thatcherism in Britain, Edgell and Duke (1991) have attempted to analyse attitudes and action with the help of a model that combines notions of social class with a recognition of the importance of sectoral cleavages derived from the Radical Voting Model.

They conclude that a combination of social class and sectoral cleavages is the basis for explaining patterns of protest in Thatcherite Britain:

> our data suggest that the structure of radicalism is influenced by sector as well as class ... attitudes and behaviour are certainly fragmented in Thatcher's Britain, but they are fragmented in a socially structured way. Class location, and to a lesser extent sectoral location, have been shown to

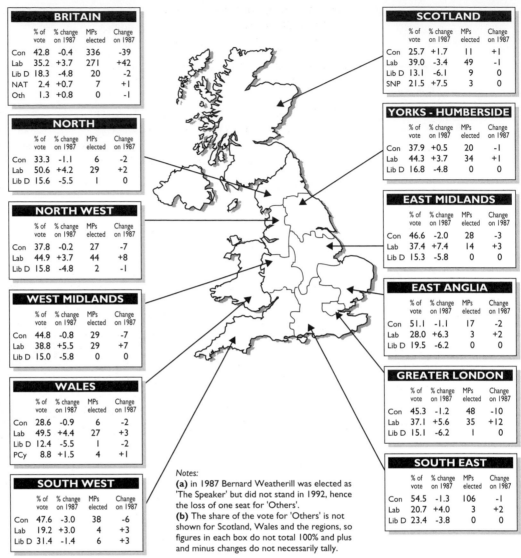

BRITAIN			
	% of vote	% change on 1987	MPs elected	Change on 1987
Con	42.8	-0.4	336	-39
Lab	35.2	+3.7	271	+42
Lib D	18.3	-4.8	20	-2
NAT	2.4	+0.7	7	+1
Oth	1.3	+0.8	0	-1

NORTH			
	% of vote	% change on 1987	MPs elected	Change on 1987
Con	33.3	-1.1	6	-2
Lab	50.6	+4.2	29	+2
Lib D	15.6	-5.5	1	0

NORTH WEST			
	% of vote	% change on 1987	MPs elected	Change on 1987
Con	37.8	-0.2	27	-7
Lab	44.9	+3.7	44	+8
Lib D	15.8	-4.8	2	-1

WEST MIDLANDS			
	% of vote	% change on 1987	MPs elected	Change on 1987
Con	44.8	-0.8	29	-7
Lab	38.8	+5.5	29	+7
Lib D	15.0	-5.8	0	0

WALES			
	% of vote	% change on 1987	MPs elected	Change on 1987
Con	28.6	-0.9	6	-2
Lab	49.5	+4.4	27	+3
Lib D	12.4	-5.5	1	-2
PCy	8.8	+1.5	4	+1

SOUTH WEST			
	% of vote	% change on 1987	MPs elected	Change on 1987
Con	47.6	-3.0	38	-6
Lab	19.2	+3.0	4	+3
Lib D	31.4	-1.4	6	+3

SCOTLAND			
	% of vote	% change on 1987	MPs elected	Change on 1987
Con	25.7	+1.7	11	+1
Lab	39.0	-3.4	49	-1
Lib D	13.1	-6.1	9	0
SNP	21.5	+7.5	3	0

YORKS - HUMBERSIDE			
	% of vote	% change on 1987	MPs elected	Change on 1987
Con	37.9	+0.5	20	-1
Lab	44.3	+3.7	34	+1
Lib D	16.8	-4.8	0	0

EAST MIDLANDS			
	% of vote	% change on 1987	MPs elected	Change on 1987
Con	46.6	-2.0	28	-3
Lab	37.4	+7.4	14	+3
Lib D	15.3	-5.8	0	0

EAST ANGLIA			
	% of vote	% change on 1987	MPs elected	Change on 1987
Con	51.1	-1.1	17	-2
Lab	28.0	+6.3	3	+2
Lib D	19.5	-6.2	0	0

GREATER LONDON			
	% of vote	% change on 1987	MPs elected	Change on 1987
Con	45.3	-1.2	48	-10
Lab	37.1	+5.6	35	+12
Lib D	15.1	-6.2	1	0

SOUTH EAST			
	% of vote	% change on 1987	MPs elected	Change on 1987
Con	54.5	-1.3	106	-1
Lab	20.7	+4.0	3	+2
Lib D	23.4	-3.8	0	0

Notes:
(a) in 1987 Bernard Weatherill was elected as 'The Speaker' but did not stand in 1992, hence the loss of one seat for 'Others'.
(b) The share of the vote for 'Others' is not shown for Scotland, Wales and the regions, so figures in each box do not total 100% and plus and minus changes do not necessarily tally.

Figure 2.5

Regional distribution of votes, 1992 General Election

Source: *Politics Review*, February 1993

be important in the fragmented social structuring of both acquiescence and protest.

(Edgell and Duke 1991, pp. 213–14)

The Class Dealignment Model

Ivor Crewe has argued that while short-term political factors contributed to the defeats of the Labour Party in the 1980s there are also longer-term social trends that are working against Labour. The most important of these are the following:

- The proportion of manual workers in the electorate fell from 63 per cent in 1959 to 54 per cent in 1983 and is continuing to fall.

- The changing composition of the working class is undermining its support for

Labour. In 1959, 62 per cent of manual workers voted Labour, but by 1983 this had fallen to 38 per cent.

- The key sectoral divisions inside the working class are based on housing, geographical region, union membership and public/private sector employment. There are similar divisions inside the middle class.

Use the Stratification section of your textbook to explain which definition of working class Crewe is working with here. What alternative definitions exist? Does it matter which you use? Which do you think is the most valid? Discuss these issues in groups and present your findings to the class.

As a result the proportion of the electorate voting along class lines has fallen in recent years (see Table 2.8).

Table 2.8 Distribution of manual and non-manual votes, 1979-92

| | 1979 | | 1983 | | 1987 | | 1992 | |
	Non-manual %	Manual %	Non-manual %	Manual %	Non-manual %	Manual %	Non-Manual %	Manual %
Conservative	55	36	51	35	49	37	49	35
Liberal/other	19	17	31	28	31	23	25	20
Labour	26	46	18	37	20	40	26	45
Non-manual Con + manual Lab as % of total vote	51		45		44		47	
Odds ratio	2.6		3.0		2.6		2.4	

Source: Crewe (1993), p. 33

This is what is meant by class dealignment. The term refers to the early orthodoxy among psephologists in Britain, best exemplified by Butler and Stokes (1974), who argued that class alignment was the most characteristic feature of voting behaviour: the working class could be expected to vote Labour and the middle class Conservative.

Crewe argues that today the working class can be divided into the traditional and the new working class and that these two groups vote in very different ways. Labour has been relatively unsuccessful in getting the new working class to vote for it. Tables 2.9 and 2.10 (see page 34) show the divisions inside the working class that appeared in the 1987 and 1992 General Elections.

Which sectoral division seems to be the most important in Tables 2.9 and 2.10? Give a concrete example of a member of the 'new working class' and the 'traditional working class'.

What differences are there between the 1992 and 1987 results? How far do these differences affect the usefulness of Crewe's theory?

Table 2.9 Voting behaviour of the 'new' and 'traditional' working class, 1987

| Party | The New Working Class | | | | The Traditional Working Class | | | |
	Lives in South	Owner Occupier	Non-union member	Works in private sector	Lives in Scotland or North	Council tenant	Union member	Works in public sector
Conservative	46	44	40	38	29	25	30	32
Labour	28	32	38	39	57	57	48	49
Lib/SDP Alliance	26	24	22	23	15	18	22	19
Conservative or Labour majority in 1987	Con +18	Con +12	Con +2	Lab +1	Lab +28	Lab +32	Lab +18	Lab +17
Conservative or Labour majority in 1983	Con +16	Con +22	Con +6	Lab +1	Lab +10	Lab +38	Lab +21	Lab +17
Category as percentage of all manual workers	40	57	66	68	37	31	34	32
Change since 1983	+4	+3	+7	+2	-1	-4	-7	-2

Source: Crewe (1987), p. 4

Table 2.10 Voting behaviour of the 'new' and 'traditional' working class, 1992

| Party | The New Working Class | | | | The Traditional Working Class | | | |
	Lives in South	Owner Occupier	Non-union member	Works in private sector	Lives in Scotland or North	Council tenant	Union member	Works in public sector
Conservative	40	40	37	32	26	22	29	36
Labour	38	41	46	50	59	64	55	48
Liberal Democrat	23	19	17	18	15	13	16	16
Conservative or Labour majority in 1992	Con +2	Lab +1	Lab +9	Lab +18	Lab +33	Lab +42	Lab +26	Lab +12
Conservative or Labour majority in 1987	Con +18	Con +12	Con +2	Lab +1	Lab +28	Lab +32	Lab +18	Lab +17
Swing to Labour 1987–92	+8.0	+6.5	+5.5	+8.5	+2.5	+5.0	+4.0	-2.5 (to Con)

Source: Crewe (1992), p. 5

Criticisms of Crewe

There have been a number of criticisms of Crewe's analysis of divisions in the working class:

- It has been said that he conflates correlation with causation. It is one thing to identify different voting patterns among different sections of the working class; it is another to prove that sectoral differences are the cause of differences in voting patterns. Parkin (1968) made a similar point much earlier. He argued that jobs in the welfare state may be sought by middle-class radicals. Their employment position is therefore a consequence of their political views rather than a cause of them.

- Heath *at al.* (1991) have argued that the effect of different housing patterns is nothing new, but is in fact a long-standing historical division. In 1964, 35 per cent of working-class house-owners voted Conservative, while in 1987 the figure was 37 per cent. People may not vote Conservative because they own their own houses; rather, they may seek to become home-owners because they are Conservatives.

- The famous C2 category is not a sociological category. As well as skilled workers it includes foremen, supervisors and small business people, so it embraces some elements of the middle class or petty bourgeoisie as well as some members of the working class. Yet it is used almost exclusively to make comments about the voting behaviour of the working class.

 What alternative method could be used to identify who are working class and who are middle class?

Party image

A final important area of Crewe's work is the notion of party image. Crewe argues that the Conservatives have won elections despite lack of public support for their policies simply because they are associated in voters' minds with prosperity. This might be called the 'feel good factor'. In relation to the 1987 election he argues that this was decisive:

> When answering survey questions on the most important issues respondents think of public problems; when entering the polling booth they think of family fortunes. 'Prosperity' is not an issue or a problem, but a blessing. By a decisive 55 per cent to 27 per cent majority the public regarded the Conservatives as more likely to bestow it. Here quite simply and obviously lies the key to Conservative victory.

(Crewe 1987, p. 7)

Figure 2.6

Some problems in studying voting behaviour

Source: *Private Eye*, 26 June 1987

What are the methodological implications of this cartoon for the study of voting behaviour?

To what extent do you agree with the centrality that Crewe gives to this point in explaining the 1987 election result? How far can the 'feel good factor' be used to explain the results of other recent elections?

The Embourgeoisement Model

A similar concern with divisions inside the working class can be seen in the re-emergence of earlier debates about embourgeoisement and the affluent worker. The embourgeoisement thesis was devised by Zweig (1961) to explain the electoral victories of the Conservative Party in 1951, 1955 and 1959.

 Use your textbooks to investigate the similarities and differences between the theory of class dealignment and the embourgeoisement theory. (Hint: Think about what changes they suggest in terms of how working-class people define themselves and the implications of this.)

Goldthorpe *et al.* (1969) sought to test this thesis by making a study of affluent workers using the case-study method. They found that 80 per cent of their sample had voted Labour, and concluded that affluence did not seem to lead to Conservative voting in the automatic sort of way suggested by the embourgeoisement theorists.

The theory that the Labour Party was condemned to perpetual opposition was dealt a further blow when Labour won the 1964 and 1966 General Elections. However, the circumstances of the 1980s (with the parallel of repeated Conservative victories) led to a re-emergence of the embourgeoisement thesis.

This link was made explicit by Peter Saunders, who wrote that 'The Conservative Party has secured three successive General Election victories since 1979 just as it did in the years from 1951 to 1959' (Saunders 1990, p. 112). He went on to argue the case for the re-emergence of embourgeoisement in the following terms:

> All this has led some sociologists to ask whether the embourgeoisement thesis was perhaps developed a quarter of a century in advance of its time. If the workers of the sixties were not shedding their class skin, what of the workers of the eighties and nineties?

(Saunders 1990, p. 112)

 How might sociologists attempt to test Peter Saunders' thesis? The original embourgeoisement thesis was tested by Goldthorpe et al. using a case study of Luton. Where might a case study be appropriately done to test Saunders' thesis? Can you think of a method other than a case study that could be used?

Fiona Devine (1992 a,b) has recently carried out a study updating Goldthorpe *et al's* 1969 study of Luton. Details of her work can be found later in this chapter on pages 39–40.

The Interactionist Model

Heath *et al.* (1985, 1991) have focused in their work on the continuing importance of class, but especially on the issue of subjective class identification. Two important methodological debates lie at the heart of their work, and underpin their disagreements with the proponents of the dealignment thesis.

First, there is a disagreement about how to measure class. Heath *et al.* argue that the popularly used advertising categories conflate important but different groups. For example, they lump together with the manual working class the manual self-employed and small business people as well as 'foremen and technicians'. This creates problems because 'It is the petty bourgeois which is the most Conservative class ... This plays havoc with the conventional manual/non-manual division' (Heath *et al.* 1985, p. 20).

Accordingly Heath *et al.* adopt a five-class model using the following categories:

1) the salariat (managers, professionals and administrators)

2) routine non-manual workers (clerks and secretaries)

3) the petty bourgeoisie (employers and the self-employed)

4) foremen and technicians

5) the working class (rank-and-file manual employees in industry and agriculture).

 *Why do you think there is no mention of the bourgeoisie in this classification?*

The effect of this reconceptualization of the classes can be seen in Table 2.11, which provides voting figures for 1987 based on Heath *et al.*'s class categories.

Table 2.11 Voting in 1987 by class using revised categories

	Salariat	Routine Non-manual	Petty bourgeoisie	Foremen and technicians	Working class
Conservative	56	52	65	39	31
Labour	15	26	16	36	48
Lib/SDP	29	23	20	24	21

Source: Adapted from Health *et al.* (1991)

Second, Heath *et al.* argue that Crewe's methodology yields figures for absolute class voting, whereas the important measure is of relative class voting. Absolute class voting is essentially calculated by adding together the middle-class Conservative voters and the working-class Labour voters and expressing this as a percentage of all voters. In contrast, relative voting refers to the relative strength of the political parties in different social classes. If Labour loses votes equally among both middle-class and working-class people, absolute voting will decline but relative voting will not. This is because the proportion of Labour's votes coming from the working class remains the same. Heath *et al.* claim this is a better measure of the extent to which support for the parties is class based. They express this measure in the form of what they call an odds ratio.

Absolute and relative figures for elections since the Second World War are given in Table 2.12. There is no difference in the figures for absolute voting provided by Crewe and by Heath *et al.*, but there is a difference in the figures for relative class voting (as can be seen by examining the 1979 and 1983 elections), and this is a function of the very different models of social class used in the two sets of research. When interpreting figures for relative class voting you need to be aware of this potential problem.

Table 2.12 Absolute and relative votes in General Elections, 1945–92

	1945	1950	1951	1955	1969	1964	1966
Absolute	62%	62%	67%	65%	61%	63%	66%
Relative (Heath)	4.8	5.5	6.3	5.9	6.1	6.4	6.4
	1970	1974	1974	1979	1983	1987	1992
Absolute	60%	55%	54%	55%	47%	48%	51%
Relative (Heath)	4.5	5.7	4.8	3.7	3.9		
Relative (Crewe)				2.6	3.0	2.6	2.4

Source: Adapted from Heath *et al.* (1985) and Crewe (1993)

You should be able to locate a copy of Heath et al.*'s* How Britain Votes *in a local reference or higher education library if your school/college library does not possess it. Refer to this to find out in detail how the odds ratio is calculated. Do you find the notion of relative class voting convincing? What other areas of sociology involve debates about absolute and relative definitions?*

According to Heath *et al.*, the relative voting figures they have produced do not show a constant decline in class voting, but rather trendless fluctuation. They reject theories of constant class dealignment, which were based on the idea that long-term social changes threaten Labour's electoral base as the old traditional working class declines. Using statistical techniques, they claim to have demonstrated that changing social factors can only account for about a quarter of the actual changes in the vote. The rest is to be explained by short-term political factors that may act to the benefit of either party at different times, hence there is no reason to believe the Labour Party is in inevitable decline. One important factor is the growth in the number of Liberal candidates: 'In the earlier elections the Liberals did not field candidates in every constituency, and Liberal candidates were particularly lacking in Labour-held working-class seats' (Heath *et al.* 1991, p. 24).

Their explanation for Labour's lack of success at the polls is squarely based on political factors that led to a decline in Labour voters but cannot be explained by social changes alone:

> The commentators had confused the decline of Labour in the 1950s with the decline of class. . . . Contemporary accounts of the decline of class are no more plausible than those of the 1950s. The commentators once again confused a decline in overall support for Labour with a decline in its relative class support. . . . Labour remained a class party in 1983; it was simply a less successful class party than before.
>
> (Heath *et al.* 1985, p. 29)

A second explanation offered by Heath *et al.* for the fall in the Labour vote is disappointment in the actual experience of Labour governments: 'Labour's working-class supporters may have been particularly disillusioned by its failures to pursue working-class interests when in office in the late 1960s and mid 1970s' (Heath *et al.* 1991, p. 79).

Heath *et al.* therefore deny that there has been a massive transformation in class self-image as portrayed in the models that emphasize increased divisions inside the working class: 'There is no direct sociological evidence that such a transformation has occurred. Certainly, classes today are much like the classes of yesterday in their self-image' (Heath *et al.* 1991, p. 78).

Criticisms of Heath et al.

Crewe (1986) has made a number of criticisms of Heath *et al's* work. He argues that their primary concentration on the salariat and the working class in their calculation of odds ratios can only explain a minority of the vote since these two classes together made up only 45 per cent of the electorate in the 1983 election. It is further argued that since their odds ratio can only look at movements between two parties it is ill suited to three-party elections. The notion of the centrality of class can only be maintained by ignoring the growth of the Alliance, whose support is not distinctively class based.

W.L. Miller provides the following example of this criticism:

> Their evidence suggests that if we could ignore the growth of Alliance voting and if we could ignore the changing class structure then there was not much evidence of class dealignment. But, of course, we cannot ignore these changes. The growth of Alliance voting meant that increasing numbers of voters opted for a party that did not represent class interests.
>
> (Miller 1992, p. 49)

In *Understanding Political Change* (1991) Heath *et al.* have responded to similar criticisms. They reject the assertion that the Liberal Democrats draw their support evenly across the class structure. On the contrary, their support is heavily skewed towards the middle class. If the Liberal Democrats' support among middle-class voters is included alongside support for the Conservatives, the decline in absolute voting is much less pronounced than it otherwise appears.

Heath *et al.* also see the rise of the Alliance as one of the key political factors that can explain the changing voting situation. In 1970 the Liberals contested only about half of all constituencies, but by the 1980s they were contesting almost every seat. In 1970 their candidates stood mainly in middle-class areas, and their expansion therefore largely took them into Labour working-class areas.

The Social Class Model

Another piece of research that has defended the continuing centrality of class is the work of Marshall *et al.* These authors also argue that the kind of divisions seen in the working class, particularly in the work of Crewe, are not new at all but have always been there. On the basis of an extensive survey Marshall *et al.* (1988) conclude that, of all the possible bases for political identification, social class remains predominant.

> Modern Britain is a society shaped predominantly by class rather than other forms of social cleavage . . . our data suggests that, in so far as identities, beliefs and values . . . are socially structured, then the source of this structuring lies in social class differences rather than more fashionable sectoral cleavages.
>
> (Marshall *et al.* 1988, pp. 183–4)

1) What evidence can you find to back up the assertions made in this passage?
2) Explain 'sectoral cleavage' and 'other forms of social cleavage'.

The Social Class Model recognizes that divisions exist; the crucial disagreement with the proponents of the idea of a fragmenting working class is over the extent to which this is a new phenomenon:

> These arguments are the probable consequence of a tendency towards dualistic historic thinking whereby a communitarian and solidaristic proletariat of some bygone heyday of class antagonism is set against the atomized and consumer-oriented working class of today. Historical data suggests a less romantic reality: sectionalism, privatism and instrumentalism have always been close to the surface of working-class life.
>
> (Marshall *et al.* 1988, p. 206)

Use your sociology textbooks to examine studies of working-class communities.
Which studies support this assertion? Which do not?
How far do you agree with Marshall?

Support for the continued importance of class comes from the recent research of Fiona Devine (1992 a, b). In order to test the salience of class and other identities in the 1980s, Devine interviewed workers in Luton to provide a qualitative update of the classical affluent worker study of Goldthorpe *et al.* She found that in the 1980s 77 per cent of her sample of Luton workers still identified with the Labour Party although some of them did not actually vote Labour (see Table 2.13).

Why might people who identify with Labour not want to vote for them? Does
this identification have any concrete political effect?

Devine concluded that, although there are a mixture of bases for social identity, social class is still predominant:

Table 2.13 Political allegiances of Devine's interviewees, 1992

Political allegiance	Interviewees
Labour Party supporters	24
Disillusioned Labour Party supporters[a]	24
Conservative Party supporters	14
Total	62

[a] This category includes voters who were previously loyal to Labour but did not vote for them in the 1980s.

Source: Devine (1992a), p. 245

> Contrary to the arguments of proponents of the class dealignment and consumption cleavages debate ... a clear association between class and party persisted in these voters' minds. ... In sum, class was clearly the salient social identity informing the interviewees' political beliefs, attitudes and voting behaviour.
>
> (Devine 1992a, pp. 246–8)

Devine also saw political factors as central to explaining why some who identified with Labour did not vote for them in the 1980s, pointing out that her respondents cited in particular the previous record of Labour governments and divisions inside the party in the 1980s.

The Class Struggle Model

Callinicos and Harman (1987) focus on the dynamics of class struggle as a key explanation for the fluctuations in working-class support for the Labour Party. They argue that the assumption that the working class automatically votes Labour is false, and ignores the importance of the dynamics of class struggle in leading the working class to vote Labour. They note that there is nothing new about divisions in the working class and the effect of affluence. They quote one of the leaders of the nineteenth-century Chartist movement, writing in 1872:

> In our old Chartist times, it is true, Lancashire workmen were in rags by the thousands; and many of them lacked food . . . You would see them in groups discussing the great doctrine of political justice . . . Now you will see no groups in Lancashire. But you will hear well-dressed working men talk, with their hands in their pockets, of co-ops and their shares in them, or in building societies.
>
> (Thomas Cooper, quoted in Callinicos and Harman 1987, p. 10)

'Affluent workers' such as these nonetheless went on to play an important part in later industrial struggles, in particular those between 1880 and the late 1930s; these struggles led their protagonists to identify with the Labour Party. Callinicos and Harman maintain that the recent decline in working-class support for Labour is the result of the experience of Labour governments since those times, which has caused widespread disillusionment. However, a rise in industrial struggle as a result of anger at current Conservative policies might lead to a resurgence of collective values and renewed interest in socialism.

Conclusion

If the proponents of partisan dealignment and the fragmentation of the working class are right, then the Labour Party faces a bleak future. On the other hand, if those who argue that social class remains central are correct, then the changing social situation need not necessarily spell oblivion for the Labour Party. If short-term political factors are crucial, future developments may well favour the Labour Party.

These issues lie at the heart of the debate over voting behaviour and also animate the debates inside the Labour Party on how (and if) to reform itself, and inside the Conservative Party in the post-Thatcher era. The next test of the theories we have examined will come in 1997 – or perhaps earlier.

Essay Questions

What do you understand by the term 'partisan dealignment'? To what extent, and why, has partisan dealignment occurred in British voting behaviour since 1964? (Oxford, June 1988)

To what extent do sociological evidence and arguments support the claim that there has been a realignment of voting behaviour in Britain? (AEB, June 1994)

To what extent has the concept of the 'deviant voter' been relevant and useful in sociological accounts of voting behaviour? (AEB, June 1995)

Coursework suggestions

1) Obtain detailed sociological data on the parliamentary constituency in which you live. You could use information from the 1991 Census for this. Then obtain detailed results of the elections, both local and general, in your area. You will need to obtain results for all the local council wards within your parliamentary constituency. You can get this by looking at local council election results for your area. Consider how the theories of voting behaviour might help explain the variations that occur within your area.

2) Devise a questionnaire to test the relative importance of social class and other possible social identities or sectoral cleavages in the formation of political identities for a representative sample of electors within your area.

Bibliography

Abercrombie, N., Hill, S. and Turner, B. (1980) *The Dominant Ideology Thesis*, London: Allen & Unwin

Butler, D. and Kavanagh, D. (1992) *The British General Election of 1992*, London: Macmillan

Butler, D. and Stokes, D. (1974) *Political Change in Britain*, 2nd edn, London: Macmillan

Callinicos, A. and Harman, C. (1987) *The Changing Working Class*, London: Bookmarks

Crewe, I. (1984) 'The electorate: partisan dealignment ten years on', in Berrington, H. (ed.) *Change in British Politics*, London: Frank Cass, pp. 183–215

—— (1985) 'Can Labour rise again?', *Social Studies Review*, September

—— (1986) 'On the death and resurrection of class voting: some comments on How Britain Votes', *Political Studies*

—— (1987) 'Why Mrs Thatcher was returned with a landslide', *Social Studies Review*, September

—— (1992) 'Why did Labour lose (yet again)?', *Politics Review*, September

—— (1993) 'The changing basis of party choice 1979–92', *Politics Review*, February

Crewe, I. *et al.* (1977) 'Partisan dealignment in Britain, 1964–1974', *British Journal of Political Science*, Vol. 7, pp. 129–90

Dearlove, J. and Saunders, P. (1991) *Introduction to British Politics*, 2nd edn, Cambridge: Polity

Devine, F. (1992a) 'Social identities, class identity and political perspectives', *Sociological Review*, May

—— (1992b) *Affluent Workers Revisited: Privatism and the Working Class*, Edinburgh: Edinburgh University Press

Downs, D. (1957) *An Economic Theory of Democracy*, New York: Harper & Row

Dunleavy, P. and Husbands, C. (1985) *British Democracy at the Crossroads*, London: George Allen & Unwin

Edgell, S. and Duke, V. (1991) *A Measure of Thatcherism*, London: Routledge

Giddens, A. (1989) *Sociology*, Cambridge: Polity Press

Goldthorpe, J., Lockwood, D., Bechhofer, F. and Platt, J. (1969) *The Affluent Worker in the Class Structure*, Cambridge: Cambridge University Press

Hall, S. and Jacques, M. (eds) (1983) *The Politics of Thatcherism*, London: Lawrence & Wishart

Heath, A. (1992) 'Social class and voting in Britain', *Sociology Review*, April

Heath, A., Jowell, R. and Curtice, J. (1985) *How Britain Votes*, Oxford: Pergamon

Heath, A. *et al.* (1991) *Understanding Political Change,* Oxford: Pergamon

Himmelweit, H., Humphreys, P. and Jaeger, M. (1985) *How Voters Decide,* Milton Keynes: Open University Press

Hoffman, J. (1988) 'The life and times of Antonio Gramsci', *Social Studies Review,* January

Leeds, C. (1986) *Politics in Action,* Cheltenham: Thornes

Lukes, S. (1984) 'The future for British socialism', in Pimlott, B. (ed.) *Fabian Essays in Socialist Thought,* London: Heinemann

Marshall, G. (1987) 'What is happening to the working class?', *Social Studies Review,* January

Marshall, G., Rose, D., Newby, H. and Vogler, C. (1988) *Social Class in Modern Britain,* London: Unwin Hyman

Miliband, R. (1985) 'The new revisionism in Britain', *New Left Review,* March

Miller, W.L. (1992) 'Voting and the electorate', in P. Dunleavy (ed.), *Developments in British Politics 3,* London: Macmillan

Parkin, F. (1968) *Middle Class Radicalism,* Manchester: Manchester University Press

Riley, M. (1989) 'Theories of voting', *Social Studies Review,* September

Saunders, P. (1990) *Social Class and Stratification,* London: Routledge

Slattery, M. (1991) *Key Ideas in Sociology,* London: Macmillan

Smith, A. (1776) *The Wealth of Nations,* 1910 edn, London: Dent

Zweig, F. (1961) *The Worker in an Affluent Society: Family Life and Industry,* London: Heinemann

Political participation, gender and ethnicity

Gender and politics

Women are notably absent from what is conventionally seen as 'politics' in Britain . . . Women are assumed to be less able at carrying out political tasks than men and less interested in politics. Political sociology has tended in the past to accept this common-sense view of women's relationship to politics and to give it scientific authority.

(Abbott and Wallace 1990, p. 184)

Refer to the politics and sociology books in your library and try to locate any concrete examples of such assumptions. You will find a number of examples in this chapter, but try to add your own.
Do you agree with the view expressed here about the approach of political sociologists in the past? How far has this situation changed?

This attitude has been seriously challenged by, among other things, the rise of feminist theory and political movements and the changed status of women in society. Criticism of earlier political sociology has focused on two key points:

1) The arguments purporting to show that women are less involved than men in 'conventional' politics are in some cases wrong, and ignore the possible causes of lower levels of participation where they do exist.

2) The definition of politics used is too narrow.

Looking at the first point, even if we accept conventional politics (meaning effectively Westminster and Whitehall) as the central arena of political activity, we cannot assume that the relative lack of women (after the 1992 General Election there were 60 women MPs out of a total of 651) is due to lack of interest and therefore personal choice on women's part; it may be due to social and political factors.

Worsley (1973) has argued that we need to make a distinction between Politics I and Politics II. Politics I refers to the exercise of constraint in any relationship, while Politics II refers to the machinery of government. It may be that the relative lack of women in Politics II is due to the effects of Politics I; in other words, the unequal position of women in their everyday relationships with men inhibits their involvement in public life. Carole Pateman's work on the sexual contract highlights the effect of the continuing oppression of women in the private sphere on their activities in the public sphere, where they have formal equality (Pateman 1988).

The issue of private and public spheres underlay the second point made by feminist thinkers when they demanded a reconceptualization of the meaning of politics. Lovenduski and Randall (1993) sum up this argument as follows: 'Feminism insists the personal is political and rejects both in theory and practice the entire distinction between private and public spheres' (p. 5)

Think about what the slogan 'The personal is political' actually means. Try to think of a number of issues that may be considered political on this basis.

Women's participation in state-oriented politics

In summarizing the claims of writers who believe there is a major gender difference in political participation and attitudes, Randall (1987) argues that the following points are consistently made:

- Women are less interested than men in politics.

- Women are less likely to vote.

- Women are more likely to be Conservative.

- Women are more moralistic than men.

- Women personalize politics.

- Women's political behaviour is strongly influenced by men.

Recent debate has focused on the validity of these statements and has also involved investigating the methodology employed by the largely male researchers whose conclusions these are.

Are women less interested than men in politics?

One example of the kind of work that has lent support to such a proposition is a study by Stradling, who found that females showed lower levels of political knowledge than males; for example, 8 per cent of girls but 15 per cent of boys showed knowledge of political institutions, and 29 per cent of girls but 51 per cent of boys showed knowledge of political office holders. This study (quoted in Wormald, 1982, p. 202) was based on a survey of 4,033 children in 100 schools.

In contrast, Dowse and Hughes (1972) found only marginal differences. In a study of a secondary modern school, 26 per cent of boys and 27 per cent of girls expressed interest in politics, while the figures for a grammar school were 44 per cent of boys and 43 per cent of girls.

Two of the most comprehensive books on women and politics are Randall (1987) and Lovenduski and Randall (1993). Both are extremely useful for source material in this area. If they are not available in your school/college library you should be able to locate them at a local higher education library.

A debate has arisen over the methodology used in such studies. Delamont (1980) has argued that there is often a 'male' bias in lists of issues presented to people in an attempt to elicit their degree of interest in and consideration of the importance of various political issues. In particular she cites the list from Butler and Stokes (1974) reproduced in Table 3.1. Delamont comments:

Table 3.1   Butler and Stokes' Feeling Thermometer

There is a slightly different way that I want to ask you how you feel towards certain places or people. This card has what we call a 'feeling thermometer'. (*Interviewer hands card to respondent.*) If you don't know too much about one of the places or people that I'm going to ask you about, or don't feel particularly warm or cold towards them, then you should place them in the middle, at the 50° mark. If you have warm feelings towards them, you should give them a score somewhere between 50° and 100° depending on how warm your feeling is. On the other hand, if you don't feel very favourable towards them you should place them somewhere between the 0° and 50° mark. First of all, I would like to ask you your feeling towards the Queen and Royal Family. Where would you place the Queen and the Royal Family on the thermometer according to your feeling towards them?

	Average Temperature	
	1969	1970
The Queen and Royal Family	77	78
Unofficial strikers	20	22
The BBC	63	—
The Common Market	46	38
Harold Wilson	45	56
The Liberal Party	48	53
The upper classes	50	—
Coloured immigrants	54	38
Edward Heath	53	58
Scottish Nationalists	42	41
Barbara Castle	45	—
Civil servants	51	—
The Commonwealth	65	65
The working classes	74	74
Enoch Powell	57	59
America	58	—
The Conservative Party	61	61
Trade Unions	49	50
Roy Jenkins	46	—
Comprehensive schools	61	62
The Labour party	48	57
The police	79	82
The middle classes	63	65
London	67	—
Jeremy Thorpe	—	58
Parliament	—	73
Other Labour leaders	—	51
Other Conservative leaders	—	56

Source: Butler and Stokes (1974), p. 454

The lists used do not include those issues which women's political campaigns have been focused on since the full granting of the suffrage in 1928. Reading history or politics, one would never know that there had been female campaigns but there have been a great many in the last 50 years, and they might reasonably be included in a researcher's definition of what constitutes politics. Yet they never are. Nor do the lists include any of the issues of particular concern to women as a whole.

(Delamont 1980, p. 174)

To what extent do you agree with Delamont's criticisms of Butler & Stoke's list? What female campaigns do you think she has in mind?

Most researchers conclude that gender differences are marginal, and Delamont argues that the contention that women show lower levels of knowledge and interest in politics is not proven.

Devise a series of questionnaires to test Delamont's hypothesis that there is a 'male' bias in the lists of issues used to test people's interest in politics, and that as a result women's interest in politics is understated. What might you expect to find if Delamont is right?

One method might be to draw up three questionnaires, one containing 'male' issues, one 'female' and one a mixture of both. You could then apply these to similar samples of people. However, this method is not without problems. Can you think what they might be?

Devise an improved method for testing Delamont's hypothesis and conduct a small survey. Report your findings back to the rest of your class.

In fact one clear theme of recent work has been the increasing participation of women. As evidence of this we can cite Table 3.2, drawn from Lovenduski and Randall (1993). These authors argue that women are participating in greater numbers in traditional political institutions partly because political parties and trade unions are becoming more hospitable to women's concerns, and they see this as a diffusion of broadly feminist demands into new quarters.

Table 3.2 Women's participation in parliamentary politics

	Women as percentage of	
	Candidates	MPs
CON		
1979	5.0	2.3
1983	6.3	3.3
1987	7.3	4.5
1992	9.8	6.0
LAB		
1979	8.3	4.1
1983	12.3	4.8
1987	14.5	9.2
1992	21.3	13.0

Source: Adapted from Lovenduski and Randall (1993), p. 156

A study of the Labour Party by Seyd and Whiteley (1992) found 39 per cent of members in their survey to be women, and an equivalent survey of the Conservative Party (Whiteley, Seyd and Richardson 1994) found 49 per cent of members to be women.

Find out how the position of the Liberal Democrats compares with that of the two other parties cited here. If you are unable to find this information in the library contact The Women's Organisation, Liberal Democrats, 4 Cowley Street, London SW1P 3NB (Tel: 0171 222 7999). If you write, enclose a SAE.

The 1992 General Election saw the election of thirty-seven women as Labour MPs, twenty as Conservative MPs, two as Liberal Democrat MPs and one as a Scottish National Party MP. These figures do show an increase in women's participation, and this may partly be explained by the success of the women's movement in campaigning for the removal of barriers to participation. This has included discussion over the timing and location of meetings, which have sometimes effectively excluded women from involvement.

Figure 3.1

Timing and location of union meetings

Source: Labour Research Department *Part-time Workers*, London: LRD; reproduced in Buswell (1989), p. 123

Why is the place meetings are held relevant to the participation of women? Are there any other groups who might be excluded by a meeting such as the one portrayed in the cartoon?
You should be able to find out where the meetings of political parties in your area are held. How far does this evidence support Lovenduski and Randall's assertion that political parties are becoming more hospitable to women's needs?

It is these barriers, rather than any lack of interest, that prevented women from becoming involved in politics. The fact that women campaigned for the removal of such obstacles undermines the notion that they are somehow not interested, and the partial success of such campaigns has allowed women to participate more fully and has thus further undermined the argument that women are indifferent to politics.

In conclusion, it seems that women are becoming increasingly active in politics as barriers to their participation are slowly dismantled, a development that is itself largely the result of women's political activity.

Are women more Conservative than men?

One of the most sweeping examples of this claim was Richard Rose's statement in 1974 that 'it is technically correct to say that an exclusively male franchise would give Labour a victory at every British General Election and an exclusively female franchise would give the Conservatives recurring victories' (quoted in Wormald 1982, p. 195).

The key to this claim was Rose's finding that there was a greater tendency for working-class women than working-class men to vote Conservative. However, Randall (1987, p. 70) has pointed out that the total gap between men and women in Rose's study amounted to only 2.5 percentage points, and Delamont (1980, p. 176) argues that the class of these women was determined by the their husbands' occupations and therefore might not reflect either their own subjective class identity or indeed their objective class identity if this had been measured independently of their husbands.

Randall (1987, p. 71) has also pointed out that class and age divisions interact with gender to provide the impression that women are more conservative than men. The elderly are more likely to vote Conservative and so are those in higher social classes, and as Milne and MacKenzie point out: 'until recently higher death rates occurred in the lower social groups and among males, so that the longer-lived tended to be women of the higher social strata' (quoted in Randall 1987, p. 71).

Wormald (1982) also notes that between 1974 and 1979 the swing to the Conservative Party was 7 per cent among men but only 4 per cent among women. Nonetheless this still left a 9 percentage point lead for the Conservatives among women while the difference was only 5 per cent for men. The gender gap was still there, but it was declining. It appears that the gap continued to reduce in 1983 and 1987, when the Conservative Party lost its advantage in attracting women's votes (see Table 3.3).

Table 3.3 Gender and age differences in voting patterns, 1987 General Election

	Men	Women	Age			
			18–22	23–44	45–64	65+
Unlikely to vote	9	8	20	9	4	5
Conservative	44	43	43	38	50	45
Labour	32	31	32	32	29	35
Alliance	22	24	20	27	20	20
Nationalist	2	2	2	2	1	1
Other	0.8	0	2	0.4	0	0

Source: Reid (1989), p. 347

 How far does Table 3.3 support the notion that the supposed greater tendency for women to vote Conservative is in fact related to age factors rather than gender?

Ironically, therefore, the period when there was a women leading the Conservative Party also saw the erosion of the Conservatives' lead among women voters, an irony underlined by the finding that in the 1992 General Election, after John Major had replaced Mrs Thatcher, 'reversing the trend of the previous two general elections,

women were apparently slightly more inclined to vote Conservative than men'
(Lovenduski and Randall 1993, p. 54).

The Report of the National Executive Committee of the Labour Party to the 1993
Labour Party Conference contains the following comment on the voting patterns
shown in Table 3.4:

Table 3.4 Gender differences in voting patterns, General Elections 1979–92

	Con percentage	Lab percentage	Lib-Dem percentage
Men			
1979	43	39	13
1983	41	30	26
1987	41	33	23
1992	39	38	18
Women			
1979	46	36	15
1983	44	28	26
1987	43	31	23
1992	43	34	18

Source: Labour Party NEC (1993), p.38

Post General Election (1992) analysis based on exit polls showed a pronounced gender gap. The difference in Conservative/Labour voting
between men and women widening from four per cent to eight per cent
since 1987. This was the biggest gender gap since 1979. Amongst the
youngest voters, the gender gap worked in the opposite direction, with a
majority of women supporting Labour. . . .

In response to the 'gender gap' a priority project was established by the
NEC . . . The gender gap project commenced in February 1993 and
agreed a programme of research and activities. These were designed to
explore the nature and the underlying reasons for the gender gap.

(Labour Party NEC 1993, p. 38)

Imagine that you are a group of researchers employed by the Labour Party on
this project. Devise a written report outlining proposed areas and methods of
research which could be conducted over six months on a budget of £40,000.
Present your detailed research proposal to the rest of the class.

Is women's political behaviour strongly influenced by men?

A number of commentators have made this assertion; a particularly striking example
is given by Duverger, writing in 1955:

While women have legally ceased to be minors they still have the mentality
of minors in many fields, and, particularly in politics, they usually accept
paternalism on the part of men. The man, husband, fiancé, lover or myth,
is the mediator between them and the political world.

(Quoted in Wormald 1982, p. 202)

Another statement embodying this assumption comes from Lazersfeld *et al.* (1968), who state: 'The almost perfect agreement between husband and wife comes about as a result of male dominance in political situations' (quoted in Randall 1987, p. 69). Randall points out that this assertion flatly contradicts the notion that women are more Conservative than men.

Goot and Reid (1975) again question the validity of such findings on the basis of a detailed analysis of the methodology employed. They point out that men and women were interviewed separately, and not as couples, by mainly female interviewers. Delamont (1980) summarizes the effect of this as follows: 'Men are unlikely to admit to women interviewers that their wives form their political judgements, whereas women can make the reverse claim with no loss of face' (p. 177).

Despite the methodological problems there have been studies that suggest women have more influence over others' views, particularly their children's, than men do. This was what Madgewick *et al.* (1973) found in a study of political socialization in Wales, for instance.

Studies that have found evidence of greater male influence do not necessarily attribute this to individual women yielding to individual men in a social vacuum, but point instead to the unequal distribution of power inside families.

Explaining the inequalities in participation

Despite increases in participation, women remain a minority at most levels of political activity. (See Figure 3.2, page 52) This needs explaining. One argument is that the professional life of a politician is not conducive to family responsibility, which is still seen as primarily a woman's task. Randall (1987, p. 125) highlights this factor when she states that 'of the 27 women MPs elected in October 1974, only two had children under 10 years of age. Nine years later, in 1983, this was still true.'

The relative underrepresentation of women in Parliament poses considerable problems for women generally. Issues of importance to women are debated in a male-dominated arena where most of the participants may be ignorant of the realities of the issue in question. A classic example is that the women's movement led the campaign for sexual equality laws, yet women had little influence over the way these laws were actually drafted and implemented since this was done by a male-dominated Parliament.

Despite the recent increase in the numbers of women entering Parliament, the UK is still well below the EC average (13.2 per cent) in this respect, as can be seen from Figure 3.3.

The figure of 7.4 per cent for women in the UK Parliament is calculated by combining figures for both the House of Commons (9.2 per cent of MPs are women) and the House of Lords (6.5 per cent of peers are women). What might be the reason for the lower representation in the House of Lords? Hint: Part of the House of Lords is composed of hereditary peers.

There is an all-party organization known as the 300 Group whose aim is to increase the number of women elected to Parliament, local government and public life. Investigate how it proposes to do this. You might be able to find copies of its newsletter, 300 Group News, *at your local reference library, or you*

Figure 3.2

Women MPs in the UK

Source: *Guardian*, 7 September 1993

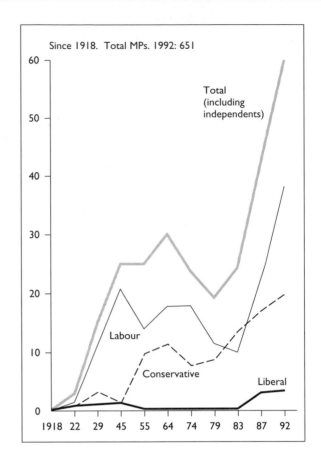

Figure 3.3

Women in parliament in the UK and other European countries

Source: *Guardian* 6 February 1993

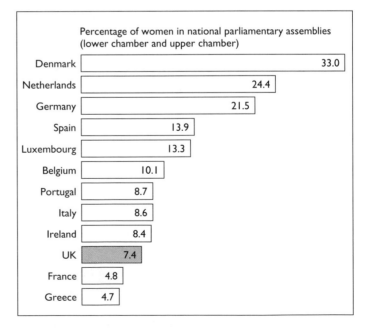

could write to them at 36–37 Charterhouse Square, London EC1M 6EA. In order to receive information you need to send an SAE.

Looking at the contemporary situation, Lovenduski and Randall (1993) argue that to some extent political parties, trade unions and other political institutions have begun to accommodate women's demands for a political voice. The greater strength of socialist ideas in the UK compared to the USA has meant that a greater proportion of feminists have tended towards socialist feminism, and radical feminism has been weaker than in the USA. Much of the 'incorporation' noted by Lovenduski and Randall has therefore taken place within the labour movement.

 The main broadly radical feminist publication in the UK before its demise in 1994 was Spare Rib. Feminist Review *presented a more socialist-feminist outlook. Locate back copies of these publications at a local higher education library. Conduct a content-analysis exercise to see if there are major differences in the views on feminism and the oppression of women presented in these journals.*

At the 1993 Conference of the Labour Party, the then Labour leader John Smith combined moves towards a one-member, one-vote (OMOV) system of selecting parliamentary candidates and electing leaders with the idea of a target of all-women shortlists in half the winnable seats that fall vacant. The reason for this move was that women candidates are more numerous in the less winnable seats at present, as shown by the figures in Table 3.5. The need for some form of positive discrimination was underlined by Barbara Follett of the pressure group Emily's List, who has calculated that if the present rate of change were to continue, it would take 200 years for Labour women to achieve equal representation in Parliament.

Table 3.5 Women MPs and candidates by party

	MPs	Cans	a	b	c
Con	17	62	4	7	42
	(5)	(10)	(8)	(8)	(15)
Lab	24	140	2	20	96
	(10)	(22)	(10)	(22)	(31)
LibDem	1	82	1	2	78
	(5)	(13)	(100)	(11)	(13)

Number (per cent in brackets) of women MPs and candidates (a) replacing retiring MPs, (b) in marginal seats and (c) in unwinnable seats.

Source: *Guardian*, 23 July 1991

However, Sarah Baxter (1993) argues that the proposal will have less impact than might be expected. The only way winnable seats fall vacant is when an MP retires, is deselected or expelled, and at the 1992 General Election there were twenty-four such vacancies created. If this trend were repeated at the next election there might be a total increase in women Labour MPs of no more than twelve.

'The personal is political': the Women's Liberation Movement

Pateman's work on the sexual contract is an attempt to explain how the distinction between a public sphere and a private sphere perpetuates the oppression of women and discourages discussion of these issues. Although women were given formal equality in the public sphere when they gained the vote in 1928, the recognition of a private sphere meant there was an area where the state would not intervene ('an Englishman's home is his castle') and therefore male oppression of women went unchallenged. It was not seen as an issue for public political discussion.

The clear inequality of power inside the private sphere continued unchecked. For example, it was not illegal for a man to have sex with his wife without her consent until 1990. What happened in the private arena was not deemed a proper topic of political debate. Yet of course political decisions were made to deem the proper place for women to be acting as a housewife in the home, and then to deem that this arrangement was a purely personal matter in which the state should not intervene.

Rejection of the distinction between public and private spheres was central in the demands of the various women's movements for a reconceptualization of 'politics', leading to perhaps the most famous feminist slogan: 'The personal is political.' As Abbott and Wallace explain:

> Feminists argue that the very division between public and private is a patriarchal idea used to exclude women and women's concerns from politics. They argue that women have been excluded from participation in politics and public life and that the state has construed the family as private – as an institution outside of state intervention. In this way, in the name of personal freedom and privacy, the arena in which women are most exploited and subordinated is exempted from political intervention.

(Abbott and Wallace 1990, p. 189)

Figure 3.4

What is feminism?

Source: Watkins, Rueda and Rodrigues (1992), p. 3

Feminism and the various strands of the women's movement enabled women to make the connection between their personal lives and political structures, and this enabled them to discuss what had previously been seen as non-political in a political way.

Anna Coote and Beatrix Campbell outline one important way this link occurred in relation to Britain:

> We asked a large number of women what they remember as being most influential in leading them to feminism in the early stage of the movement. We were struck by how many mentioned in almost the same breath the Ford strike and a paper written by an American, Anne Koedt, which had begun to circulate on ill-typed roneoed sheets among British women in 1969.

> (Campbell and Coote 1987, p. 10)

The Ford strike in question took place in 1968 when women sewing machinists in Dagenham and then Halewood went on strike for equal pay with male workers. This was the first equal pay strike in British history and led eventually after another strike to a victory in April 1985. The paper written by Anne Koedt, entitled 'The myth of the vaginal orgasm', showed that the clitoris and not the vagina was the centre of sexual pleasure for women and described how this fact had been suppressed in favour of an emphasis on penetrative sex. The impact of this paper underlines the concern of the women's movement with oppression in both the public and the private spheres of life.

Randall (1987, p. 234) quotes figures for the British feminist movement in 1983 as comprising about 300 groups, composed of 10,000 activists with another 20,000 sporadically active. The core of the movement consisted of about 2,000 each of radical and socialist feminists. How does this compare with other political movements and organizations in terms of membership?

While feminists might share a desire for autonomy from men, this issue created a division inside the women's movement. Radical feminists argued that all men oppressed all women through a system they entitled patriarchy, based on the way reproduction is organized and also on male physical violence. They held that the oppression of women could not be entirely explained on economic grounds. It follows from such a view that socialism will not necessarily liberate women, and secondly that women must organize separately from men.

Socialist and Marxist feminists placed a greater emphasis on the oppression of women as it derives from their secondary position in the workplace and the economic sphere. They argued that under the capitalist system the workforce must be reproduced at the cheapest possible cost, and it was to this end that women's role was defined as primarily related to the home, which in turn affected their position in the labour market. One implication of this view is that both working-class men and women suffer from capitalism and they have a common interest in fighting it together.

Debates between these two positions dominated the early women's movement in this country, and this is reflected in the slogans that were adopted.

The first four aims of the Women's Liberation Movement adopted as the slogans for marches in London and Liverpool on International Women's Day in March 1971 were:

- *Equal pay*
- *Equal education and job opportunities*
- *24-hour nurseries*
- *Free contraception and abortion*

In 1975 and 1978 the following were added:

- *An end to discrimination against lesbians and the right of all women to define their sexuality*
- *Freedom from violence and sexual coercion, regardless of marital status*
- *An end to all laws, assumptions and institutions that perpetuate male dominance and men's aggression towards women*

Consider the extent to which each of these demands reflects a broadly radical feminist or socialist/Marxist feminist position.

Lovenduski and Randall (1993) believe that feminism in the 1980s and 1990s can be seen as having the following features:

- greater diversity

- a decline

- deradicalization

- growing involvement in state agencies, notably local government.

They argue that although the women's liberation movement in this country consisted in the beginning mainly of women inside socialist organizations it grew quickly and drew in women who had no such involvement, and this contributed to the splits between radical and socialist feminists. In the 1980s this split has continued, with socialist feminists focusing on the Labour Party as a result of the increasing influence of feminist ideas in that organization. In particular, Lovenduski and Randall cite the growth of women's committees in Labour councils, notably the GLC. At the same time radical feminists have organized mainly around various autonomous women's centres.

One of the problems the women's movement came to face, according to Lovenduski and Randall, was the question of difference. The idea of the difference between men and women was central to the movement, but 'The recognition of competing political identities – the acknowledgement of difference – was a watershed for British feminism, marking clearly its fragmentation. It undermined the basic premise of Feminism, that all women share some common political interests' (Lovenduski and Randall 1993, p. 89). There were, for example, differences between black and white women, and lesbians and heterosexual women.

Explain in your own words the reasons given by Lovenduski and Randall for the fragmentation of the women's movement.

Despite these problems, the ideas generated by feminism and the women's movement have had a broad impact in recent times. We can see their influence, for instance, in the Greenham Common women's peace camp, the miners' wives support groups and campaigns against pornography. Lovenduski and Randall make an overall assessment of the gains and losses of recent years as follows:

Gains

- The institutionalization and professionalization of the movement, with an increasing involvement in state agencies.

- A general diffusion of feminist values, bringing about changing attitudes towards women and their position in society.

Losses

- The decline and fragmentation of the movement and the growth of internal conflicts.

- The deradicalization of the movement.

Race and politics

If we react to white racism with a violent reaction, to me that's not black racism. If you come to me and put a rope around my neck and I hang you for it, to me that's not racism. Yours is the racism, but my reaction has nothing to do with racism.

(Malcolm X, speaking in 1963)

There were Africans in Britain before the English came here. They were soldiers in the Roman imperial army that occupied the southern part of our island for three and a half centuries.

(Fryer 1984, p. 1)

What point do you think Fryer is making in this statement?

John Solomos (1989) has pointed out that the issue of black people's participation in politics was largely ignored until the 1970s. The first significant mention came after the 1974 General Elections. Shamit Saggar makes broadly the same point: 'This apparent discovery of race within the world of psephology was largely initiated by the publication of an empirical study by the Community Relations Commission which concluded that black voters played a pivotal part in helping to elect a majority Labour Government in the October 1974 General Election' (Saggar 1993, p. 9).

Since that time debate has focused on the extent to which race and ethnicity are a distinctive factor influencing voting and political participation generally.

One way of considering how ethnic minorities think about politics is to look at the issues they are concerned about and make comparisons with the views of the ethnic majority. Information on this subject is contained in Table 3.6.

Table 3.6 The two most important issues for voting in the 1987 General Election, by ethnic group (%)

Issue	White percentage	Afro-Caribbean percentage	Asian percentage
Unemployment	45	70	65
Health	32	25	34
Education	19	13	17
Defence	37	18	32
Law and order	6	4	11
Pensions	9	7	6
Housing	5	21	–
Prices	7	15	10
Race	1	–	1

Table 3.6 helps us to consider whether there are differences between whites and ethnic minorities, and also whether differences exist between ethnic minority groups. Table 3.7 addresses the second question in more detail but in relation to a slightly earlier period.
Compare and contrast these two pictures of ethnic minorities' political concerns.

Table 3.7 Political priorities of Asian and Afro-Caribbean voters in 1983 (%)

The most important election issues*	Asians intending to vote (%)						Afro-Caribbeans intending to vote (%)					
	All	Con	Lab	Alliance	18–24	45+	All	Con	Lab	Alliance	18–24	45+
Unemployment (1)	71	39	79	72	70	73	67	57	72	56	72	67
Immigration/Nationality (4)	36	13	40	31	27	47	17	13	18	22	12	19
Cost of living (2)	19	34	16	19	17	11	27	30	28	39	34	30
Education (3)	17	26	14	19	23	10	23	30	21	28	28	13
Health Service (7)	13	12	13	19	11	13	13	17	14	–	9	18
Police/Law & Order (5)	8	29	6	14	9	11	16	13	17	6	14	13
Housing (5)	9	5	8	17	11	9	16	17	15	22	16	15
Nucl. weapons/defence (8)	9	5	9	8	17	7	8	17	8	17	9	11
Taxation (9)	5	24	3	3	3	6	3	4	3	11	2	5
Trade unions (10)	4	5	3	–	3	4	2	–	3	–	–	5

* listed by Asian ranking: Afro-Caribbean ranking in brackets
Source: Harris survey for *Black on Black/Eastern Eye* Election Special, May 1983: quoted in O'Donnell (1991), p. 107

The conclusion drawn by the authors who produced both Tables 3.6 and 3.7 was that ethnicity does not appear to produce distinct outlooks on political issues. Saggar (1993) maintains that 'the empirical evidence of black political attitudes appears to point to a remarkable degree of similarity between black and white outlooks' (p. 11), and O'Donnell (1991) concludes that 'Even allowing for the importance of immigration, black voters appear to have similar concerns as white voters' (p. 106).

Immigration was an important issue in 1983 because of the 1981 Nationality Act, which was seen by some as racist. Investigate the controversy over this piece of legislation and write a short report of about 300 words.

However, we cannot assume that it is possible to read off people's voting behaviour from their attitudes, so we need to investigate this area of political activity directly to see if ethnicity does affect voting behaviour.

The first point to note is that overwhelmingly ethnic minorities appear to prefer the Labour Party. Table 3.8 summarizes the voting intentions of Asian and Afro-Caribbean voters in 1983 and 1987. One interesting difference between Asians and the rest of the population in this period relates to their greater swing to voting Conservative. While among the population as a whole there was a swing away from the Conservatives of 1.7 per cent between 1983 and 1987, among Asians there was a swing towards the Conservatives of 14 per cent. Several factors might help to explain this phenomenon.

Table 3.8   Voting intentions of Asian and Afro-Caribbean voters

	Asians		Afro-Caribbeans	
	1983	1987	1983	1987
Conservative	9	23	7	6
Labour	81	67	88	86
Alliance	9	10	5	7

Source: *Guardian*, 19 June 1987, quoted in Solomos (1989), p. 147

First, there is a high level of self-employment among some sections of the Asian population in this country. Geddes (1993, p. 49) states that while the workforce as a whole contains 16 per cent self-employed, among Indian men it rises to 23 per cent.

Second, Saggar (1993) makes reference to a study of social mobility among ethnic minorities conducted by Robinson (1990) which suggests that ethnic Indians may have experienced dramatic change in the 1980s, generally in an upward direction, whereas such changes were more modest for other ethnic groups, and this is reflected in changed voting intentions.

A third explanation invokes the alleged cultural conservatism of Asians in the UK. This point was made most forcefully by Nirj Deva, Conservative MP for Brentford and Isleworth, when he stated: 'Asians are naturally Conservative with a capital and a little "c". They believe in profits, in enterprise, home ownership, religious education, children and families – all of it is conservative and all the things that the party is talking about' (quoted in Geddes 1993, p. 44).

Devise a questionnaire to test this statement.

One problem with this type of analysis is that it does not explain why the majority of Asians still vote for the Labour Party, even taking into account the recent 14 per cent swing to the Conservatives. Solomos argues that this fact undermines the idea that ethnic minority voters are divided along class lines: 'although during both the 1983 and 1987 General Elections there was much speculation about a major move towards the Conservative Party by middle-class Asians and Afro-Caribbeans, the scale of the change does not support such generalizations' (Solomos 1989, p. 147)

Imagine that you are employed as a researcher by Conservative Central Office to investigate the 'ethnicity gap' revealed by voting figures for ethnic minorities.

Your employers are concerned at the large lead for Labour among ethnic minorities revealed by these figures. Draw up a research proposal outlining potential areas for investigation.

The class position of ethnic minorities as a whole does seem to offer a possible explanation for their bias towards Labour because their populations are relatively skewed towards the working class. Brown (1984) reported that the proportion of white men in the professional and managerial class was 19 per cent compared to 5 per cent of Afro-Caribbeans and 13 per cent of Asians, while the proportion of whites in semi-skilled or unskilled manual employment was 16 per cent compared to 35 per cent for Afro-Caribbeans and 40 per cent for Asians.

Another possible factor may be the age structure of ethnic minority populations. Ethnic minorities are generally younger than the population as a whole, and the young are more likely to vote Labour than older people. This point can be seen from Figure 3.5 and Table 3.9.

Figure 3.5

Ethnic minorities as a proportion of each age group of the population, Great Britain (average, spring 1984, 1985 and 1986)

Source: O'Donnell (1991), p. 120

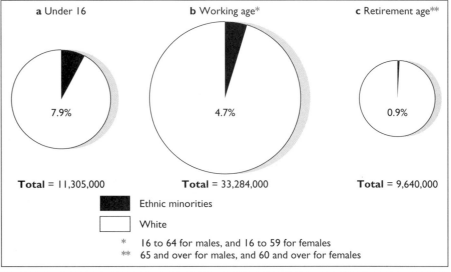

a Under 16	**b** Working age*	**c** Retirement age**
7.9%	4.7%	0.9%
Total = 11,305,000	**Total** = 33,284,000	**Total** = 9,640,000

■ Ethnic minorities
□ White

* 16 to 64 for males, and 16 to 59 for females
** 65 and over for males, and 60 and over for females

Table 3.9 Voting by age group in the 1992 General Election (all voters)

Age Group	% of votes			
	Con	*Lab*	*Lib-Dem*	*Con lead*
18–21	35	40	25	-5
22–29	43	41	16	-2
30–44	39	39	21	——
45–64	44	35	21	+9
65+	48	37	14	+11

Source: Adapted from Crewe (1992)

In conclusion, it seems that with the possible exception of views on immigration (which may be a factor deterring middle-class Asians and Afro-Caribbeans from voting Conservative) ethnic minorities do not have distinctive political views, and the ways their voting patterns diverge from those of whites can largely be explained in terms of their age and class structure.

Ethnic minority candidates for Parliament and local government

In the late 1970s and early 1980s there were demands for greater representation for ethnic minorities within the Labour Party. Solomos (1989) argues that among the factors fuelling this development were the inner-city riots in the early 1980s and the anti-racist policies of left-wing Labour councils. Out of this pressure crystallized a demand for Black Sections inside the Labour Party.

The black community (similarly in this respect to the women's movement) finds itself operating in two, not necessarily linked, arenas: there are community-based groups that are largely resisting incorporation, and there are increasing numbers of black activists elected as representatives through the conventional political parties.

In terms of Westminster politics, 1987 witnessed a major change. The four black MPs elected then (see Table 3.10) were the first black MPs since 1924. When Nirj Deva was elected in 1992 he became the first black Conservative MP since 1900. Nonetheless the six MPs elected in 1992 represent a mere 0.9 per cent of all MPs compared to an ethnic minority population of 3,005,050 or 5.9 per cent of the total for England and Wales, according to the 1991 Census.

Table 3.10 Black MPs

Name	Constituency	Party	Date first elected
Diane Abbott	Hackney N. & Stoke Newington	Labour	1987
Paul Boateng	Brent South	Labour	1987
Nirj Deva	Brentford & Isleworth	Conservative	1992
Bernie Grant	Tottenham	Labour	1987
Piara Khabra	Ealing Southall	Labour	1992
Keith Vaz	Leicester East	Labour	1987

It seems that the majority of blacks aspiring to a parliamentary career face similar hurdles to women candidates. In the 1987 election 75 per cent of black candidates were standing in effectively unwinnable seats (five of the six Conservatives, eight of the fourteen Labour and all seven Alliance candidates).

Geddes (1993) provides a comprehensive picture of ethnic minority representation in local government on the basis of a survey conducted in 1992. He discovered that there are 342 ethnic minority councillors in England and Wales, which is 1.6 per cent of the total of 21,065. This is a rise from 170 (0.7 per cent) in 1985. He found the following:

• There are now more Asian and Afro-Caribbean councillors than ever before.

• However, ethnic minorities are still under-represented in local government.

• Ethnic minority councillors are highly concentrated in urban areas, and crucially London. Some 57.3 per cent of ethnic minority councillors are in London (see Table 3.11), a city with a little over 40 per cent of the UK's ethnic minority population.

• There are clear differences in representation among different ethnic minority groups.

Table 3.11   Asian and Afro-Caribbean councillors in London by party

	Total	Labour	Conservative	LiberalDemocratic	Independent
Afro-Caribbean men	31	29	0	1	1
Afro-Caribbean women	24	20	2	0	2
Asian men	59	50	4	4	1
Asian women	10	8	0	2	0
Total	124	107	6	7	4

Source: Geddes (1993), p. 54

The group most likely to be councillors is Asian men (52.4 per cent of ethnic minority councillors), and Asians as a whole form 70 per cent of ethnic minority councillors.

- A clear majority of ethnic minority councillors are elected under the Labour Party banner – 85 per cent of the total.

Other forms of political participation

The black civil rights movement in the USA arose in response to oppression. In the Southern states of the USA black people faced legalized discrimination in the form of the 'Jim Crow laws' which enforced an effective system of apartheid. Black people were also frequently denied the right to vote, either through education or property qualifications designed to exclude them, or through physical harassment from the Ku Klux Klan. The effect can be seen in Figure 3.6. Black people in the Northern states were spared much of this direct repression, but still faced racism.

Figure 3.6

The American South in 1964

Source: Fairclough (1990), p. 135

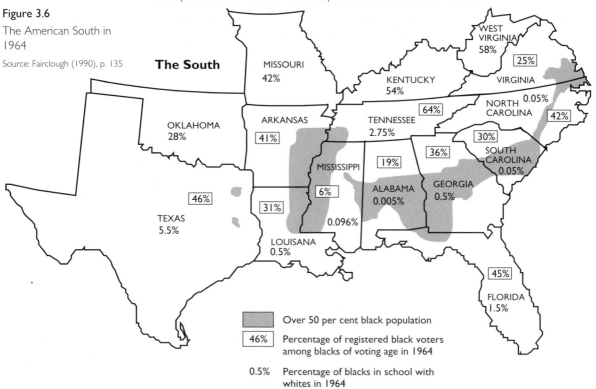

According to the figures provided on this map, which state appeared to have the worst record on civil rights for black Americans?

The civil rights movement secured victories with the passing of the 1964 Civil Rights Act and the 1965 Voting Rights Act by which blacks in the South eventually got the vote. The focus of the movement then shifted to the struggle against economic inequalities, and Martin Luther King launched the Poor People's Campaign, which attempted to unite white and black people against poverty. He made his last appearance at a rally in support of this campaign in Memphis, Tennessee; the following evening, 4 April 1968, he was assassinated.

Figure 3.7

The sharp end of bigotry: National Guard bayonets confront civil rights marchers in Memphis, Tennessee, 1968

Source: *Times Higher Education Supplement*, 10 June 1994

 How would you feel if you were on this march?

From the mid-1960s King's emphasis on non-violent direct action and the philosophy of integrating white and black which underlay the civil rights movement had been challenged by the rise of the slogan of 'black power'. This was partly a response to the hostility black people marching in Northern cities had faced from whites, and secondly sprang from a feeling that while the civil rights movement had brought gains for black people in the South, it had bypassed those in the North.

 The differences within the black civil rights movement are explored in Fairclough (1990) and Ovenden (1992), and in The Autobiography of Malcolm X *(1985). Use these books to write a short report outlining the major differences.*

The anger that fuelled the black power movement erupted in the Los Angeles district of Watts in 1965, where riots lasted six days and involved something like 15 per cent of the population. This was urban unrest on a scale not seen in the USA for decades. Despite King's opposition to violence, many black people saw riots as the only effective form of protest, and they continued: there were 38 in 1966, 128 in 1967 and 131 in the first half of 1968.

The slogan 'black power' suggested that the aim of integrating whites and blacks was unrealistic, and instead called upon blacks to organize separately. This black nationalist tradition found expression in several movements. The first was the Nation of Islam, whose most famous minister, Malcolm X, explained the philosophy of black nationalism in the following terms:

> The political philosophy of black nationalism means that the black man should control the politics and the politicians of his own community . . . The economic philosophy of black nationalism is pure and simple. It means only that we should control the economy of our community.
>
> (Quoted in Ovenden 1992, p. 69)

Towards the end of his life Malcolm X seems to have changed his views on the role of white people in the struggle against racism, but the black nationalist tradition continued through the Nation of Islam and then also the Black Panther Party.

There are several films now on video release that offer an insight into the rise of the black civil rights movement. Try to watch some of the following:

- *The title of* Mississippi Burning *is frighteningly descriptive of the film's content. The film itself aroused controversy when it was released because it deals with the fight against bigotry in Mississippi yet the leading characters are mostly white. Some critics suggested that this portrayed blacks in a passive way. Watch the film and see if you agree.*
- *Look out for Spike Lee's* Malcolm X, *which provides a detailed portrayal of the development and ideas of black nationalism.*
- *For an insight into contemporary life in black America watch John Singleton's* Boyz N the Hood.

Today black nationalism still thrives in the USA, as is evidenced by the continuing growth of the Nation of Islam whose current leader is Minister Louis Farrakhan. In the UK there is a branch of the Nation of Islam led by Minister Wayne X.

Some elements of the black political leadership have, however, been incorporated into mainstream political institutions. There has been a large rise in the number of black mayors in the USA, and Jesse Jackson, a former follower of Martin Luther King, ran a presidential campaign in 1984 and gained 26 per cent of the vote for the Democratic Party nomination.

Contemporary responses to racism

The issue of race and politics has become an important focus in political sociology in recent years for several interconnected reasons.

In the late 1980s and early 1990s across the whole of Europe there was a resurgence of neo-fascist movements with explicitly racist agendas. One of the key reasons adduced to explain this phenomenon is the re-emergence of mass unemployment to levels not seen since the 1930s, particularly in Europe.

In France the Front National led by Jean-Marie Le Pen gained 12.4 per cent of the vote in national elections in 1993, up from 9.6 per cent in 1988. In the UK Derek Beackon, a member of the neo-Nazi British National Party (BNP), was elected as a councillor in a by-election in September 1993 in Tower Hamlets. Although he lost his seat in subsequent council elections in May 1994, and none of the other fifty-one far-right candidates managed to win a seat, the vote for the far right remained quite high in some places, reaching 32 per cent for the BNP in parts of Newham and 28 per cent in parts of Tower Hamlets.

In Russia Vladimir Zhirinovsky obtained a large vote on an essentially fascist platform, and in Italy the new government of Silvio Berlusconi included five members of the neo-fascist Alleanza Nazionale in its cabinet.

These developments fuelled a major debate over how to respond to the growth of racism, partly reflecting the growing influence of members of ethnic minorities in traditional political organizations, and partly also the dissemination of the ideas of black nationalism.

 In an article in New Statesman and Society, 15 April 1994, John Pilger argues that we are witnessing the growth of respectable fascism. Obtain a copy of this article and answer the following questions:

    A) According to Home Office figures, how many times more likely are Asians to be attacked than any other racial group?

    B) How many racial attacks are there in Britain each year?

    C) What points does Pilger make about the role of the media?

    D) How far do you agree with the conclusions he reaches?

Perspectives on responses to racism

We have alluded to the growth of black nationalism in the UK. There have been calls for black self-defence groups, first heard after the urban riots of 1981 and 1985.

Besides the Labour Party Black Sections, another organization set up to combat racism is the Anti-Racist Alliance (ARA). This movement emphasizes that the strategy and tactics of how to fight racism must be determined by black people, but it does not exclude white people from participation. It has a large degree of support among Labour MPs and trade union leaders.

A different response has come from Marxist writers who have stressed that black people form a disadvantaged and oppressed part of the proletariat, and as such can combine with white workers to campaign against racism. Szymanski (1976) studied workers in the Southern states of the USA and found that where the levels of racism were highest, there was the greatest income inequality among whites. As a result he concluded that the white workers lost out from racism because it allowed the capitalists to divide the workforce.

Alexander (1987) argues there is no reason to doubt that the conclusions drawn by Szymanski apply to Britain too. He also points out that black people constitute 11 per cent of the population of the USA yet black nationalism did not succeed there, so it is unlikely to do so in the UK where black people constitute only about 5 per cent of the population. He concludes that a united working-class campaign against racism offers better prospects for success.

The largest organization espousing this idea is the Anti-Nazi League (ANL), whose slogans such as 'Black and white, unite and fight' are based on a Marxist understanding of the relationship between race and class. One indication of the support for the ANL's aims was the attendance of approximately 100,000 people at its carnival held in South London in May 1994 (see Figure 3.8).

Figure 3.8

ANL carnival, May 1994

Source: *New Musical Express*, 11 June 1994

Derek Beackon, briefly BNP councillor in Tower Hamlets, has been quoted by the Anti-Nazi League (ANL, 1994) as saying the following:

- On the Holocaust: 'Well no, I don't think anybody was deliberately exterminated by the Germans. It certainly wasn't six million Jews – maybe a couple of hundred thousand, but so what? Lots of others died in that war, didn't they?' (Today, 16 September 1993)
- On democracy: 'I am only going to represent the white people. I will not represent Asians. I will not do anything for them. They have no right to be in my great country.' (London Evening Standard, 17 September 1993)
  The Anti-Nazi League believes that parties such as the BNP can be identified as Nazi parties. Use any textbook to investigate the German Nazi party and consider whether you agree with the view of the BNP taken by the Anti-Nazi League.

Conclusion

There are increasing numbers of ethnic minority representatives in local and national government, but this still falls far short of representation proportionate to the demographic structure of the population as a whole. The main avenue for this increased representation appears to be the Labour Party and its Black Sections.

In the 1990s the re-emergence of racism and fascist movements has in response stimulated support for two contrasting organizations opposed to these views, the ARA and the ANL, with very differing views and strategies.

As we have noted, the spectre of mass unemployment across Europe appears to lie behind the Europe-wide rise of the far right and racist sentiment, and as a result it seems likely these issues will continue to be important for some time to come.

Essay Questions

1) What evidence is there that ethnic minorities are increasingly active in political life? What are the likely political consequences of such involvement? (Oxford, 1987)

2) 'One of the best researched findings in British politics is that women participate less and declare lower levels of interest than do men . . . women are less likely to vote than men. In general, women are more conservative politically and are usually less politically interested than men' (Dowse and Hughes, 1972, pp. 192–3). To what extent does sociological evidence support these contentions

Coursework suggestions

1) When considering the patterns of political participation of women, the relative importance of gender, class, and age are matters of considerable debate that affect the conclusions one draws. Devise a survey to test the levels of interest in politics among various social groups and then apply this questionnaire to a sample.

You will need to consider carefully the various problems involved in the construction of a sample, namely how to ensure you select a sample of women that will provide you with data on all these variables and whether to include a sample of men for comparison purposes.

Use your findings to test the various theories relating to the involvement of women in political activity. You could also include questions that aim to investigate the relative importance of the structural barriers to the involvement of women mentioned by many researchers in this area.

2) Find out about the representation of women and/or ethnic minorities in positions of political authority in your local area. The reference library will be able to supply you with lists of councillors and MPs. You also need to consider what other positions might be included in such a survey, and how you will determine whether these groups are under-represented or over-represented in positions of authority.

Consider how effective any equal opportunities policies are in relation to this area. The local offices of the Equal Opportunities Commission or the Commission for Racial Equality might be able to provide you with useful information for this project.

Bibliography

Abbott, P. and Wallace, C. (1990) *An Introduction to Sociology: Feminist Perspectives*, London: Routledge

Alexander, P. (1987) *Racism, Resistance and Revolution*, London: Bookmarks

Anti-Nazi League (1994) *Fighting the Nazi Threat Today*, London: ANL

Baxter, S. (1993) 'The Nimbies in the Labour Party', *New Statesman and Society*, 26 November

Brown, C. (1984) *Black and White Britain*, London: Heinemann

Buswell, C. (1989) *Women in Contemporary Society*, Walton-on-Thames: Nelson

Butler, D. and Stokes, D. (1974) *Political Change in Britain*, London: Macmillan

Campbell, B. and Coote, A. (1987) *Sweet Freedom*, 2nd edn, Oxford: Basil Blackwell

Delamont, S. (1980) *The Sociology of Women: An Introduction*, London: George Allen & Unwin

Dowse, R.E. and Hughes, J.A. (1972) *Political Sociology*, Chicester: Wiley

Fairclough, A. (1990) *Martin Luther King*, London: Cardinal

Fryer, P. (1984) *Staying Power: The History of Black People in Britain*, London: Pluto Press

Geddes, A. (1993) 'Asian and Afro-Caribbean representation in elected local government in England and Wales', *New Community*, October

Goot, M. and Reid, E. (1975) *Women and Voting Studies*, London: Sage

Labour Party NEC (1993) *Report of the National Executive Committee to the 1993 Labour Party Conference*, London: Labour Party

Lovenduski, J. and Randall, V. (1993) *Contemporary Feminist Politics*, Oxford: Oxford University Press

Madgewick, P.J. *et al.* (1973) *The Politics of Rural Wales*, London: Hutchinson

O'Donnell, M. (1991) *Race and Ethnicity*, London: Longman

Ovenden, K. (1992) *Malcolm X: Socialism and Black Nationalism*, London: Bookmarks

Pateman, C. (1988) *The Sexual Contract*, Cambridge: Polity Press

Pilger, J. (1994) 'The rise of respectable fascism', *New Statesman and Society*, 15 April

Randall, V. (1987) *Women and Politics*, 2nd edn, London: Macmillan

Reid, I. (1989) *Social Class Differences in Britain*, 3rd edn, London: Fontana

Robinson, V. (1990) 'Roots to mobility: the social mobility of Britain's black population, 1971–87', *Ethnic and Racial Studies*, Vol. 13, No. 2

Saggar, S. (1993) 'Analysing race and voting', *Politics Review*, February

Seyd, P. and Whiteley, P. (1992) *Labour's Grassroots*, Oxford: Clarendon Press

Solomos, J. (1989) *Race and Racism in Contemporary Britain*, London: Macmillan

Szymanski, A. (1976) 'Racial discrimination and white gain', *American Sociological Review*, Vol. 41, No. 3

Watkins, S.A., Rueda, M. and Rodrigues, M. (1992) *Feminism for Beginners*, Trumpington: Icon

Whiteley, P., Seyd, P. and Richardson, J. (1994) *True Blues: The Politics of Conservative Party Membership*, Oxford: Oxford University Press

Wormald, E. (1982) 'Political participation', in I. Reid and E. Wormald (eds) *Sex Differences in Britain*, London: Grant McIntyre

Worsley, P. (1973) 'The distribution of power in industrial society' in J. Urry and J. Wakeford (eds) *Power in Britain*, London: Heinemann

X, Malcolm (1985) *The Autobiography of Malcolm X*, Harmondsworth: Penguin

4 New social movements

The concept of the social movement is as old as sociology itself. Most people would agree that the workers' movement was the most important of the first social movements. It gave birth to many elements of the contemporary social and political structure, notably the right to vote, the trade unions and both Marxist and socialist parties.

The political organizations that arose in the UK and elsewhere during the nineteenth and twentieth centuries, especially political parties and pressure groups, came to occupy the central position in sociological analyses of politics and society. Social movements themselves appeared to be in decline. In recent times, however, they have returned to the centre stage of social and political activity. Many writers therefore refer to the rise of *new* social movements, although the extent of their newness is very much a matter of debate.

Simon Hallsworth provides the following summary of the type of movements usually classified under the heading of new social movements:

> The term is most often used to refer to those movements which may be held to pose new challenges to the established cultural, economic and political orders of advanced (i.e. late twentieth century) capitalist society. As such the term is usually applied to cover the feminist movement; anti-racist groups such as Black Power; the radical students' movement of the 1960s; anti-war groups such as CND; environmental movements such as Greenpeace and Friends of the Earth; animal rights groups such as the Animal Liberation Front; and Gay Rights organizations such as Outrage and more recently Queer Nation [Hallsworth 1994, p. 7].

It is argued that several key factors lay behind the rise of the new social movements, among them the following:

- There have been fundamental changes in society, usually characterized as a move from industrial to post-industrial society.

- The post-industrial economy has stimulated the growth of what has been called the 'new middle class', who often form a key social base for the new social movements.

- The working class, the key social base for older social movements, now appears to be in decline and can no longer bring about social and political change.

- There has been growing disillusionment with attempts to effect change by reforming the state as a result of the economic crisis of the 1970s and the consequent crisis of the Welfare State.

- Many people came to feel that traditional political debate, based for instance on assumptions about the role of women in the structure of the Welfare State, excluded significant groups and perpetuated the oppression of others.

- A greater emphasis on cultural and ideological struggle developed under the . influence of the work of Antonio Gramsci.

- Much of the Left distanced itself from Marxism because of the experience of Stalinism in Eastern Europe. Opposition movements in those countries stressed autonomy from the state and indeed were forced to organize independently from any state organization. Groups such as New Forum in East Germany inspired social thinkers in the West.

- Direct-action type movements flourished in the 1960s in the wake of the Black Civil Rights Movement in the USA, and more recently in the form of the environmental and peace movements.

- Finally, in the late 1980s postmodemist ideas became extremely influential. These ideas have been nurtured by, and in turn have reinforced, the new social movements.

> *'We may define a social movement, in broad terms, as a collective endeavour to promote or resist change in the society of which it forms a part; but this statement needs to be qualified in some way if we are to retain a clear distinction between a "movement" and a "party". One way of doing this is to point out the less organized character of a movement, in which there may be no regular or easily identifiable membership (no "party card" or dues), and little in the way of a central office or staff' (Bottomore 1993, p. 28).*
> *Try to think why movements should adopt such a form.*

The turn away from class and the state

The main characteristic of the new social movements is a critique of two features of the original workers' movement, namely: (1) using the state to effect transformation, and (2) viewing social classes as the central political actors. The new social movements often organize themselves in conscious repudiation of a politics based on class, or at least feel that such an approach is concerned with too narrow a range of interests. An example of this is the feminist view that the oppression of women cannot by fully explained on the basis of a class analysis.

> *Beatrix Campbell has written that 'men and masculinity, in their everyday, individual manifestations, constitute a systematic bloc of resistance to the women of their own community and class. Both individual men and the political movements men have made within the working class are culpable' (Campbell 1984, p. 5).*
> *Explain what you think she means by this statement. How far do you agree with her assessment of the basis of women's oppression?*

One approach to understanding the new social movements may be to apply Weber's concept of status groups and his views about the increasing bureaucratization of the world. The debate about the significance of new social movements therefore touches on the debate about the extent to which it is possible to explain political mobilization on the basis of class.

Several thinkers, for example Inglehart (1990), have suggested that the focus of politics has now shifted from a concern with materialist issues, crucially the distribution of economic resources, towards post-materialist values, by which they mean a concern with the quality of life. The emphasis placed by postmodernists on difference fits in with the themes of autonomy and separatism that are central to many of the new social movements.

The rise of the new social movements

The separation between the older class-based movements and the new social movements can be traced to the events of the late 1960s. The Black Civil Rights Movement in the USA stressed that only the oppressed could fully understand their oppression and fight against it. This idea inspired a series of movements based on 'separatism', most notably the various women's movements that grew up in the late 1960s and 1970s.

These movements were organized largely outside the existing Labour and socialist movements and valued their sense of autonomy in terms of organization and tactics of struggle. They often considered the old bureaucratic, hierarchical structures of political parties to be part of the problem, and instead argued for more informal, participatory styles of organization. They were also based on the idea of direct action outside the formal traditional structures of political power. Table 4.1 summarizes the main differences between old and new social movements.

Table 4.1   Contrasts between the old and new social movements

	Workers movement	*New social movements*
Location	Increasingly within the state	Civil society
Aim	Political integration/ Economic rights	Changes in values and lfestyles/ Defence of civil society
Social Base	Economic class/ Industrial society	Non-economic forms of identity/ Post-industrial society
Theme	Citizenship	Autonomy
Organization	Formal/hierarchical	Network/grassroots
Medium of action	Political mobilization	Direct action/cultural innovation

Source: Adapted from Scott (1990), p. 19, and Scott (1992), p. 142.

The examples of new social movements most often cited are:

- the Black Civil Rights Movement

- the women's liberation movement

- the gay liberation movement

- the student movement

- the environmental movement

- the peace movement.

As can be seen, these are all movements based around groups whose identity is not determined by their place within the sphere of production. The crucial question to be asked is whether the struggles engaged in by these groups and the methods they use represent a radically new form of political action.

> *Divide into groups and investigate the arguments for and against rejecting class analysis in relation to the struggles against (a) racism, (b) the oppression of gays and lesbians, (c) the destruction of the environment, (d) nuclear warfare, (e) sexism. Take one issue per group and use this book and other resources available in the library to compile a report of about 1,000–1,500 words. Present your report to the rest of the class.*

Contemporary applications of new social movement theory

Post-Marxism

In the 1980s and 1990s there was a shift away from Marxism on the part of a group of thinkers who were attempting to develop a new radical politics based largely on the adoption of the theories of postmodernism and an orientation towards the new social movements. They were influenced by the following factors:

- The acceptance among some Marxists, notably those aligned with the Communist Party and its journal *Marxism Today*, that there had been a major shift in society which they characterized as the shift from Fordism to post-Fordism, and this linked into the idea of the decline of the working class. This view was also taken by André Gorz in his book *Farewell to the Working Class* (1982).

- The re-emergence in the 1980s of mass social movements such as the peace movement, and the rise of the environmental movement, which could be contrasted with the lack of success of the Labour Party in fighting against the Thatcher governments. This also encouraged the rise of protest based on direct action.

- The rise of protests in Eastern Europe and the eventual collapse of the East European regimes and the Soviet Union. There were Marxists who, although for a long time critical of these states, still in some way identified with them, and their collapse left them looking for alternatives. Political movements based on civil society were highly formed in Eastern Europe precisely because the totalitarian nature of those states left little alternative for opponents of the regimes.

> *The term 'civil society' denotes all the institutions in society that are not specifically part of the 'state'. Try to think of some concrete examples of what struggle in civil society might entail.*

Hall and Jacques - New Times

One of the most important expositions of post-Marxist ideas in the UK has been the analysis that we are living in 'new times' developed by a group of thinkers associated with *Marxism Today*, crucially Stuart Hall and Martin Jacques. They claim that there have been fundamental changes in society which demand a new politics. They also argue that while the post-war settlement centred on the Welfare State benefits certain groups, notably white male workers, it has excluded others:

[T]he labour and democratic movement was a parent to these settlements, but it was also a child of them . . . It largely co-operated in the conservative gender and racial settlement . . . and was wedded to an ideal of progress which did not question the industrialism which exploited nature and the modernism which created the tower block . . .

The poles of the political map in the 1990s will be the politics of race and the underclass in the inner city, and the growth of new industrial regions such as the M4 corridor, and within them growth towns like Swindon and Basingstoke. The labour movement is present in these towns. But it is not central to the spirit emerging within them, in the way that it was in Sheffield in the early part of the century or Coventry during the heyday of engineering. [Manifesto for New Times, in Hall and Jacques 1989, pp. 29–35]

These passages illustrate the themes that the working class was complicit in the continued inequalities of the post-war period, and that it can no longer be at the centre of politics. Hope for the future is placed in movements dedicated to democratic, sustainable and humane development. Hall and Jacques also emphasize informal networks and express a distaste for hierarchy: 'These are not formal policies or parties. They are moods, currents and forces in society' (*ibid.*).

Ernesto Laclau and Chantel Mouffe: developing radical democracy

In their book *Hegemony and Socialist Strategy* (1985) Laclau and Mouffe clearly align themselves with the post-Marxist attempt to base a new vision of politics on the new social movements. They argue that notions of revolution are now outdated and produce bureaucratic nightmares, and that the diverse identities on which new social movements are based enable a new politics that avoids the trap of attempting to provide an all-embracing total theory.

The totalizing element in Marxism is held to lead to the totalitarianism of socialist states. Laclau and Mouffe thus join postmodernism in rejecting total theories, and therefore also theories that see the working class as the basis of political struggle. The working class is only one possible element in the struggle, which must embrace the multiplicity of bases of oppression and therefore of action.

The struggle for hegemony is very important for Laclau and Mouffe, since they argue that 'many of these forms of resistance are made manifest not in the form of collective struggles, but through an increasingly affirmed individualism' (Laclau and Mouffe 1985, p. 164). Such struggles are not inherently progressive: one manifestation of such a struggle that they cite is the populism of Thatcherism, based as it was on individualistic ideas. What allows the various forms of struggle to come together into a collective struggle is adherence to the idea of democracy. The task of the left 'therefore cannot be to renounce liberal-democratic ideology, but on the contrary, to deepen and expand it in the direction of a radical and plural democracy' (*ibid.* p. 176).

New social movements and black communities in Britain

Paul Gilroy (1987) has argued that the ideas of Touraine and Melucci (see pages 77 and 79), combined with the notion of an urban social movement and the goals identified by Castells (see page 75), can be applied to the black communities of Britain.

Community is central to Gilroy's notion that cultural resistance can become a form of political resistance: 'There are good grounds on which to argue that the language of community has displaced both the language of class and the language of "race" in the political activity of black Britain' (p. 230). In particular he argues that such an emphasis allows us to understand the distinct strands that have emerged within the black communities and the way in which their activity has often been organized around defence of the community against attempts by the police and the state to criminalize blacks. Rejection of the universal category of class based on production allows us to recognize the development of black cultures that prize non-work time – a theme that Gilroy develops into a critique of work and capitalism in general. In this respect he echoes Gorz's critique of the traditional centrality of production and his exposition of how new movements often now mobilize around issues of consumption rather than production.

Two approaches to the new social movements

As we have already noted, there has been much debate about how 'new' the new social movements really are, and varying positions are offered on their extent, nature and significance. In a wide-ranging review of the significance of these movements and debates about them, Alan Scott (1992) suggests that it is possible to distinguish between writers who adopt a structural approach and those who adopt a social action approach.

Writers who take the structural approach argue that new social movements are qualitatively different from other political forms because they reflect fundamental changes in the underlying structure in society, most notably the change from industrial to post-industrial society; external social conditions thus determine their character. They are also new in that their aims are very different from those of the old social movements. The latter strove to become part of the political decision-making process, but the new social movements are more concerned to free themselves from the state than to get involved with it. Their main aim is to develop a sphere of autonomy free from the state in which they can develop alternative ways of living. These writers have therefore stressed the cultural dimension of these struggles and their wariness of incorporation into the state.

Writers who take the social action approach see these movements as developing, not as a result of broad structural changes in society, but as a consequence of their interactions with conventional institutions such as the state. Crucially, certain groups have felt excluded from the decision-making process, and their aim is to overcome their exclusion. The non-institutional nature of their actions merely reflects the fact that as yet they have not gained entry to institutions. This argument is in clear contrast to the structural emphasis on autonomy from the state.

For social action theorists these movements are new in the sense that they are of recent origin, but they question whether they are really 'new' in another sense. They maintain that all organizations have a life-cycle; social movements are at first excluded, but as their demands are noted they gradually become incorporated. In its early stages the labour movement also largely relied upon non-institutional action. Thus these thinkers believe that at some stage in the future the 'new' social movements will evolve into more formal institutionalized forms of politics. They would regard this evolution as a sign of their success, while for structural thinkers such an eventuality would represent the death or neutering of the movement.

These two strands of opinion are summarized in Table 4.2.

Table 4.2 Two approaches to the new social movements

	Structural	Social action
Reason for their rise	Change in social structure	Exclusion of some groups from decision-making processes
Arena where they operate	Civil society	State/civil society boundary
Key aims	Defence of autonomy from state Development of new values and form of life	Political and cultural integration
Nature of action	Direct action Anti/non-institutional	Direct action but potentially institutional

Source: Adapted from Scott (1992), p. 140

1) *The following section outlines the views of some of the leading theorists of new social movements. Once you have worked through the section, form yourselves into groups and try to identify which thinkers follow a broadly structural approach and which a social action approach. Write a small summary of the views of each writer and explain why they fit into the category you have assigned them. Copy out Table 4.2 and add a heading 'Key thinkers'; write in your list of thinkers who adopt each approach. Discuss your findings with other groups and try to arrive at a consensus.*

2) *Allocate the structural writers to half the groups and the social action writers to the rest. Within your group try to identify any important differences that emerge between writers within the same overall approach. It is important to do this since any process of classification inevitably sometimes involves glossing over such differences. For example, I hope you have put Alain Touraine and Alberto Melucci in the same category (I'm not saying which), but there are nonetheless important differences between them. Construct a spider diagram with the words 'Structural approach' or 'Social action approach' in the middle and then add all the names of the writers you have identified, pointing out the differences between them.*

Key theorists of the new social movements

Manuel Castells

Castells (1983) considers the development of new social movements in an urban setting. He argues that their contemporary significance is due to structural changes in society which have led to the key arena for political conflict moving from the production sphere (marked by conflict between the bourgeoisie and the workers' movement) to conflict based on collective consumption, cultural identity and political self-management.

This is because, in the face of the growing global scope of production, the labour movement appears powerless, and efforts to control production and consumption through the state no longer seem convincing. However, there are still conflicts and, faced with a growing distance between themselves and the realms of the state and production, people try to control their lives by controlling their locality. The urban social movements are thus a defensive reaction to structural change in the world which has made the old forms of movement obsolete.

Castells cites the gay movement in San Francisco, which mobilized around the reconstruction of neighbourhoods in the city and succeeded in getting them refashioned to reflect their cultural values. A local economy of gay bars and clubs flourished. Gay activists struggle to retain their cultural identity and autonomy from the local state, but there is a danger that they will become incorporated into the local decision-making process, and as a result lose their distinct identity and their potential for social change. 'In fact, all social movements are unable to fully accomplish their project since they lose their identity as they become institutionalized, the inevitable outcome of bargaining for social reform within the political system' (Castells 1983, p. 328).

An event often cited as the birth of the gay liberation movement was a protest that occurred at the Stonewall Bar in Greenwich Village, New York, in June 1969. In an article in the Guardian *(14 June 1994) Bruce Bawer investigated the legacy of this protest. He argued that 'the time has come to move beyond the Stonewall sensibility'.*
Obtain a copy of this article and summarize Bawer's arguments. Is his view broadly in line with a structural or a social action approach to new social movements? Explain your answer.

In February 1994 the British House of Commons voted on a proposed amendment to reduce the age of consent for gay men from 21 to either 18 or 16. Gay rights pressure groups such as Outrage and Stonewall were lobbying for the age of consent to be equalized for both homosexuals and heterosexuals at 16.
Use newspaper and magazine articles from that period to find out what actually happened and what arguments were used by those for and against change.
In your opinion, should there be a universal age of consent or not?

Jürgen Habermas

In the last ten to twenty years, conflicts have developed in advanced western societies that, in many respects, deviate from the welfare-state pattern of institutionalized conflicts over distribution . . . The question is not one of compensations that the Welfare State can provide. Rather, the question is now to defend or reinstate endangered life styles, or how to put reformed life styles into practice. [Habermas 1981, p. 33]

Habermas believes we are living in the stage of late capitalism, distinct from classical capitalism. The key difference between the two stages is the enhanced importance of the state in late capitalism. This has two important effects:

- The increased role of the state in the economy undermines the market. The distribution of income is therefore no longer seen as the act of impersonal market forces but arises directly from the actions of the state. The state attempts to steer the economy in a way which provides economic growth but also benefits the mass of the population and thus secures their continued loyalty. There are problems with this since business desires tax cuts, but this would lead to cuts in welfare provision which could provoke popular protests. Thus the state attempts to steer a course between conflicting interests, but sometimes this may result in what Habermas calls 'legitimation crises'. One possible basis for protest by new social movements is therefore when the state is seen to favour one group rather than representing the interests of all.

- The increase in the role of the state in monitoring previously private spheres of society, notably the family, extends the area of what is considered political. The state encroaches on the autonomy of civil society. This sometimes leads to the attempt to reassert a private sphere free from this process of 'colonization' by the state.

These twin effects lead to the rise of new social movements, which try to ensure that economic rewards are rationally distributed and also resist the extension of sphere intervention in private areas of social life by emphasizing democracy, participation and autonomy. The new social movements undermine the previously unchallenged traditional structures of society and in so doing extend the scope of modern participatory democracy. Habermas therefore sees the new social movements as a key element of modern rationality extended beyond its merely technical application.

 What evidence is there to support Habermas's notion of legitimation crises? How can the concept be applied to contemporary Britain? There was a useful summary of Habermas's view in New Society, *22 March 1979.*

Alberto Melucci

According to Melucci (1989), the structure of society has changed and we are now living in a post-industrial era. This has transformed the character of social movements. Modern movements differ crucially from their predecessors in that they are not concerned with citizenship (meaning access to the state) but are defined by a desire for autonomy. There has been a move away from the emphasis on formal organization typical of class-based movements towards a search for an alternative identity which may take a religious or spiritual form. The new movements are largely cultural rather than political phenomena. Melucci calls this a vision of a democracy of everyday life, in which social movements challenge the dominant codes of society, and by defining alternative identities change society.

Another reason underlying Melucci's emphasis on the 'non-political' aspects of social movements is his belief that moves to politicize them encourage the development of grand-scale programmes, which lead to totalitarianism. This idea is directly linked to the postmodernist rejection of totalizing theories. Unlike Touraine or Habermas, Melucci holds that the new social movements cannot become a new universal actor, as for example the old workers' movement was for socialists.

Claus Offe

According to Offe (1985, p. 819), new social movements arise because 'The conflicts and contradictions of advanced industrial society can no longer be resolved in meaningful and promising ways by etatism, political regulation and . . . bureaucratic authorities'. The failure of social democratic organizations, notably the Welfare State, has led to the growth of new social movements that can represent groups formerly left out because they were not organized as workers.

The bureaucratic nature of the Welfare State and the fact that it provided benefits for certain groups but not for others have been combined into a rejection of the idea that state-led reforms can solve contemporary problems. New social movements also wish to politicize the institutions of civil society, and in so doing create a new definition and arena for political activity.

In Offe's view the new social movements represent a new type of non-institutional politics. He believes they can be distinguished from other movements in that they are seen as legitimate and they attempt to make their views binding on others and thereby bring about societal change. These differences are summarized in Table 4.3.

Table 4.3 New social movements: a new type of non-institutional politics

Ends	Not binding	Binding
Means		
Not legitimate	Private crime	Terrorism
Legitimate	Religious practices	Sociopolitical movements

Source: Offe (1985), p. 827

Offe has also argued that new social movements may develop in a pattern whereby they start out mobilizing around specific issues and using direct action tactics but later develop to a point where they or the issues they mobilize around are incorporated into the institutionalized decision-making process.

Alan Scott

Scott (1990) not only provides a comprehensive summary of debates on the new social movements but develops his own view that they need to be considered in a political framework, utilizing the concepts of political science to understand their emergence and role in society.

Scott stresses that there 'are important continuities between new and older social movements' (p. 35). This is in clear contrast to the view of some writers that the older movements are now irrelevant or at best ineffective due to the radically changed nature of society. He maintains that 'no categorical distinction can be drawn between social movements, pressure groups and parties. Social movements are best understood in terms of a continuum stretching from informal network-like associations to formal party-like organizations.'

Scott studied the West German Green movement and found that there were important ideological divisions within it that mirrored the old divisions between left and right; thus there were continuities between the old and the new. He holds that both old and new groups fulfil both political and cultural functions, and therefore an over-emphasis on one aspect of their identity exaggerates the extent of change. Older movements are frequently portrayed as exclusively political and new groups as exclusively social or cultural, and this is a view he rejects.

Scott focuses on the way the activities of the new social movements expand the scope of citizenship and achieve the inclusion of formerly excluded groups in the policy-making process. One key group is the highly educated but politically marginalized middle class. Scott comments that the new social movements are 'typically either predominantly movements of the educated middle classes, especially the "new middle class", or of the most educated/privileged section of generally less privileged groups' (p. 138).

Scott sees an orientation on the state as an important component of both old and new social movements. This leads him to believe that integration into the state decision-making process does not lead to the disappearance or obliteration of a movement, as some argue. Instead it can be seen as a measure of success:

> [W]hile integration does typically mean the disappearance of the movement as movement, it is at the same time the criterion of the movement's success . . . The disappearance, or dormancy, of the women's movement after the political franchise had been won, and its reappearance during the 1970s illustrates both the 'partial' nature of political integration, and also how this very success highlighted other forms of discrimination and exclusion, giving rise to new demands and analysis [p. 150].

Thus Scott also emphasizes the cyclical nature of social movements, underlining continuities with the past rather than seeing the new movements as qualitatively different from their predecessors.

 What are the implications of Scott's views for the future of new social movements?

Alain Touraine

Touraine is one of the most influential writers working to develop a new sociology based upon an analysis of social movements. He believes that the concept of social movement should now be substituted for social class as the basic unit for social analysis.

His starting point is a study of the process by which movements come together and achieve an identity: '[T]he working class cannot be defined "objectively", and therefore . . . the concept governing the analysis is no longer one of class position, but of social movement' (Touraine *et al.* 1987, p. 21).

He also argues that the nature of these social movements has changed as society has experienced structural change from an industrial to a post-industrial stage. The main form of production is no longer manufacturing but the production of knowledge, and the crucial role in the production and coordination of that production of knowledge lies with the modern technocratic state. Unlike in industrial times, therefore, the main arena of conflict is against this technocratic state. This shift is summarized in Table 4.4 (page 80).

Table 4.4 Characteristics of the industrial and post-industrial periods

Industrial period	Post-industrial period
Manufacturing production	Knowledge production
Conflict at the workplace	Conflict in other arenas as other actors notably as consumers
Conflict against the owners of capital	Conflict against the controllers of knowledge, information and technology (the technocracy)
Concentrated state power	Fragmented power structure, state no longer all-powerful

Source: Adapted from Touraine (1982) and Scott (1992)

Explain in your own words the distinction between 'conflict against the owners of capital' and 'conflict against a technocratic state'. How do these link up with Marxist theories of capitalism and Weberian theories of the bureaucratization of society?

Since Touraine believes that there can only be one form of social movement appropriate to the concrete societal circumstances at any one time, his argument that we have moved into post-industrial society means that the old workers' movement can no longer fulfil its former function. The new social movements therefore arise to fill the vacuum. For Touraine there is a clear distinction to be drawn between the old and the new social movements since they relate to very different periods. The time for the workers' movement has passed, and instead a single movement able to transform the system will have to arise from other groups.

Touraine is crucially concerned with the process by which movements achieve recognition of their identity, and he links this to their need to develop a notion of their own interests. They must recognize who their enemy is. Touraine believes the French ecology movement failed to do this and instead lapsed into a utopian existence based on shared lifestyle. Although it had the potential to become a social movement, in the end it did not. In contrast, he argues that the Solidarity movement in Poland represented a successful social movement since it avoided the two dangers of degeneration that threaten potential social movements: (1) lapsing into a utopian lifestyle existence, and (2) orienting exclusively on the state.

Guarding their autonomy and a focus on civil society are thus crucial determinants for Touraine in the success or failure of a social movement. On this basis some have argued that he is very reluctant to define the peace movement as a social movement because it is based on making criticisms of the state and its expenditure patterns. Touraine prefers to emphasize a different side of this movement: 'The anti-nuclear movement cannot be reduced to a political action. It is a voluntary action, and above all a different way of living, acting and thinking' (Touraine 1983, p. 178). Again this passage reflects his belief that there is only one appropriate social movement for each type of society. He believes political movements were linked to industrial society, and in post-industrial society a more cultural orientation is appropriate.

Critical views on the politics of new social movements

Although the idea of new social movements has gained currency on the left, there are alternative views that challenge the theory that the nature of society has fundamentally changed, and also question the effectiveness of the new social movements in bringing about social change.

Neo-pluralism/corporatism

In many ways the new social movements arose in opposition to the rise of the corporate state (central negotiations including the state, labour and employers' interest groups). Although those who extol the new social movements as a new model for action often emphasize action in civil society and reject involvement with the state, some critics suggest that this is untenable.

Paul Hirst argues that the state is so strong today that organizations based in civil society will be unable to challenge it, and he believes the new social movements do not provide a strategy because they remain fragmented minorities.

> Movements in civil society cannot supplant or occupy the place of the state, precisely because in developed societies civil society is neither homogenous nor closed against the state. Britain, for example, is not remotely like Poland. Its civil society is diverse, characterized by many competing and contrary interests. Of these interests, the 'new social movements' form no more than a minority. Gay or black activists, for example, can't hope to beat or supplant the state. [Hirst 1990a, p. 20]

He believes that those associated with these theories have generalized too much from the experience of Eastern Europe:

> [I]n the East, the state lacks both legitimacy with the broad mass of the people and refuses to concede full representative government. Whilst that continues to be true, then opposition based on 'civil society' can work. Once full representative democracy is conceded and the state is not chronically lacking in legitimacy such strategies of opposition within 'civil society' can have at best local and single-issue effect. In Western representative democracies the state is neither weak nor lacking in the means to legitimate its policies. [Hirst 1990b, p. 5]

Critical Marxist responses

One important reason for the emergence of an emphasis on new social movements and cultural struggle was a concern among many Marxist thinkers with trying to avoid the 'economic reductionism' so characteristic of Stalinism. Perry Anderson sees this as a key element of Western Marxism, which as a result 'came to concentrate overwhelmingly on study of superstructures' (Anderson 1984, p. 75), and culture in particular became the main focus of concern. This, allied with the eventual collapse of the regimes in Eastern Europe, has led large numbers of now mainly ex-Marxists to adopt wholesale the 'new politics'.

Those who continue to consider themselves Marxists have generally not been associated with the Communist Parties and the regimes of Eastern Europe. One such form of Marxism is based on the work of Leon Trotsky. Contemporary Marxist writers recognize and support the emphasis on direct action which is so central to the new social movements, but differ with them over their evaluation of the potential of movements based on the working class. They reject the theory that we now live in a post-industrial society and that the working class is a spent force, and they do not believe the new social movements offer an effective way to change the overall structure of society because of their fragmented nature.

Ralph Miliband (1985) argues that many of the people involved with the new social movements do not share the hostility to the workers' movement often expressed by the theorists. In fact, many of them might be quite happy to describe themselves as workers and to see this as part of their identity. He also argues that there is still a need for the workers' movement because of its potential power.

> '[T]he primacy of organized labour in struggle arises from the fact that no other group, movement or force in capitalist society is remotely capable of mounting as effective and formidable challenge to the existing structures of power and privilege as it is in the power of organized labour to mount. In no way is this to say that movements of women, blacks, peace activists, ecologists, gays, and others are not important, or cannot have effect, or that they ought to surrender their separate identity. Not at all. It is only to say that the principal (not the only) "gravedigger" of capitalism remains the organized working class' (Miliband 1985, p. 13).
> How might Alain Touraine and other theorists of new social movements view this statement?
> What evidence is there to support the views of Miliband or Touraine? Which position do you feel is stronger, and why?

Alex Callinicos (1989) rejects the thesis of the post-industrial society and also rejects the postmodernist analysis that often goes along with it. He argues that on an international level the working class is more numerous than ever and that the working-class movement can and does fight against the oppression of marginalized groups, contrary to the contention that underlay the calls for separatism in the original new social movements (notably the Black Civil Rights Movement and the women's liberation movement).

Case study of a new social movement

The environmental movement has perhaps attracted the greatest interest as a potential unifying force for radical change. It is also the movement where the postmodernist rejection of the idea of progress is often seen most clearly, since it focuses explicitly on the negative effects of industrial production and some environmental speakers have an almost catastrophic vision of the end of the planet.

Many former socialists have radically altered their opinions as they have moved towards the environmentalist movement. For instance, in his book *From Red to Green* (1983) Rudolf Bahro remarks: 'The metropolitan working class is the worst exploiting class in history' (p. 184).

> What do you think Bahro could mean by this remark?

For Bahro the working class is in no sense a solution but instead part of the problem.

He argues that workers have a stake in continued economic growth, and socialism is based on such a belief; it is this belief that we need to reject as there is a real danger of exterminating the planet. Instead he proposes the development of small-scale production.

The idea that the environmental movement transcends class lines is also outlined in Ulrich Beck's *Risk Society* (1992). Beck rejects the concept of postmodernity and instead argues that we live in a distinct new era of modernity, which he calls 'reflexive modernity'. Sociologists need to abandon the evolutionary belief in progress that underlay classical sociological theories because of the increased risks associated with modern industrial production.

Beck argues that such risks are not distributed in the same way as class inequalities. Class inequalities have not disappeared, but they have been joined by these new forms of risk that affect everyone: '[I]n the water supply all the social strata are connected to the same pipe . . . poverty is hierarchic, smog is democratic . . . Risks display a social boomerang effect in their diffusion: even the rich and powerful are not safe from them' (pp. 36–7). Class politics cannot provide the basis for mobilization to deal with the risks arising from environmental problems. Science and the environment, Beck claims, provide a new arena for political action which is amenable to everyone since all are affected. Whether the risks of pollution are in fact equally distributed has been the subject of much debate, and critics reject Beck's contention.

The debate about the validity of science and the scientific view of progress is of central importance to the environmental movement, though some do emphasize science as a basis for the movement. Steven Yearly argues:

> Many social movements in this century have been based on moral or reli-
> gious claims: for example, that abortion is morally wrong, that civil rights
> should be extended to minority populations or that God meant women to
> join (or be excluded from) the priesthood. While there are moral claims
> associated with the Green case, it is also highly dependent on specifically
> scientific and technical considerations. [Yearly 1992, p. 9]

The environmental movement appears to have been very successful in raising its concerns to national and international political status, but this has also led to splits between those prepared to engage in parliamentary or more conventional politics and those who adopt an approach more concerned with lifestyle, autonomy and civil society. In his study of the West German environmental movement Scott argues that, as the possibility of governmental power approached, splits inside the movement were exacerbated between the 'realos' and the 'fundis'.

In the UK similar tensions have been evident. In the 1989 European elections the Green Party won 15 per cent of the vote, and arguments inside the movement soon followed. At the 1989 party conference Sara Parkin advocated electoral pacts – a suggestion denounced as an accommodation to conventional politics by more fundamentalist members – and there was talk of those who were 'Deep Greens' and those who were not. The party subsequently suffered a loss of electoral support, and in the 1994 European elections they gained only 3 per cent of the vote.

How important are votes for the Green Party as an indication of the strength of the environmental movement?

The core policies of the British Green Party are arguably the following: for unilateral nuclear disarmament, against nuclear power, for stringent limitations on pollution, a decrease in economic inequalities, decentralization of economic and political power, and a sustainable level of both economic growth and population growth. While this presents a clear critique of industrial/capitalist society, it also underlines the fact that the key debates are still about economics and production rather than more directly cultural issues, though of course it could be argued that the green notion of a different way of living is the central overriding philosophy.

Although the Green Party now seems to operate as an organized political party, there is a direct action aspect to the movement in the form of Greenpeace, an organization formed in 1971, originally to protest about US nuclear testing. The group espouses the philosophy of non-violent direct action. Its first method of protest, which it has continued to use to this day, was to sail a boat into the area of the test to disrupt the testing. The same tactics were adopted to protest against nuclear testing in the South Pacific and then also in protests against whaling, seal culling, the slaughter of dolphins and the dumping of toxic waste.

By the early 1980s Greenpeace had attracted large-scale support, largely financial. However, probably the most publicity it gained was as a result of the sinking of its ship, *Rainbow Warrior,* in 1985. Greenpeace was protesting about French nuclear testing in the South Pacific, and while the ship was moored in Auckland harbour in New Zealand it was blown up by the French secret service, causing something of a political scandal.

Figure 4.1

The sinking of the *Rainbow Warrior*

Source: *Sunday Times,* 10 October 1993

As a result of the publicity surrounding this event, the membership of Greenpeace rocketed to 3.5 million worldwide with 270,000 in the UK. This success has not been without tensions, however. A Channel 4 documentary entitled *Greenpeace: End of an Era?,* shown in May 1994, included interviews with members and/or ex-members, previously in leading positions in the organization, who felt that Greenpeace had become too concerned with survival as an organization, leading it to downplay the type of direct action it had become famous for.

This reflects a familiar debate about whether the success of the organization has transformed and partly institutionalized it, at the cost of its radicalism. The issue was further underlined by the involvement of Greenpeace in negotiations with whaling companies, which also attracted criticism in some quarters.

> *'Planet Earth is 4,600 million years old. If we condense this inconceivable time-span into an understandable concept, we can liken the Earth to a person 46 years of age . . . Modern humans have been around for four hours. During the last hour, we discovered agriculture. The industrial revolution began a minute ago. During those sixty seconds of biological time, humans have made a rubbish tip of Paradise'* (Greenpeace leaflet).
> *How far do you think this is a fair summary of industrial society?*

Mike Robinson has written about the growing emphasis on the quality of life and post-materialist values linked with concern for the environment, for example in the rise of green consumerism. He quotes figures suggesting that the main environmental groups had about 3 million members by 1983, but he also points out that there is a second strand to the movement – the attentive public:

> Although they may not be held together by any sense of communal purpose and ideology, they still participate in and share the ideologies of the formal groups at given times and for given issues. Put another way, one does not have to be a member of Friends of the Earth (FoE) or the Council for the Protection of Rural England (CPRE) to be an environ-mentalist. [Robinson 1992, p. 36]

He maintains that underlying this diffusion of green values is the new morality of life developed by the Green Party, and in particular its notion of ecological interconnectedness which allows it to develop links with other movements:

> The ecological thinking of the Greens which stresses diversity and social equality has helped attract other movements seeking to alter some aspect of social organization and the direction of socio-economic policy . . . Two of the more distinct and established groups which have to some degree merged with the green dimension of environmentalism have been those which advance the causes of feminism and peace. [*Ibid.*, p. 53]

He sees the Greens as part of the wider movement: 'The Greens are frequently seen as constituting a social movement, as though they were separate from the rest of the environmental movement. Perhaps a more appropriate interpretation is to see the Greens as the radical wing of environmentalism' (*ibid.*, p. 48).

One aspect of the environmental movement that has grown considerably in recent years in Britain is the anti-roads campaigns. Alarm UK, which acts as a umbrella organization for anti-road groups, calculated that by 1993/4 there were 250 community groups up and down the country, including protests at Twyford Down in Hampshire and the anti-M11 protests in East London.

> *Investigate whether there are any protests about road-building in your area. You might find reports of them in your local newspaper. Compile a list of the arguments for and against new roads. Try to find out about the social backgrounds of those for and against.*

Bored? Pessimistic? Depressed?
Looking for more from life?

The No M11 Link Campaign

invites you to visit ..... the Independent Free Area of

CLAREMONTÉ

(otherwise known as Claremont Road, London E11)

A STATEMENT OF DEFIANCE

a theatrical experience   a street design for the future
a tourist attraction   a caring community

a situation comedy   and a **PARTY!**

see it, participate in it, add your own contribution to this
ever-changing work of performance art!

- Art House and outdoor sculptures
  open at all times
- Barricading/painting/tree-house building on Saturdays
  or weekdays by prior arrangement - ring 0956 300676 or 081-558 2638
- Carnival from 3pm on Sundays
  performers ring "the Man from Claremonté on 0956 300676 or 081 558 2638
- Temporary & long-term housing
  is always available for helpful and open-hearted visitors

GET CONNECTED
! GET ON THE "NO M11" PHONE FREE!
Details overleaf

Cheques, made out to "WAM 11", always welcome - please sent to:
No M11 Link Campaign, Arch 211, Grove Green Road, E11 4AJ

"This continuing celebration of human imagination, potential and diversity urgently
needs & deserves your support". Bill Clinton

VISIT CLAREMONTÉ
The State of the Art

Claremont Road in Leyton, East London, was for a time declared by its residents the Republic of Claremonté. This protest received large amounts of support from the local community and led to escalating police costs for the motorway builders.

To what extent might the following be viewed as examples of new social movements? Consider the different answers that the main theorists of new social movements might give to this question. (Whether religious groups can be counted as new social movements, for example, is a matter of debate.) What do you think yourself?

- *Squatters*
- *Labour Party Black Sections*
- *Greenham Common Women's Peace Camp*
- *The Branch Davidian sect in Waco, Texas*
- *The Nation of Islam*
- *Greenpeace*
- *Aerobics classes*
- *Counselling and psychotherapy*
- *New Age travellers*
- *National Abortion Campaign*
- *Friends of the Earth*
- *Green Party*

- *Thatcherism*
- *Campaign for Nuclear Disarmament (CND)*
- Time Out *magazine*
- *Worker cooperatives*
- *Alternative medicine*
- *London Rape Crisis Centre*
- *Outrage*

If you are not sure about the 'aims' and 'focus' of any of these groups, ask your teacher or look them up in the library. Try to add some examples of your own.

Essay Questions

1) What are the main features of a 'new social movement'? (4 marks)

   Choose one of the following and show how it displays the features of a 'new social movement':
   feminism
   environmentalism
   the peace movement. (4 marks)

   What factors might explain the development of new social movements? (7 marks)

   Evaluate the usefulness of sociological theories of 'new social movements' in understanding any one such movement with which you are familiar. (10 marks)
   (InterBoard Syllabus – Specimen Exam Paper, 1994)

2) Evaluate the argument put forward by some writers that the disappearance of a new social movement can be a key indicator of its success.

3) How new are 'new social movements'?

4) 'New social movements are exclusively social phenomena based in civil society.' Explain and evaluate this statement.

5) 'Political life . . . is no longer rooted in a conception of a qualitatively better world. Even social movements, which in the 1970s accused the political parties, left and right, of operating without vision, have ceased articulating their utopias and sunk into Realpolitik' (Aronowitz 1992, p. 255). How far do sociological evidence and arguments support this view?

Coursework suggestions

1) Conduct a detailed study of the difference between an 'old' social movement and a 'new' social movement, and evaluate whether it is possible to draw such a distinction.

2) Choose one new social movement and interview members of it to discover the importance of the movement in their lives. What do they think are its aims, and how do they set about deciding on those aims and achieving them?

3) To what extent are political actions in the UK today best described using a framework developed by new social movement theorists? How important and how effective can new social movements be?

Bibliography

Anderson, P. (1984) *Considerations on Western Marxism,* 2nd edn, London: Verso

Aronowitz, S. (1992) T*he Politics of Identity,* London: Routledge

Bahro, R. (1983) *From Red to Green,* London: Verso

Beck, U. (1992) *Risk Society,* London: Sage

Bottomore, T. (1993) *Political Sociology,* 2nd edn, London: Pluto

Callinicos, A. (1989) *Against Postmodernism,* Cambridge: Polity

Campbell, B. (1984) *Wigan Pier Revisited,* London: Virago

Castells, M. (1983) *The City and the Grassroots,* London: Edward Arnold

Gilroy, P. (1987) *There Ain't No Black in the Union Jack,* London: Hutchinson

Gorz, A. (1982) *Farewell to the Working Class,* London: Pluto

Habermas, J. (1981) 'New social movements', *Telos,* No. 49, pp. 33–7

—— (1987) *The Theory of Communicative Action,* Cambridge: Polity

Hall, S. and Jacques, M. (eds) (1989) *New Times,* London: Lawrence & Wishart

Hallsworth, S. (1994) 'Understanding new social movements', *Sociology Review,* September

Hirst, P. (1990a) 'The state we're in', *New Statesman and Society,* 19 October

—— (1990b) *Representative Democracy and Its Limits,* Cambridge: Polity

Inglehart, R. (1990) 'Values, ideology and cognitive mobilization in new social movements', in Dalton, R.J. and Kuechler, M. (eds) *Challenging the Political Order,* Cambridge: Polity

Laclau, E. and Mouffe, C. (1985) *Hegemony and Socialist Strategy,* London: Verso

Melucci, A. (1989) *Nomads of the Present,* London: Hutchinson

Miliband, R. (1985) 'The new revisionism in Britain', *New Left Review,* March

Offe, C. (1985) 'New social movements: challenging the boundaries of institutional politics', *Social Research,* Vol. 52, No. 4

Pusey, M. (1987) *Jürgen Habermas,* London: Tavistock

Robinson, M. (1992) *The Greening of British Party Politics,* Manchester: Manchester University Press

Scott, A. (1990) *Ideology and the New Social Movements,* London: Unwin Hyman

—— (1992) 'Political culture and social movements', in Allen, J., Braham, P. and Lewis, P. (eds), *Political and Economic Forms of Modernity,* Cambridge: Polity

Touraine, A. (1982) *The Voice and the Eye,* Cambridge: Cambridge University Press

—— (1983) *Anti-nuclear Protest,* Cambridge: Cambridge University Press

——, Wieviorka, M. and Dubet, F. (1987) *The Workers Movement,* Cambridge: Cambridge University Press

Yearley, S. (1992) *The Green Case: A Sociology of Environmental Issues, Arguments and Politics,* London: Routledge

5

Political parties and pressure groups

Political parties

Political parties are an important category of contemporary political organizations. The rise of mass parties resulted from the extension of the franchise during the period of democratization. To become a Member of Parliament or a councillor today it is generally necessary to become active in one of the main political parties.

Sociologists have been concerned to see whether the political parties act as the guardians of democracy that they claim to be, and whether they are internally democratic.

Some commentators also suggest that the age of mass political parties may be coming to an end. They argue that political interests are becoming increasingly fragmented, the membership of the traditional parties is declining, and in their place we are witnessing the growth of alternative forms of political organization such as the new social movements.

The great spur for the rise of political parties was the extension of the franchise, which increased the size of the electorate. In the UK two Acts stand out, the 1832 Reform Act ('The Great Reform Act') and the 1867 Reform Act, which had the effect of doubling the electorate. The reason for the link between the extension of the franchise and the rise of political parties was the need for organizations to ensure that their supporters were registered to vote. As Sir Robert Peel put it: 'there is a perfectly new element of political power – namely the registration of voters . . . That party is strongest in point of fact which has the existing registration in its favour' (quoted in Bulmer-Thomas 1953).

The dominance of the three main parties

Elections in the twentieth century have reflected this new element of political power. In general elections since 1900 there have only been three occasions (1918, 1922 and 1931) when the combined votes for the Conservative, Labour and Liberal parties did not represent 94 per cent of the total votes cast, and if we look at figures for the three most recent general elections shown in Table 5.1 we can see that this still holds.

 These figures are for the United Kingdom. Find out the percentage voting figures for these three parties in your region. Does the proposition hold true for your region?

Table 5.1 Percentages of votes cast in general elections, 1983-92

Party	1983	1987	1992
Conservative	42.0	42.2	42.8
Labour	27.6	30.8	35.2
Liberal/SDP	25.4	22.6	18.3
Total, big three	95.0	95.6	96.3

Are there any regions of the country where this proposition is unlikely to be true? Why might this be the case? Does it matter?

According to the pluralist point of view, political parties are crucial to the operation of democracy because they act as channels of influence controlled by their members. Elite theory, in contrast, sees parties as vehicles for elites who compete for power but are in no real sense accountable to their members. In order to assess the merits of these opposing viewpoints, sociologists can examine the nature of the membership and the candidates who run for these parties to see whether there appears to be any consistent pattern in the type of people who join or who are selected as candidates. This also involves a consideration of the changing nature of the parties in recent years.

Let us look at each of the main parties in turn.

The Labour Party

'Contrary to what is frequently said, under John Smith's leadership Labour has been an extraordinarily effective opposition. Its limitations arise not from a failure to oppose, but from being in opposition.'

Tony Blair, quoted in New Statesman and Society, 16 July 1993

'The party is being dismantled. It is hard to escape the conclusion that everything is being wound up, just at the moment when everything the party said is needed. We are being driven back into the nineteenth century. Labour's so-called modernizers are really Victorian liberals. They're in favour of market forces, not very keen on trade unionism.'

Tony Benn, quoted in New Statesman and Society, 16 July 1993

The rise and fall of the Labour left

The last fifteen years of the Labour Party have witnessed sharp reversals in the fortunes of the Labour left. After the 1974–9 Labour government tensions between the left and right were evident, and the influence of the left rose sharply. The continuing importance of these differences of opinion can be grasped from the two quotes at the head of this section.

One of the key left organizations inside the party was the Campaign for Labour Party Democracy (CLPD), which had only 60 members in 1974 but by 1981 had grown to 1,016 members and also had 118 Constituency Labour Parties (CLPs) and 113 trade union branches affiliated to it. This group argued that the previous Labour government had not implemented party policy and sought to prevent any future Labour government from behaving in the same way. Its chosen method was constitutional change, in particular the automatic reselection of Labour MPs before every election to ensure that they would take the views of their constituency parties seriously. The CLPD won this constitutional amendment and also a change in the way the leader and deputy leader were elected at the Special Labour Party Conference at Wembley in 1981.

However, by the late 1980s the Labour left had been almost completely routed, and in 1993 its eclipse was symbolically shown by the failure of Tony Benn to gain election to the NEC.

Seyd (1987) argues that this reversal of fortunes occurred as a result of splits in the Labour left which first surfaced when sixteen members of the Tribune Group, including Neil Kinnock, failed to vote for Tony Benn in the contest for deputy leader. The origins of what later came to be termed the 'soft left' and the 'hard left' lay in this division. In December 1982 twenty-three Labour MPs launched the Campaign Group as an alternative left group. This group, along with a declining CLPD, came to constitute the 'hard left', while Tribune and the Labour Coordinating Committee (LCC) formed the core of the 'soft left'.

Labour in the 1990s

The key elements of the ongoing struggle inside the Labour Party can be traced to the shift towards what has been labelled 'new realism' when Neil Kinnock was leader. A number of factors underlay the policy changes adopted at that time:

- Most notable was the debate about whether the working class was in decline and later the argument that class as a category was becoming irrelevant. These arguments were advanced in a variety of ways by certain psephologists and in some influential journals, especially *Marxism Today* and *New Statesman and Society*.

- There were repeated calls for the incorporation of new policy initiatives inspired by the new social movements, particularly ecology and feminism.

The composition of the Parliamentary Labour Party has certainly changed over time, as shown in Tables 5.2 and 5.3 (page 92).

> *Identify the trends indicated in these tables. Compare and contrast them with the trends shown in Burch and Moran's comparative table for the Conservative Party included later in this chapter (page 98). Write a short summary of any differences and similarities.*
> *The figures in these tables provide information only up to 1983. Use your local reference library to update these figures. You can find information on the social*

Table 5.2 Background of all Labour MPs, 1945–83 (%)

	1945	1950	1951	1955	1959	1964	1966	1970	Feb. 1974	Oct. 1974	1979	1983
All public schools	19.4	22.2	23.4	23.5	24.6	24.0	22.8	19.4	15.7	16.4	17.0	13.4
Oxbridge	14.5	15.4	16.8	16.4	17.2	17.7	19.3	20.4	19.3	20.8	20.4	14.4
Public/Oxbridge	10.4	14.5	13.7	13.1	12.9	12.9	12.7	12.8	9.7	10.4	11.2	9.1
State sec./univ.	18.7	18.6	18.8	18.6	20.3	24.6	29.8	35.0	39.0	40.3	37.1	38.2
Elem./sec. only	52.4	49.2	36.9	59.9	47.2	39.4	35.5	31.0	26.5	24.4	28.9	21.5
All universities	34.2	37.7	38.7	38.2	39.5	43.9	48.5	51.2	53.0	55.7	57.0	54.1
Manual workers	27.6	27.6	26.2	25.3	21.1	18.4	16.6	13.2	12.3	12.0	19.8	15.3
Teachers/lecturers	12.1	13.9	14.8	14.3	14.9	16.5	20.1	20.9	25.8	28.1	24.2	25.8
Local government	43.5	41.4	40.8	40.8	39.3	42.9	43.7	41.3	46.6	46.4	37.6	47.8
Numbers	393	315	295	277	258	317	363	287	301	319	269	209

Source: Burch and Moran (1987), p. 142

Table 5.3 Background of new Labour MPs, 1945–83 (%)

	1945	1950	1951	1955	1959	1964	1966	1970	Feb. 1974	Oct. 1974	1979	1983
All public schools	21.5	27.4	13.3	15.4	11.9	19.8	15.3	12.5	6.5	18.2	18.0	22.5
Oxbridge	17.7	19.4	13.3	7.7	4.8	17.9	23.6	18.8	15.2	22.7	5.0	11.8
Public/Oxbridge	12.2	16.1	6.7	7.7	2.4	11.3	8.3	9.4	6.5	9.1	2.5	11.8
State sec./univ.	19.4	19.4	26.7	26.9	26.2	29.2	48.6	43.7	41.3	50.0	52.5	38.2
Elem./sec. only	51.9	38.7	46.6	50.0	59.5	32.3	22.2	23.4	26.0	13.6	40.0	20.6
All universities	37.6	43.6	40.0	34.6	31.0	45.3	63.9	56.2	47.8	72.7	52.5	55.9
Manual workers	19.7	17.6	20.0	19.2	23.8	18.9	12.5	6.2	19.6	4.6	20.0	20.6
Teachers/lecturers	13.3	17.7	20.0	23.1	9.5	18.9	34.7	29.7	19.9	50.0	15.0	17.6
Local government	42.2	45.2	40.0	53.0	54.7	51.9	43.1	39.1	56.5	45.4	62.5	64.7
Numbers	227	62	15	24	42	105	72	64	46	22	40	34

Source: Burch and Moran (1987), p. 142

background of MPs in the following sources: Who's Who, The Times Guide to the House of Commons *and* Dod's Parliamentary Companion.

Ingle (1993) found that the Parliament elected in 1992 contained 271 Labour MPs, of whom 186 had university degrees (including 58 from Oxbridge) and 18 polytechnic qualifications. The most common occupation was journalists/authors (50), followed by lecturers (48), trade union or party officials (46), teachers (43) and barristers (21). Ingle concludes that the Labour Party is now less representative of the working class than the Liberal Party it replaced as representative of the working class nearly 100 years ago.

> *Dunleavy (1993, p. 135) has argued that 'Labour now is a fairly straightforward piece of machinery, dominated by the party leadership and parliamentary party, but housed in a shell of an older and larger labour movement which grows less relevant as the years go by.' To what extent does the evidence support this view of the contemporary Labour Party?*

Traditionalists and modernizers

The social composition of the Parliamentary Labour Party certainly seems to have changed; and it is arguably as a result of this change, as well as reflecting the debates mentioned above, that a new division has sprung up inside the party between 'traditionalists' and 'modernizers'.

The 1993 Labour Party Conference bought to a head clashes between the 'modernizers' and the 'traditionalists'. One of the key areas of dispute concerned the links between the party and the trade unions. The conference abolished the trade union block vote. Now instead of each union casting its vote in one block equivalent to the number of its affiliated members, union delegates vote individually on resolutions. The size of the union vote was also limited to 70 per cent of the total conference vote, and it will eventually drop to 50 per cent. The size of the unions' vote in leadership contests was also reduced from 40 per cent (as decided in 1981) to 33 per cent.

There was a major argument over the proposed shift to the one member, one vote (OMOV) system in the selection of parliamentary candidates and Party leaders. Eventually the OMOV resolution was carried by 47.509 per cent to 44.388 per cent of the vote. Subsequently the death of John Smith led to OMOV being used for the first time, and the victor was the modernizer Tony Blair.

> *You can find a detailed explanation of the organizational changes to the Labour Party enshrined in the decisions of the Special Conference at Wembley in 1981 in Cordell (1992). Further details on the organizational changes and the new OMOV procedures can be found in Kelly and Foster (1991) or Coxall and Robins (1994). Use these books and the information contained here to write a report of about 500 words summarizing the changes introduced at the 1993 Labour Party Conference and explaining their significance.*

A critical view of the new voting system has been taken by Marqusee, who argues that '"one member, one vote" it is not. One MP's or MEP's vote may be worth the votes of 600 individual members or 14,000 trade unionists' (Marqusee 1994, p. 9). Figure 5.1 explains this surprising result graphically.

Figure 5.1

Labour's new electrocal system

Adapted from the *Guardian*, 17 June 1994

Choosing the Winner

Labour's electoral college gives a third of the vote to MPs and MEPs, a third to paid-up party members and a third to political levy payers in unions affiliated to the Labour Party.

Labour MPs and MEPs	Party members
Political levy payers	

- A total of 271 Labour MPs and 62 MEPs will be entitled to vote, thereby giving each MP and MEP precisely 0.1 per cent of the vote of the total electoral college.
- There will be 260,039 individual party members entitled to vote, giving each 0.00013 of a percentage vote.
- In the union section, 4.1 million political levy payers will be entitled to vote from 38 different unions and a dozen socialist societies (each vote worth 0.000008 of a percent).

Who are the Labour Party's members?

One of the key arguments in recent years has been that activists inside the Labour Party are unrepresentative of either the membership of the party or the wider electorate. A second, much older argument is that associated with the elite theorist Robert Michels (1962) known as the Iron Law of Oligarchy which asserts that in any organization the views of the leaders become paramount. This view of political parties was also broadly endorsed by McKenzie (1963). He argued that although the Labour Party constitution stipulated that the members via the annual conference were the ultimate arbiters of party policy, in reality the party leaders dominated, as in the Conservative Party.

The findings of a 1990 survey of Labour Party membership by Seyd and Whiteley are summarized in Table 5.4. These authors comment: 'There is an almost perfect reversal of occupational groups among party members and voters. Whereas one-half and one-fifth of Labour voters belong to the manual working class and salariat respectively, the opposite is the case among Labour members'(Seyd and Whiteley 1992, p. 38).

Table 5.4 Social characteristics of Labour Party members and voters

	Members percentages	*Voters percentages*
Gender:		
Male	61	48
Female	39	52
Age:		
18–21	2	8
22–25	3	10
26–35	17	20
36–45	26	18
46–55	17	14
56–65	16	16
Over 66	19	15
Social class:		
Salariat	49	14
Routine non-manual	16	19
Petty bourgeoisie	4	4
Foreman and technician	5	6
Working-class	26	57
Housing tenure:		
Owner	75	53
Rented from local authority	18	39
Private renting	4	6
Housing association renting	2	3
Household income (£p.a.):		
Under 5,000	17	36
5,000–10,000	21	31
10,000–15,000	18	18
15,000–20,000	15	9
20,000–25,000	10	4
25,000–30,000	8	1
30,000 and over	12	1

Source: Seyd and Whiteley (1992), p. 39

How far do you agree that the figures provided back up the conclusion drawn by Seyd and Whiteley?

1) In relation to membership figures for the Labour Party nationally there are a number of specific problems regarding their validity. Use a politics textbook to investigate what these are.

2) Find out the up-to-date figures for national membership of the Labour Party. These should be available from the party itself at 150 Walworth Road, London SE17 1JT (Tel. 0171 703 0833). Enclose an SAE if you are writing to them, and ask nicely.

The changing composition of the Labour Party is reflected at the parliamentary level. All of the twenty-nine MPs elected on the Labour ticket in 1906 were from working-class origins, but by 1945 teachers outnumbered miners as the largest occupational group inside the parliamentary party. Coates points out that the Wilson Cabinet in 1969 contained only one former manual worker, and there were only three in the Callaghan government of 1976. He comments: 'the embourgeoisification of the parliamentarians has been paralleled recently by a similar social shift among party activists in the constituencies (a recent survey suggested that 57 per cent of all Labour Party activists were now in white-collar occupations)' (Coates 1985, p. 198).

Thus there is general agreement that the Labour Party has become more middle class. A variety of explanations have been offered for this:

* Hindess (1971) argued that the key reason was social change and the consequential decline of the traditional working class. He also maintained that the more diverse nature of modern society contributed to a weakening of the link between social class and political parties – a phenomenon he detected in all the advanced industrial countries.

* Whiteley (1983) also argued that the decline in membership of the Labour Party was due to a loss of working-class members. He felt, however, that while this might be an effect of social change, it was also due to the disappointment that instrumental working-class supporters felt at the policies and actions of Labour governments.

* Seyd and Whiteley (1992) have argued that historically the individual membership was largely ignored due to the importance within the party of the affiliated organizations, notably the trade unions. The leadership could be sustained by the block votes wielded by these organizations. As a result, the mass individual membership base of the party withered away. The shift to a one-member, one-vote system is an attempt to reverse this decline and to rebuild a mass party based on individual membership. However, given the increasingly middle-class nature of the constituency parties and the weakening of the role of the trade unions, there is a danger that working-class members will be even further marginalized, and they may leave the party as a result.

Which of these arguments do you find most convincing as an explanation for the increasingly middle-class social composition of the Labour Party?
To what extent does the changing social composition of the Labour Party lend support to the embourgeoisement thesis, which was concerned with the effects of change on working-class voters?

Further light on the changing nature of Labour Party membership is shed by Seyd and Whiteley (1992), who found that 43 per cent of members saw themselves as less active than five years ago compared to only 20 per cent who saw themselves as more active. The average age of the Labour Party member is 48, and 50 per cent of the membership is entirely inactive (see Table 5.5).

Table 5.5 The amount of time devoted to party activities by Labour Party members in an average month (% of members)

Question: How much time do you devote to party activities in the average month?

None	50
Up to five hours	30
Five to ten hours	10
Ten to fifteen hours	4
Fifteen to twenty hours	2
More than twenty hours	4

Source: Seyd and Whiteley (1992), p. 88

The Conservative Party

'We offered a complete change in direction – from one in which the state became totally dominant in people's lives and penetrated almost every aspect to a life where the state did do certain things, but without displacing personal responsibility. I think we have altered the balance between the person and the state in a favourable way.'

Margaret Thatcher, interview in The Times, 5 May 1983

'The political cutting edge of Conservatism is its commitment to the free market. That has provided the hard intellectual core of modern Conservatism. It has given the Conservative Party its drive and purpose, and it has played a large part in the Conservatives' recent political success: the slogans of freedom, choice, opportunity, ownership meet the mood of the times and the mood of the electorate.'

David Willets, MP, Modern Conservatism (1992)

It is not at all clear who the members of the 'Conservative Party' are, and this confusion extends to the party's legal status. Conservative Central Office is legally the private office of the leader and has no formal connection with the constituency associations. Not surprisingly, therefore, it is somewhat difficult to obtain detailed information about party membership and activities. There are no accurate records for the simple reason that the relevant figures are not kept centrally, and such information as is available is very seldom published.

Why do you think the Conservative Party does not publish such information?
What methodological problems for researchers does this pose?
You might try asking Conservative Central Office for their comments. They can
be reached at 32 Smith Square, London SW1P 3HH (tel. 0171 222 9000). As
always, if you write to them, enclose an SAE and ask nicely.
Alternatively, try to obtain up-to-date figures for membership from your local
Constituency Conservative Association. You should be able to locate their
address in the local phone directory or from your reference library. Try to find
out how their membership figures have changed in recent years.

A rare accurate figure for the peak of Conservative Party membership put it at
2,805,832 in 1953, but since that time it has declined. A survey conducted in 1992
indicated a membership in the region of 750,000 (Whiteley, Seyd and Richardson
1994); however, since the average age of party members was 62 and a quarter were
66 or over, the party stood to lose more than 40 per cent of its membership within
a decade. Combined with the party's present unpopularity, this could lead to a
withering of its roots.

Much more information is available about the background of Conservative
candidates. In 1983 there were forty women candidates, of whom only thirteen were
elected. Forty-seven per cent of candidates were from the professional class while
less than 1 per cent were drawn from the working class. Seventy-five per cent of
candidates had been to public school, of whom 18 per cent had been to Eton; and
63 per cent of candidates were university graduates, and 82 per cent of these were
Oxbridge graduates.

Burch and Moran (1987) provide figures for the social backgrounds of Conservative
MPs in the period 1945–83, and of new Conservative MPs, as shown in Tables 5.6
and 5.7. They comment:

> Throughout the 29 years following the Second World War Conservative
> MPs thus conformed to a narrow and exclusive pattern of recruitment
> based on public schools and Oxbridge. The 1979 and 1983 figures,
> however, show a decisive change from this established pattern. . . . These
> . . . suggest that in terms of educational background the Conservative
> Party has become more open and less exclusive in its sources of recruit-
> ment. [Burch and Moran 1987, p. 134]

The figures in Tables 5.6 and 5.7 provide information only up to 1983. Use your
local reference library to update these figures. Write a short report of 400 words
and present your findings to the rest of the class.

The rise and fall of Margaret Thatcher

1979 was of course a significant year for another reason. It marked the rise to the
position of Prime Minister of the first woman in the UK to hold that office, Margaret
Thatcher. If the recent past of the Labour Party can be described as being about the
rise and fall of the Labour Left, the recent past of the Conservative Party can be
similarly described as the rise and fall of Margaret Thatcher.

Thatcher rose to the leadership of the Conservative Party in 1975 after the defeat of
the Heath government of 1970–74. One of the questions often considered is the
degree of continuity and change she brought to the Conservative Party.

Table 5.6 Background of all Conservative MPs, 1945–83 (%)

	1945	1950	1951	1955	1959	1964	1966	1970	Feb. 1974	Oct. 1974	1979	1983
All public schools	83.2	83.1	70.2	79.7	75.8	77.9	78.9	74.2	75.0	74.6	73.0	64.1
Eton	27.1	26.7	23.7	23.1	19.4	22.2	21.8	19.0	18.2	17.0	15.0	12.4
Oxbridge	53.3	54.0	54.3	53.7	50.6	54.3	57.1	51.3	55.7	55.1	49.2	45.7
Public/Oxbridge	50.3	51.9	51.0	51.3	46.5	49.3	51.6	44.7	48.3	47.5	37.4	37.1
Elem./sec. only	3.7	5.3	6.4	7.2	7.9	8.2	5.1	7.5	7.7	7.2	8.2	8.8
State sec./univ	7.0	6.0	6.8	6.6	8.2	7.8	9.0	10.0	11.4	11.9	16.2	17.9
All universities	64.7	64.7	64.6	65.9	60.7	63.8	67.0	63.5	66.9	67.4	68.0	71.7
Local government	14.1	16.8	16.6	20.7	25.5	27.2	28.9	30.4	32.0	31.0	35.0	38.1
Numbers	213	298	321	344	365	304	253	330	297	277	339	396

Source: Burch and Moran (1987), p. 141

Table 5.7 Background of new Conservative MPs, 1945–83 (%)

	1945	1950	1951	1955	1959	1964	1966	1970	Feb. 1974	Oct. 1974	1979	1983
All public schools	81.2	76.5	68.7	70.5	73.1	82.9	84.5	67.0	85.6	87.5	53.2	47.0
Eton	26.1	21.4	25.0	20.5	16.3	21.9	15.4	12.1	14.5	–	13.2	6.0
Oxbridge	42.1	46.9	53.1	50.0	45.2	56.3	46.1	40.7	59.7	62.5	36.0	35.0
Public/Oxbridge	43.5	44.9	43.8	47.4	39.4	50.0	46.1	34.1	53.2	62.5	30.4	25.0
Elem./sec. only	6.9	9.8	11.7	10.3	5.7	3.1	7.6	11.1	1.6	12.5	16.0	12.0
State sec./univ	2.7	8.8	11.7	7.7	9.6	9.3	–	13.3	11.2	–	22.6	30.0
All universities	50.8	61.3	56.3	66.3	53.8	70.4	62.0	57.2	72.6	75.0	73.2	72.0
Local government	10.8	22.5	22.1	35.9	36.5	34.4	38.7	32.5	27.4	25.0	41.2	52.0
Numbers	72	102	34	77	104	64	13	90	62	8	75	100

Source: Burch and Moran (1987), p. 141

Working in groups, write a report evaluating the success of Thatcherite policies and ideas, using the following headings. Take one section per group:

- *Privatization*
- *Public expenditure cuts*
- *Tax changes*
- *Europe*
- *The family*
- *Enterprise*

Incorporate a discussion of how these ideas and policies are viewed today, and how sociological debate has considered them.

On one level it is clear there was a massive change. Thatcher had a very clear ideological agenda that came to be referred to as 'Thatcherism'. Its origins have been described as follows:

> The New Right is the seedbed from which Thatcherism has grown, and is composed of two rather different strands. There is the revival of liberal political economy, which seeks the abandonment of Keynesianism and

any kinds of government intervention; and there is a new populism – focusing on issues like immigration, crime and punishment, strikes, social security abuse, taxation and bureaucracy. [Gamble 1983, p. 113]

The fact that Thatcher based her arguments squarely on the ideas of the New Right represented a shift away from the old Conservative idea of being a 'broad church' without any coherent ideology. As for her popularity, she was of course elected party leader, but her victory was not overwhelming. In the decisive ballot for the leadership in 1975 when 139 MPs' votes were required for victory, Thatcher won 146 votes and the other four candidates got a combined vote of 133. Blake (1985, p. 320) comments that 'Mrs Thatcher was victorious, though not by much.'

Thus when she came to power in 1979 it was not certain that Thatcher's ideas were wholeheartedly supported by the Conservative Party or even the government. Many members of her first Cabinet were Heath-style Conservatives, and the ideological struggle within the party continued to sharpen over the following years.

The high point of Thatcherism inside the Conservative Party was undoubtedly her second term of office between 1983 and 1987, when the party seemed largely united behind her. The main exception to this, and quite an important one, was the split over the future of the Westland helicopter company which led to the resignation of Michael Heseltine from the Cabinet; this was the one time Thatcher is alleged to have said she might be forced to resign.

J. Kingdom (1992, p. 1) has argued as follows:

When Margaret Thatcher made her imperious declaration that 'there is no such thing as society' she captured the essence of a political mission. . . . Thatcher challenged the notion that Britain could be a community; at a stroke people were to be relieved of any responsibility for one another, the biblical maxim 'love thy neighbour' exposed as ill-conceived post-war funk.

Although the era saw legislation specifically discouraging homosexual relationships, Thatcherite doctrines offered little encouragement to love anyone at all – anyone, that is, other than oneself. This was to be the masturbatory society, offering a solitary view of fulfilment, free of the complications arising from tiresome moral demands by others.

This presents a fairly critical view of Thatcherism. Imagine that you are a supporter of the New Right. Research and write a response to this critical comment about Thatcherism.

However, Thatcher's third term, after the 1987 General Election, began to reveal differences and divisions that led ultimately to her downfall. There were two central issues. First was the introduction of the Poll Tax. Thatcher described this as her flagship, though in the country at large it met with an extremely hostile reception. As a result the popularity of the Conservative Party fell sharply, and the Labour Party gained a 15 per cent lead in the opinion polls. Nonetheless Thatcher claimed that the Poll Tax did the Conservatives more electoral good than harm. Smith and McLean (1994) concede that there is some truth in this claim because a large number of people dropped off the electoral roll to avoid detection by the Poll Tax authorities

Figure 5.2

Whose baby?

Source: Cummings cartoon in the
Daily Express, 24 March 1991

"*Begone! I'M not the father!*"

and therefore lost their right to vote; the great majority of these were likely to be
Labour voters.

The second issue was the growth of divisions over the future of Britain's relations
with Europe. Kelly (1993) emphasizes that the differences that emerged follow from
the logic of the two traditions inside the Conservative Party, the Tory and Whig (or
market liberal) positions. In the early Thatcher years both groups could unite around
a strategy to revitalize the British economy, but as the 1980s rolled on the 'Whigs'
(whose leading representatives he considers to be Geoffrey Howe, Nigel Lawson
and Leon Brittan) came to believe that economic revival now required greater
integration with Europe; in contrast the 'Tories' (Nicholas Ridley, John Biffen, Norman
Tebbit, Margaret Thatcher) felt that national independence and sovereignty were the
most important considerations.

Dunleavy (1993) argues that over both Europe and the Poll Tax Thatcher moved
sharply to the right after 1987, and it was this that opened up divisions in the party.
These differences erupted into the open with the resignations of Nigel Lawson and
Geoffrey Howe, who implicitly attacked Thatcher in his resignation speech. Michael
Heseltine then challenged Thatcher for the leadership. She did not win enough votes
in the first round, and after first declaring 'We fight on' she resigned, leaving John

Figure 5.3

A resigned Mrs Thatcher

Source: *Sunday Times*, 17 October
1993

Major as her preferred candidate to beat Heseltine. This he duly did, winning 185 out of 372 votes in the second round.

Which leader received the greater percentage of votes for the leadership, Margaret Thatcher in 1975 or John Major in 1990?

The question of continuity between Major and Thatcher is also a matter of debate. We have noted that he was her preferred successor, yet over Europe and the Maastricht treaty most of the opposition to his policies has come from Thatcherite MPs. Edward Leigh, a Thatcherite Minister who was sacked in 1993, argued that 'The left of the Tory Party has now achieved its ambition to control economic, foreign and industrial policy. The right sits beleaguered in isolated fortresses in the Home Office, Social Security and Wales' (*Spectator*, 5 June 1993).

Kelly (1993, p. 140) suggests that Major represents an important change in terms of his background: 'Major's social origins and background were starkly different from any previous Tory leader, even the "meritocratic" Heath and Thatcher had been Oxford graduates.' He argues that one possible reason for the continuing divisions is that most of the new MPs first elected in 1992 are Thatcherites. Twenty-four of the sixty-three MPs who signed a motion critical of Major's stance on Europe and the Maastricht treaty were new MPs.

An alternative view which stresses more of the continuities between Thatcher and Major has been put forward by Hall (1993, p. 14):

> It was surprising at the time of the election how relatively successful Major was in fronting a kind of alternative to Thatcherism – Thatcherism with a human face – which represented no profound political philosophical investment of his own . . . Because there is no authentic language of Majorism, as there was an authentic language of Thatcherism, when in difficulties in mobilizing political support, Major is driven back to the old themes of the Thatcherite project, in order to fill the void.

Hall argues that this is clearly seen in the 'Back to Basics' campaign with its emphasis on crime, family breakdown and social disintegration.

The question of what John Major really stood for became increasingly important in the context of increasing divisions within the Parliamentary Conservative Party; particularly over bad election results and Europe. In an attempt to silence his critics, John Major resigned his leadership in June 1995 to force a contest, challenging his critics to 'put up or shut up'. In a surprise move, right-wing Cabinet Minister, John Redwood, resigned his Cabinet post in order to challenge John Major, presenting himself as the true Thatcherite heir. The election in July 1995 led to a clear victory for John Major, winning by 218 votes to 89. This effectively means he will lead the Conservative Party at least up until the general election. Whether the result will heal the divisions remains to be seen.

The Conservative Party outside Parliament

As already noted, it is not clear if such a thing exists, but Conservatives outside Parliament there certainly are. Whiteley, Seyd and Richardson conducted a survey shortly before the 1992 General Election using a very similar set of questions to that used for their 1989 survey of Labour Party members. This is useful for purposes of comparison. They found that the average age of Conservative Party members was 62, and only 5 per cent were under 35. In terms of educational qualifications 31 per cent had none, while 12 per cent had a university degree. In contrast to Conservative MPs, only a quarter of Conservative members were educated at non-state schools. Their summary of the social characteristics of Conservative members and voters is shown in Table 5.8.

Table 5.8 Social characteristics of Conservative Party members and voters (percentages)

	Members *(N = 2467)*	*Voters* *(N = 2779)*
Gender:		
Male	51	45
Female	49	55
Age:		
25 and under	1	9
26–35	4	20
36–45	11	18
46–55	17	18
56–65	24	14
66 and over	43	21
Social class:		
Salariat	55	38
Routine non-manual	18	24
Petty bourgeoisie	13	12
Foreman and technician	6	5
Working-class	8	22
Housing tenure:		
Own property	91	86
Rented from council	3	7
Other rented	5	7
Age at end of full-time education:		
16 and under	55	64
17–18	25	19
19 and over	19	14
Household income (£p.a.):		
Under 10,000	26	25
10,000–15,000	19	14
15,000–20,000	15	16
20,000 and over	42	44

Source: Whiteley, Seyd and Richardson (1994), p. 50

Seyd and Whiteley's findings on the social characteristics of Labour Party members are summarized in Table 5.4 (on p.94). Use that table and Table 5.8 on Conservative party membership and voters to write a short report on the similarities and differences in the social characteristics of the members of the two parties.

Which party shows a greater similarity between the social characteristics of its members and its voters? Does this matter?

The lack of a clear legal basis for the party was revealed in the newsletter of a pressure group operating inside the party known as the Conservative Charter Movement. Since 1980 this group has campaigned for democratic reforms in the party. At present there are no real mechanisms for party members to have an effective say in the formulation and implementation of party policy, nor are ordinary members involved in leadership elections. This aspect led Robert McKenzie to describe it as 'a tightknit system of oligarchical control' and the Charter Movement stated in 1982 that 'There is no element of democracy in the running of the party for the simple reason that the party was never intended to be democratic' (*Crossbow*, Summer 1982).

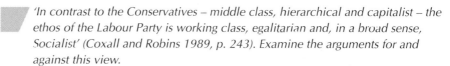

An article detailing the views of the Conservative Charter Movement appeared in New Statesman and Society, *1 October 1993. Obtain a copy of this article and write a summary of the changes this movement is calling for.*
There is a detailed outline of the structure of the Conservative Party in Cordell (1992). Use this to assess the validity of the points made by the Conservative Charter Movement.

Concern over the running of the party has reached high levels for a combination of reasons: the party is running a massive financial deficit, which by the end of 1992/3 stood at £19 million; membership numbers are falling; and there is unease over the provenance of some of the party's funds following the revelation that money supplied by businessman Asil Nadir (£440,000) was considered by his accountants to have been stolen. The Charter Movement commented: 'We don't know what Central Office had to concede in return for this money, but we can be absolutely sure that the interests of party democracy are not enhanced' (*Guardian*, 13 December 1992). The party's heavy reliance on this sort of donation is shown by the fact that the annual income from constituency associations had fallen from 14 per cent of total income in 1987 to 7 per cent in 1991 (Ingle, 1993).

'In contrast to the Conservatives – middle class, hierarchical and capitalist – the ethos of the Labour Party is working class, egalitarian and, in a broad sense, Socialist' (Coxall and Robins 1989, p. 243). Examine the arguments for and against this view.

The Liberal Democrats

'I have the highest ambition, and that is to lead the country.'

Paddy Ashdown

'The tally of seats in Parliament is only one reflection of nationwide Liberal strength. In local government, the Liberal Democrats have a base far larger than their Liberal predecessors of the 1950s or 1960s.'

Chris Cook, A Short History of the Liberal Party *(1993)*

The Liberal Democrats have succeeded to the mantle of the Liberal Party as the third party in the British parliamentary system, quite a way behind the other two. It is generally seen as occupying the centre ground.

The Liberal Party was once a dominant political force, but its electoral success declined dramatically after the 1918 General Election as the Labour Party grew in strength. However, its share of the vote rose significantly in the 1974 elections, which have come to be seen as something of a watershed; since that time commentators have predicted greater things for them.

The Liberal Party and the SDP campaigned together as the Alliance in the 1983 and 1987 general elections, although there were evident tensions between the two leaders, David Steel and David Owen. The immediate effect of the Alliance was to boost the centre's share of the vote from 13.8 per cent in 1979 to 25.4 per cent in 1983 and 22.5 per cent in 1987. In terms of MPs their number rose from 11 in 1979 to 23 (1983) and then 22 (1987). Despite this improvement, because there were large Conservative majorities the Alliance failed to hold the balance of power.

Using information available in your library, write a short summary of the social composition of Liberal Democrat voters.

By the time of the 1987 election there were clear pressures for a merger between the two parties. The new merged party chose the name Liberal Democrats, and in the leadership election of July 1988 Paddy Ashdown decisively defeated Alan Beith. The rump SDP under David Own continued as a separate party but received a decisive blow in the Bootle by-election in May 1990 when its candidate received 155 votes compared to 418 for the Monster Raving Loony Party. At the 1992 General Election its two remaining MPs were defeated.

The first electoral results for the Liberal Democrats were not promising. In the May 1989 local elections they gained only 83 seats while losing 190. In the European elections in the same year they won only 6.4 per cent of the vote, overshadowed by a massive vote for the Green Party. Cook (1993, p. 204) comments that 'the Greens had done best in the south of England and those middle-class constituencies in which Liberals had formerly prospered'.

The Liberal Democrats made a better showing in the local elections of May 1991 when they gained 750 seats and lost only 230, and this encouraged them in a more upbeat approach. However, the 1992 General Election brought them mixed fortunes. Although they gained four seats, most notably defeating the Conservative Party Chairman, Chris Patten, in Bath, their share of the vote went down from 22.6 per cent in 1987 to 17.8 per cent, and all the seats won in by-elections between 1987 and 1992 were lost.

The party's support seems to be rooted only in certain regions. In 1987 thirteen of the twenty-two Alliance seats were in rural Wales or Scotland, and three more were in the West Country. In 1992 the Liberal Democrats won seats in the South West (six) and in Scotland.

Other parties

There are of course other parties, notably the Scottish National Party and Plaid Cymru which represent nationalist aspirations in their countries. They are discussed in the section on nationalism in Chapter 9. The other main party which caused

Figure 5.4

Splitting images

Source: *New Statesman and Society*, 17 December 1993

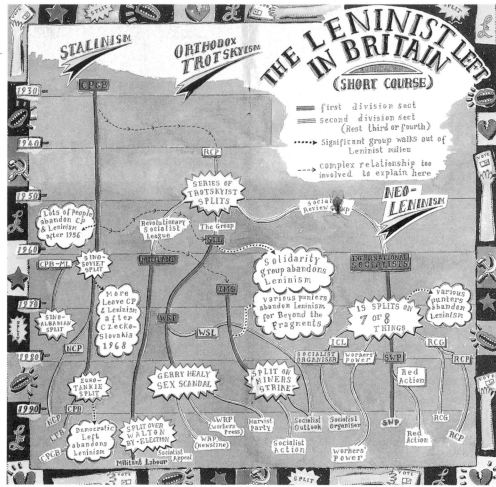

comment in the 1980s was the Green Party which achieved a spectacular rise in its vote in the 1989 European elections but has since declined as an electoral force. This party can also be seen as part of the environmental movement considered in the previous chapter on new social movements. The 1990s have seen a revival of fascist parties such as the National Front and the British National Party.

The 1980s also saw the final decline of the Communist Party of Great Britain, and the main parties of the revolutionary left are now the Socialist Workers Party and Militant Labour.

What view of the Leninist Left do you think the author of Figure 5.4 holds?

The function of mass parties

The place of political parties in theories of political sociology varies. Pluralist writers consider them an important channel for communicating the wishes of the people to government. Elite writers have generally seen them as oligarchical organizations formed to organize electoral support in the wake of democratization. The most famous exponent of this point of view is Robert Michels, who argued that there is an

Iron Law of Oligarchy, as mentioned earlier: 'The formation of oligarchies within the various forms of democracy is the outcome of organic necessity, and consequently affects every organization' (Michels 1962, p. 419). Marxist writers, on the other hand, generally view the main parties as representatives of distinct class interests, and seek to explain their actions on this basis.

Figure 5.5

Companies love Tories.
Donations to the
Conservative Party and
'front' organizations

Source: *Economist* (1984), p. 7

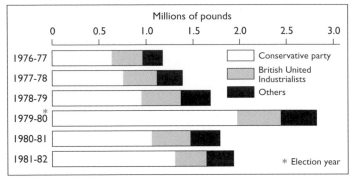

Table 5.9 Sponsored Labour candidates, 1992

	Total	Elected
Transport and General Workers Union (TGWU)	44	38
General Municipal and Boilermakers Union (GMBU)	22	17
National Union of Mineworkers	14	14
Amalgamated Engineering Union	15	13
Manufacturing Science and Finance Union (MSF)	13	13
National Union of Public Employees (NUPE)	15	12
National Union of Rail Maritime and Transport Workers (RMT)	13	12
Confederation of Health Service Employees (COHSE)	6	6
Graphical Paper and Media Union (GMPU)	7	5
Electrical Electronic Telecommunications and Plumbing Union (EETPU)	10	3
National Communication Union (NCU)	4	3
Union of Shop Distributive and Allied Workers (USDAW)	3	3
Transport Salaried Staffs Association (TSSA)	2	2
Associated Society of Locomotive Engineers and Firemen (ASLEF)	2	1
National Association of Colliery Overmen Deputies and Shotfirers (NACODS)	1	1
Iron and Steel Trades Confederation (ISTC)	1	–
Union of Communication Workers (UCW)	1	–
Trade Union sponsored	173	143
Co-operative Party	26	14
All sponsored candidates	199	157

Source: Butler and Kavanagh (1992), p. 227

How far do Figure 5.5 and Table 5.9 support the notion that the two main parties represent distinct class interests? What other information would you need to help you answer this question fully?

If finance is seen as a key factor, the similarity noticed by McKenzie begins to break down. Research by Pinto-Duschinsky, reported in Butler and Kavanagh (1992, p. 260), shows that there are important differences in the level of financial support each receives, as Table 5.10 shows.

Table 5.10 Indicators of financial support for the three major parties

Party	Income (1991)	Expenditure (1991)	HQ Staff (1991)	Campaign expenditure (1992)
Conservative	13.0m	18.1m	200	10.1m
Labour	7.9m	6.8m	152	7.1m
Liberal Democrats	1.6m	1.3m	17	2.1m

Source: Butler and Kavanagh (1992), p. 260

A facet of inequality related to finance is the number of poster sites each party used in the 1992 General Election. The Conservatives used 4,500 (at a cost of £1.5 million), Labour 2,200 (£0.5 million) and the Liberal Democrats 500 (£170,000).

How might such inequalities in financial resources be explained? What implications, if any, do they have for the operation of British democracy?

The end of mass parties?

Some writers, such as Mulgan (1994), have suggested that the era of mass parties is over. He argues that in the post-modern environment, with its fragmenting identities, they no longer fit and are like political dinosaurs whose style of politics is no longer appropriate and no longer motivates people.

To what extent does sociological evidence support the notion that the era of mass parties is now over?
What, if anything do you think might replace them?

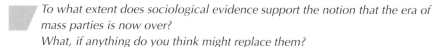

Pressure groups

It has often been argued that British society is becoming more diverse, and this argument has been extended into the political sphere, as we have seen. The political parties, it is said, are too blunt an instrument to represent such diverse interests; people are now looking for more precise instruments to represent their interests and affiliations, and they are finding what they want in pressure groups.

It has been suggested that, since political parties aim to form the government and pressure groups do not, political parties such as the Scottish National Party and Plaid Cymru should really be classified as pressure groups.
What is the basis for this suggestion? How valid do you think the argument is?

Pressure group activity is central to pluralist views of power in society since it is held that pressure groups are now the most important means of articulating the views of the people in the decision-making process. McKenzie (1974, p. 280) argued that they had become 'a far more important channel of communication than parties for the transmission of political ideas from the mass of the citizenry to their rulers'.

There are a number of what might be called pressure groups or factions inside each major political party. The following can be cited as examples: the Bow Group, the Manifesto Group, the Tribune Group, the Campaign Group, the No

Turning Back Group, the Monday Club, the Tory Reform Group, the Labour Coordinating Committee and the Young Liberals.
Find out which political party each of these groups is linked with and how they differ from other groups associated with that party. You should be able to find information on these in any politics textbook.

It has been suggested that by the late 1960s people had become disillusioned with the established political parties, and this led to the growth of the new social movements and also of pressure groups. Coxall (1981) argues that the 1960s and 1970s witnessed an explosion of pressure group membership. He cites the examples of Shelter, which by 1969 had more than 220 affiliated branches, and the Child Poverty Action Group, which by 1970 had over forty. He argues, however, that despite this growth they still mobilized a minority of the population. Coxall and Robins (1994) suggest that in the 1980s some groups, such as the poverty lobby and CND, suffered decline, but others, notably those concerned with the environment and animal welfare, rose to take their place; overall, promotional group membership continued to grow.

However, pluralists would argue that there is still a considerable degree of legitimacy in the system. Their assumption of inertia means they believe people only become involved in pressure group activity if the issue affects them personally. The fact that only a minority of the population is involved in pressure group activity is taken by pluralists as evidence that most people are happy with the existing governmental arrangements.

 How might Marxists, elite theorists and the New Right view the present status of pressure groups? Write a short report on the role of pressure groups in the analysis of power in society offered by these groups of writers.

Pressure group politics – three contrasting models

Elite pluralism

This term has been used to describe the views of writers such as Richardson and Jordan (1979), but it might also be said that some of the modifications Dahl (1971, 1982) has made to his own views bring him very close to this position. Dahl has argued, for instance, that while not all groups gain access to government and some citizens are under-represented in the pressure group process, their interests are nonetheless represented by the government as the individuals concerned make up a large number of voters.

This view remains pluralist because it emphasizes the competition between the groups that do gain access, and because it sees the government as remaining independent of any one group. Elite pluralists believe that as a result the system remains largely democratic.

Richardson and Jordan have argued that governments act to minimize conflict between groups and to secure agreement. They nonetheless recognize inequalities between groups, which they argue can best be described by the insider/outsider division. Certain groups appear to have greater access to government than others. One oft-cited insider group is the National Farmers Union, which has clear access to and close links with the Ministry of Agriculture. (However, it might be argued that the increasing importance of government at European level in this area serves to maintain a competitive and changing environment.) In contrast, an example of an outsider group would be the Campaign for Nuclear Disarmament, whose views are not welcomed inside the Ministry of Defence or any other department of government.

Elite pluralists argue that, despite the division between insider and outsider groups, the government remains fundamentally pluralist because those that are excluded react to their exclusion and this leads to their views being taken seriously. The classic example of this, according to Richardson and Jordan, is the way environmental views have now been accepted into the mainstream of political debate, although most of the pressure groups involved, such as Greenpeace and Friends of the Earth, would certainly be classified as outsider groups.

Fragmented elitism

Marsh (1983) argues that the closest approximation to corporatist arrangements occurred in the economic/industrial field in the 1950s and 1960s, while in other areas a greater plurality of groups has been involved. He argues that there is an elitist element to the system since the various elites in government and in pressure groups are only marginally influenced by the rest of the population. This contrasts with the continuing emphasis in the elite pluralist model on the government as representative of all interests.

The fragmented elitism model sees decisions being taken that reflect particular interests: 'Decisions are taken with little coherence and with little concern for the national interest. The policy adopted on any issue reflects not the national interest but rather the aims of the strongest coalition of groups and interests on that issue' (Marsh 1983, pp. 12–13). This view differs from the classical elite model in seeing the elite groups who run society as fragmented and lacking in cohesion.

Marsh argues that there are important divisions inside the government, for example between departments and between ministers. As a result, a number of key pressure groups are able to use power for their own ends. Because of their weight in the economy, the government cannot afford to ignore powerful interests such as the CBI and the TUC. These groups are powerful because of their structural position rather than their level of activity. In contrast, ideological groups such as CND enjoy no such structural advantage, and therefore any contest between economic and ideological groups will be unequal.

Marsh maintains, however, that whatever its structural advantages no group is guaranteed continuing dominance because the fragmented nature of the elites involved, both in government and in the pressure groups themselves, leads to continual shifts in the power hierarchy.

Veto group model

Lindblom (1977) has argued that there are certain groups whose power is such that they have an effective veto over policy initiatives in their area. He points to one group in particular, namely business, which enjoys a privileged position inside the decision-making process because of the importance of business for the economy and therefore for the political fate of governments.

This emphasis on the privileged position enjoyed by a particular group is in line with the elitist view of power, and espousing such a view represents a shift for Lindblom, who originally endorsed a pluralist analysis. His current views contrast with the insistence (seen even in elite pluralism) that the government takes decisions which do not reflect particular interests.

Marsh has criticized Lindblom's model from a fragmented elitist position by arguing that there are important divisions within business, so Lindblom exaggerates the power of business, which he argues does not enjoy the power of veto over government policy.

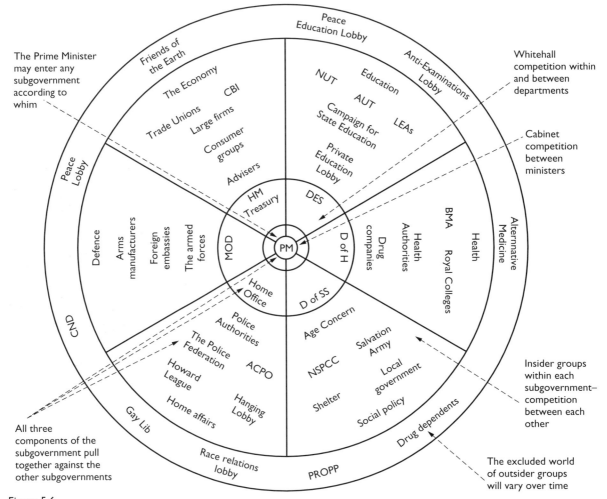

Figure 5.6

Pressure groups and policy communities

Source: Kingdom (1991), p. 421

Which view of the way power is distributed among pressure groups is depicted in Figure 5.6?

Draw a similar diagram to show the policy communities related to other government departments, for example, Agriculture, Environment, the Welsh Office, the Foreign Office and Transport.

Explain how the three models of pressure group politics outlined in this section compare with classical pluralist and elite theory views on the distribution of power in society.

Insider and outsider groups

An important dichotomy developed to investigate inequalities between pressure groups in terms of access to government is the division between 'insiders' and 'outsiders'. Grant (1985) argues that this is a better typology because it takes into account the actions of government as well as those of the pressure group in analysing the extent of influence on policy a group might have. The government itself is held to be an important actor in deciding whether pressure groups are given insider status, providing them with good access to possible positions of influence. Outsider groups, on the other hand, are forced to rely rather more on gaining sufficient public support for their campaigns to force action from the government, though it should not be supposed that they are totally excluded, as Table 5.11 shows.

Table 5.11 Percentages of pressure groups in contact with various levels of government

| | Percentage of groups in contact on a weekly/monthly basis | | | |
| | Weekly | | Monthly | |
	Outsider	Insider	Outsider	Insider
Prime Minister	--	2	10	14
Cabinet ministers	5	12	37	45
Junior ministers	10	14	38	67
Senior civil servants	12	25	45	49
Junior civil servants	12	55	62	76
House of Commons	20	39	51	72
House of Lords	8	23	36	63
Political parties	13	27	34	51
Media	74	86	84	94

Source: Baggott (1992), p. 21

Which of the following pressure groups would you consider 'insiders' and which 'outsiders'?
- *Friends of the Earth*
- *Animal Liberation Front*
- *The British Medical Association*
- *The National Farmers Union*
- *Age Concern*
- *Campaign for Nuclear Disarmament*
- *Confederation of British Industry*

Explain your choices in a short report. Draw up a list of other 'insider' and 'outsider' pressure groups.

An interesting study of a recent successful outsider group is that of the All-Britain Anti-Poll Tax Federation. Barr (1992) argues that this is an excellent example of an ideological outsider group that was successful because its demand for the abolition of the Poll Tax was non-negotiable, and it was able to mobilize large numbers of people around its central strategy of non-payment which exposed weaknesses in the political system concerned with the enforcement of local taxation.

The success of this group has spurred on other outsider groups, notably the Campaign Against the Child Support Agency and the various groups to be found under the broad umbrella of the Anti-Roads Movement. Much of this movement may indeed be classified as a new social movement with an emphasis on lifestyle. The occupants of Claremont Road in east London who formed part of the anti-M11 campaign created a festival atmosphere in their road which acted both as a blockade and as a basis of building further support. The publication of the Criminal Justice Bill which some feel is designed to criminalize alternative lifestyles and direct-action protests also led to the creation of a new campaign linking together a number of groups in ways very similar to the anti-Poll Tax movement.

Essay Questions

1) 'Whatever the role granted in theory to the extra-parliamentary wings of the parties, in practice final authority rests in both parties with the parliamentary party and its leadership. In this fundamental respect the distribution of power within the two main major parties is the same' (McKenzie 1963). How valid is this view in the light of contemporary sociological evidence and argument?

2) 'As the central organizing force of democracy, it is hard to see the decline of the party reversing' (Mulgan 1994). Evaluate the validity of this statement with reference to contemporary sociological evidence.

3) To what extent does sociological evidence support the notion that the importance of pressure groups in the political process has declined in recent years?

Coursework suggestions

1) All three major political parties have experienced major organizational change in recent years. The Liberal Democrats emerged from the Liberal/SDP Alliance, and the method of electing the leader has changed in both the Labour and Conservative parties. (For more on the Labour Party's reforms, see Kelly and Foster 1991, Coxall and Robins 1994 or Cordell 1992; and for information on changes in the Conservative electoral process, see Kelly 1992, Coxall and Robins 1994 or Cordell 1992.) Consider how these changes have tested the validity of theories about the distribution of power inside political parties such as those developed by Michels and McKenzie.

In order to do this you will need to study the array of secondary material available and then investigate in further detail through the use of a questionnaire sent to the HQs of these parties or interviews with party members in your locality. If you are conducting interviews you

might seek responses from local office-holders in the parties as well as ordinary members to see if they have different perceptions of the effect of these changes.

2) Most analysts of pressure groups utilize the insider/outsider distinction. Conduct a case study of one insider group and one outsider group to consider how important this distinction is to the success of a pressure group. Choose two pressure groups that deal with broadly the same policy area, one of which you would characterize as an insider group and one as an outsider. Analyse the important ways in which they differ.

You could start by looking at the different methods of operation adopted by the groups you select. For example, the survey by Baggott (1992) suggests very different patterns of contact. His categories could provide the basis for a questionnaire to use in your case study, but you also need to consider other forms of action the group engages in. Conduct a content analysis of newspapers to assess the amount of coverage your groups receive in the media. Try to obtain information on the sociological characteristics of the membership of the two groups and consider the extent to which there are significant differences. Finally, consider how successful the two groups have been in achieving their aims. Consider how useful the insider/outsider dichotomy is in explaining any differences revealed by your research.

Bibliography

Baggott, R. (1988) 'Pressure group politics in Britain: change and decline?', *Talking Politics*, Autumn

—— (1992) 'The measurement of change in pressure group politics', *Talking Politics*, Autumn

Barr, G. (1992) 'The anti-Poll Tax movement: an insider's view of an outsider group', *Talking Politics*, Summer

Blake, R. (1985) *The Conservative Party from Peel to Thatcher*, London: Fontana

Bulmer-Thomas, I. (1953) *The Party System in Great Britain*, London: Phoenix House

Burch, M. and Moran, M. (1987) 'The changing political elite', in M. Burch and M. Moran (eds) *British Politics: A Reader*, Manchester: Manchester University Press

Butler, D. and Kavanagh, D. (1992) *The British General Election of 1992*, London: Macmillan

Coates, D. (1985) 'Parties in pursuit of socialism', in D. Coates, G. Johnston and R. Bush (eds) *A Socialist Anatomy of Britain*, Cambridge: Polity Press

Cook, C. (1993) *A Short History of the Liberal Party*, London, Macmillan

Cordell, J. (1992) *Essential Government and Politics*, London: Collins Educational

Coxall, B. (1981) *Parties and Pressure Groups*, London: Longman

Coxall, B. and Robins, L. (1989) *Contemporary British Politics*, London: Macmillan

—— (1994) *Contemporary British Politics*, 2nd edn, London: Macmillan

Dahl, R. (1971) *Polyarchy*, New Haven, CT: Yale University Press

—— (1982) *Dilemmas of Pluralist Democracies*, New Haven, CT: Yale University Press

Dunleavy, P. (1993) 'The political parties', in P. Dunleavy (ed.) *Developments in British Politics 4*, London: Macmillan

Economist (1984) *Political Britain Today*, London: Economist

Gamble, A. (1983) 'Thatcherism and Conservative politics', in Hall and Jacques (1983)

Grant, W. (1985) 'Insider and outsider pressure groups', *Social Studies Review*, September

Hall, S. (1993) 'Thatcherism today', *New Statesman and Society*, 26 November

Hall, S. and Jacques, M. (eds) (1983) *The Politics of Thatcherism*, London: Lawrence & Wishart

Hindess, B. (1971) *The Decline of Working-Class Politics*, London: MacGibbon & Kee

Ingle, S. (1993) 'Political parties in the nineties', *Talking Politics*, Autumn

Jessop, B. (1992) 'From Social Democracy to Thatcherism: twenty-five years of British politics', in N. Abercrombie and A. Warde (eds) *Social Change in Britain*, Cambridge: Polity Press

Kelly, R. (1992) 'Power in the Conservative Party', *Politics Review*, April

—— (1993) 'After Margaret: the Conservative Party since 1990', *Talking Politics*, Summer

Kelly, R. and Foster, S. (1991) 'Power in the Labour Party', *Politics Review*, September

Kingdom, J. (1992) *No Such Thing as Society?*, Buckingham: Open University Press

Kingdom, P. (1991) *Government and Politics in the UK*, Cambridge: Polity

Lindblom, C. (1977) *Politics and Markets*, New York: Basic Books

McKenzie, R.T. (1963) *British Political Parties*, revised edn, London: Heinemann

—— (1974) 'Parties, pressure groups and the British political process', in R. Kimber and J. Richardson (eds) *Pressure Groups in Britain: A Reader*, London: Dent

Marqusee, M. (1994) 'Double-edged democracy', *Red Pepper*, July

Marsh, G. (ed.) (1983) *Pressure Politics: Interest Groups in Britain*, London: Junction

Michels, R. (1962) *Political Parties*, New York: Free Press

Mulgan, G. (1994) 'Party-free politics', *New Statesman and Society*, 15 April

Richardson, J.J. and Jordan, G. (1979) *Governing Under Pressure*, Oxford: Martin Robertson

Seyd, P. (1987) *The Rise and Fall of the Labour Left*, Basingstoke: Macmillan

Seyd, P. and Whiteley, P. (1992) *Labour's Grassroots: The Politics of Party Membership*, Oxford: Clarendon Press

Smith, J. and McLean, I. (1994) 'The Poll Tax and the electoral register', in A. Heath, R. Jowell and J. Curtice (eds) with Bridget Taylor, *Labour's Last Chance? The 1992 Election and Beyond,* Aldershot: Dartmouth

Whiteley, P. (1983) *The Labour Party in Crisis*, London: Methuen

Whiteley, P., Seyd, P. and Richardson, J. (1994) *True Blues: The Politics of Conservative Party Membership,* Oxford: Oxford University Press

Willetts, D. (1992) *Modern Conservatism*, Harmondsworth: Penguin

6

Revolution and political change

Louis XVI of France: 'My God! It's a revolt!'

The Duc de La Rochefouchard-Liancourt: 'No, Sire, that is a revolution.'

Conversation, Paris, 1789

'Revolutions are not made, they come. A revolution is as natural as an oak. It comes out of the past. Its foundations are laid far back.'

Wendell Phillips

Any attempt at a social analysis of political structures and political change in society must consider the important role that revolutions play. This is particularly true of sociology, a subject whose foundations lay in the attempt to explain and consider the implications of the two most important revolutions of Europe at the time, namely the French and Industrial Revolutions.

This point is made clear by Michael Kimmel:

> Classical sociological theorists were preoccupied with the question of revolution. For one thing, they all lived and wrote during eras of revolution . . . Marx and Tocqueville wrote their major works in response to the calamitous upheavals of 1848, when no fewer than fifty revolutionary movements vied for political power in the major states and the smaller countries of Western Europe. Weber and Freud were each deeply affected by the First World War (as well as the Russian Revolution to a lesser degree) and Durkheim responded directly to both socialist revolutionary organizing and the crisis in France precipitated by the Dreyfus affair. [Kimmel 1990, p. 15]

It was thus in a revolutionary context that these writers developed their general theories about society. Those who saw society as generally orderly and consensual were forced to consider how their theories could incorporate an explanation of revolution and social change. On the other hand those who saw social change and conflict as the normal course of events were concerned whether revolutions did actually bring about change or merely substituted one leadership for another. It is this question that underlay debate between Marxists and Weberians over the legacy of the Russian Revolution of 1917.

1) Make notes on the reflections of Marx, Weber and Durkheim on the revolutions of their times. The following books provide in-depth accounts of these three key sociologists: Gerth and Mills (1948); Lukes (1973); Worsley (1982).
2) Draw up a table to show the differences between these key sociologists.

Revolutionary movements have played an important part in the development of democracy and the nation-state. In France one of the key causes of the revolution was an attempt to extend control to the people and wrest it from the hands of the absolute monarch, Louis XVI.

In Britain, there is today a statue of Oliver Cromwell in the grounds of the Palace of Westminster where MPs conduct their business. The statue is there because it was the revolutionary struggle led by Cromwell (culminating in the beheading of Charles I) in the English Civil War in the 1640s that won for Parliament some control over events. But revolutions are not merely interesting historical events; they are very much a part of the contemporary political scene. One of the most important phenomena of recent years has been the revolutionary transformations that swept through Eastern Europe in 1989, bringing down the Stalinist regimes there. The causes and implications of this movement are a central concern of political sociology today.

3) In what ways was the English Civil War concerned with democracy?
4) What changes brought about by the English Civil War are still a part of contemporary political structures in Britain? What has been abandoned?

Reflections on revolution

Psychological theories

Freud argued that collective behaviour is the result of the inadequate development of individual egos, which induces affected individuals to follow a leader like an obedient herd. Collective action is thus an expression of individuals' neurotic needs.

This view has been applied to revolutionary movements, most famously by Gustav Le Bon (1913, 1960), who emphasized the pathological nature of revolutionary action. Essentially Le Bon argued that collective action was irrational and that in the throes of this irrational act people can be led to undertake acts of terrible violence. Le Bon was attempting to explain the outbreak of the Terror during the French Revolution, but the idea has been more widely applied.

In rebuttal, critics point out that revolutions are not necessarily very violent. In relation to the Russian Revolution of 1917, Sukhanov (1955, p. 620) notes that 'the decisive operations that had begun were quite bloodless', and Cliff (1976, p. 374) puts the total loss of life in Petrograd in the revolution at five, all during the assault on the Winter Palace. Proponents of this psychological theory also seem to ignore the repressive force used by governments against revolutionary movements. Viewing violence as irrational overlooks the important fact that the use or threat of force underpins the authority of all states.

An alternative psychological approach, derived from the work of Wolfenstein (1971), claims that the roots of the revolutionary personality lie in problems in the father–son relationship. This idea is derived from Freud's notion of the Oedipus complex, according to which young boys experience desire for their mothers, which may bring them into conflict with their fathers, but if ultimately resolved leads them to break with their mothers and identify with their fathers. Wolfenstein argues that if this complex remains unresolved the adult male may displace feelings for the father onto the main symbol of authority, the state. Revolutionaries are therefore really angry with their fathers.

This view has been strongly criticized on two grounds. First, in effect it views the authority of the state as legitimate since revolutionary behaviour is held to be caused by psychological disturbance rather than by the actions of the state. Second, because the Oedipus complex concentrates on the father–son relationship, 'such a model is, by definition, uninterested in and incapable of explaining revolutionary activity and leadership by women, such as Rosa Luxembourg, Emma Goldman, or Alexandra Kollontai' (Kimmel 1990, p. 72).

An overall criticism of psychological views is that they attempt to explain large-scale social movements and social structures in terms of the state of mind of individuals. Lenin, for instance, may have been a leading figure in the Russian Revolution, but he did not make it all by himself.

Functionalist views

The functionalist school of sociology considers the normal state of society to be social equilibrium; social change and revolution are thus anomalies for which an explanation must be found. In this search functionalists draw particularly upon the work of Durkheim and Pareto.

Durkheim (1947) argued that as society moved from being based on mechanical to organic solidarity, there was an increasing division of labour, and as a result the integrating mechanisms of society began to break down. Economic change was moving faster than the structures of social regulation, leading to a state of anomie, characterized by the collapse of social order. Revolutions may be one outcome of this process. Revolution is therefore an effect of the disruption caused by modernization.

 What other social phenomena did Durkheim use his theory of anomie to explain?

Chalmers Johnson (1964) saw revolution as arising from destabilization introduced into a system in equilibrium from a number of sources, such as technological change and the effects of other revolutions. The key internal danger is a change in the societal value system, such as might be caused by the process of secularization. These long-term factors lead to what Johnson calls 'multiple dysfunction'. However, in order for revolution to occur it is also necessary that societal elites have lost political authority. If they can restore their legitimacy they might adapt to the changed circumstances and avert revolution. This points to the importance of the quality of political leadership. Here the functionalists draw upon Pareto's theory of the circulation of elites, in which he suggested that the key process of history was a continual cycle whereby the existing elite becomes weak and decadent and is replaced by another. The functionalists adopt this to suggest that the quality of the leadership is an important element in determining whether revolution occurs.

A third element of the functionalist analysis of revolution is that it suggests revolutions are simply temporary deviations from a condition of political stability and equilibrium. In analysing peasant revolutions, Huntingdon (1968) claimed that where they are successful they merely result in urban elites imposing their will on the peasants. The implication is that no revolution can truly succeed. As a result, functionalist views have been deployed prominently to argue that revolutions are essentially utopian and irrational. But since the strains that lead to revolutionary upsurges are real enough, functionalist writers argue that there is a need to implement key reforms of societal institutions to assist the process of modernization and avoid the danger of revolution.

Critics have charged that the functionalists' insistence that societies are based on consensus means they see all political authority as legitimate, and this leads them to underestimate the use of repressive force as an element in the power structure of most states which may act as a spur to the development of revolutionary movements.

The functionalists' generally negative view of revolutionary change has at times been influential in determining US policy towards social and political change in the world.

 One example of this can be seen in the involvement of US social scientists in Project Camelot. This is reported in detail in Bilton et al. (1987, p. 607).

    1) How might a functionalist view of revolution and society lead social scientists to engage in such research?

    2) What concerns were raised about their involvement?

Marxist theories

Marx is the social thinker most readily associated with revolution. In Marx's writing the whole history of humanity can be seen as the succession of class rule of one sort or another bought to power by revolutionary upheavals. This idea is perhaps best expressed in the opening passage of the *Communist Manifesto*:

> The history of all hitherto existing society is the history of class struggles. Freeman and slave, patrician and plebeian, lord and serf, guildmaster and journeyman, in a word, oppressor and oppressed, stood in constant opposition to one another, carried on an uninterrupted, now hidden, now open fight, a fight that each time ended, either in a revolutionary re-constitution of society at large, or in the common ruin of the contending classes. [Marx and Engels, 1968 edn, pp. 35–6]

The key ideas here are that society changes by means of revolutions, in other words thoroughgoing transformations, and that the basis of such revolutions is the class struggle.

Marxists have therefore consistently analysed revolutions in class terms. The French Revolution was a bourgeois revolution, according to this view, and the Russian Revolution was a proletarian one. This underlines the centrality of the sphere of production to Marxist theories. Marx's theory of society stresses that the economic base of society to some degree determines its social, political and ideological structures.

Marxism has been criticized as a form of economic determinism which sees social and political change as dependent upon and caused by economic processes. Marx

Figure 6.1

Scenes from the Russian Revolution

himself rejected such an automatic link while insisting that the sphere of production is ultimately the decisive factor:

> One thing is clear: the Middle Ages could not live on Catholicism, nor could the ancient world on politics. On the contrary, it is the manner in which they gained their livelihood which explains why in one case politics, in the other case, Catholicism, played the chief part. [Marx, 1976 edn, Vol. 1, pp. 175–6]

What do you understand by the term 'economic determinism'? To what extent do you consider this to be a valid criticism of Marxism?

Instead of focusing in the traditional Marxist manner on urban classes, Moore (1966) emphasized the class struggle in the countryside during the commercialization of agriculture. The outcome of the struggle may be democracy, fascism or socialism, according to Moore, depending on the line-up of class forces in the countryside, crucially the peasantry and the landlords. On this basis, he argued, it is possible to explain why England developed towards bourgeois democracy, while in Germany and Japan fascism developed, and in France, China and Russia there were revolutionary transformations of society.

Moore's work has been helpful in reminding us that the development of capitalism does not automatically lead to democracy (as claimed by modernization theorists in debates about the sociology of development). In showing that development in Japan and Germany led in the direction of fascism, Moore undermined this simple equation.

A persistent criticism of Marxist theorists has been that they assign little significance to extra-economic factors such as the state and the realm of ideas. None of them excludes these factors altogether, but their critics argue that they nonetheless treat them as mere epiphenomena.

A second, linked criticism is that, in focusing on class conflicts internal to societies, many Marxist theories miss out on the international context which often plays an important role in revolution. This is less true of Wallerstein's world systems theory (1974), but that is still a theory about the international economic order and thus remains open to the accusation of economic reductionism.

Neo-Weberian views

Several influential neo-Weberian writers have argued that Marxists cannot defend themselves against the charge that their theory is a form of economic determinism, no matter how they may qualify it. Even the neo-Marxist conception of the state (see Chapter 7), which grants it relative autonomy from the economy, still ultimately views the economy as a more important determinant of social change than other sectors of society.

 One of the key debates touching upon the causes of revolutions is about the origins of the modern state. For a Marxist account of this see Anderson (1974); for an alternative, broadly Weberian view see Poggi (1978). If you can locate these, write a report outlining the differences in the explanations offered.

The neo-Weberians consider that there are several autonomous spheres of society, any of which may at a given time be the most important determining element in social change. Crucially, they argue that the state is not dependent on the class structure, but an active agent in its own right.

One exponent of this type of analysis is Theda Skocpol, who states her objections to the Marxist theory as follows: 'classical Marxism failed to foresee or adequately explain the autonomous power, for good or ill, of states as administrative and coercive machineries embedded in a militarized international states system' (Skocpol 1979, p. 292).

According to this approach, the causes of revolution lie either in divisions within the state bureaucracy or in the effects of military competition. This analysis reflects the great emphasis on power in the works of Max Weber, who in turn leaned heavily on ideas developed by Friedrich Nietzsche, who argued that there existed a general 'will to power' (Nietzsche 1969).

Weber located the immediate cause of revolution in the breakdown of the capacity of the state to use the means of violence at its disposal – the police and the armed forces. He held that as societies develop they become increasingly bureaucratic. Unlike Marxists, he believed that revolutions offered no respite from this process. He argued that the type of authority most suited to revolutionary movements, the charismatic, was transitory. After a successful revolution this type of authority does not persist because the leader becomes part of a bureaucratic structure. The institutionalization of a revolution therefore leads to a strengthening of the bureaucratic power of the state.

In the models deriving from this analysis the underlying driving force of history is not purely economic competition but competition between states to gain power in the international arena. This often leads to a focus on war as the basis of states and therefore of revolutions (since revolutions can only occur when there are states). For instance: 'It was war, and preparations for war, that provided the most potent energizing stimulus for the concentration of administrative resources and fiscal reorganization that characterized the rise of absolutism' (Giddens 1985, p. 112). War, not capitalism, is seen as the key basis of political power, and wars existed before capitalism. The point is therefore to deny that the contemporary state is a creation of capitalism. These theorists therefore argue that revolutions cannot be explained on the basis of a purely class analysis, as Marxists attempt to do.

In his theory of structuration Giddens argues that the modern world is organized by both capitalism and the nation-state, and the state is not reducible to capitalism. The contradictions in the modern world may be generated as much by the state as by capitalism. The thrust of this is to deny that an economic crisis of capitalism would inevitably lead to revolution, as some Marxist models seem to imply.

However, perhaps the most consistent attempt to analyse revolutions using the state as the primary causal ingredient has been made by Skocpol (1979). She argues strongly that revolutions are to be explained in structural terms, by which she means that they are not amenable to explanation on the basis of the mobilization of actors (as for example in Lenin's notion of a conscious revolutionary party). Put another way, revolutions come about, they are not made.

The key cause of revolutions, according to Skocpol, is the collapse of the existing state structure, not as a result of conscious action by those opposed to it, but because of structural factors, especially military and economic competition in the international arena. In order to deal with military defeat or fiscal crisis, the state may attempt reforms. If these are unsuccessful political crises may follow, out of which a revolution might arise if there is a large-scale mass uprising. This, however, is dependent on the political autonomy of the masses from the state. A successful revolution leads to the construction of a more powerful state. States are therefore both the cause and the consequence of revolutions. Skocpol illustrates these arguments with case studies. France, Russia and China had all suffered defeats in war prior to their revolutions, and in all these cases the peasant villages had some degree of autonomy from the state. In contrast, revolution did not occur where countries had not suffered serious military defeat, or where there were strong bureaucratic controls over the local communities, as in England, Prussia and Japan.

The model firmly locates revolution in an international context. However, in contrast to Wallerstein (1974), who argues in his world systems model that international economic competition makes countries in the semi-periphery most likely to experience revolutionary change since, unlike countries in the core and the periphery, their class structure is formed by the process of 'combined and uneven development' described by the Russian revolutionary Leon Trotsky, Skocpol points to the primacy of the international state structure: 'Although uneven economic development always lies in the background, developments within the international state system as such – especially defeats in wars or threats of invasion and struggles over colonial controls – have directly contributed to virtually all outbreaks of revolutionary crises' (Skocpol 1979, p. 23).

An emphasis on the international political/military context is central to the work of another writer broadly in this tradition, Michael Mann. He argues that there are four sources of social power, namely the economic, the political, the military and the ideological (Mann 1986, 1993). He claims that the rise of the English state cannot be explained in terms of the rise of capitalism, as some Marxist accounts suggest, but instead there is a need to concentrate on the international geopolitical environment, and in particular wars.

Figure 6.2 correlates growth in British state expenditure with periods of war. Mann (1988) argues that the trends illustrated in the figure led to the increasing militarization of the state, and emphasizes that this militarization was primarily a response to external foes and not internal disorder; the use of the army for purposes of internal control is only occasioned by the increased burden of taxation needed to pay for military expenditure whose initial spur is the threat of external enemies.

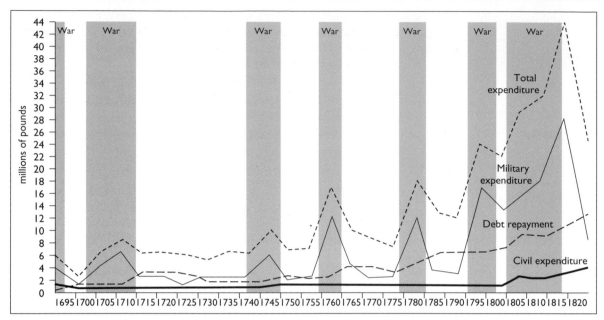

Figure 6.2

British state expenditure, 1695–1820 (at constant prices: 1690–99 = 100)

Source: Mann (1988), p. 106

1) *Explain how war and preparation for war can be considered a key element in the development of revolutionary situations in: (a) Russia, 1917, (b) the Soviet Union, 1989.*

2) *Consider the periods surrounding the two world wars. Research whether there were greater numbers of revolutions in these periods.*

Marxist critics of this emphasis on war and the state have argued that the ability to wage war depends upon production and therefore class relations, so the outcome of wars can be affected by the class structure. Brenner (1986) argues that the key reason for the rise of military expenditure in the pre-capitalist states was the need to shift the burden of taxation onto the peasantry. The feudal system of production was unable to produce increased returns for the owners of production. The only way they could increase their income was to redistribute wealth away from the peasants, and this required the building up of means of coercion, leading to the creation of military machines.

Callinicos, drawing on the work of Lenin and Bukharin and the notion of the fusion of the state and capital in the system of state capitalism, has argued that this point can be generalized for more recent times:

> The war-making capacities of early modern states came to depend increasingly on whether or not they were able to draw on the intensive development of the productive forces made possible by capitalist production relations . . . In the course of the nineteenth century two competitive logics – the military struggle between the great powers and the economic interaction of accumulating capitals – fused. . . . The history of the past 150 years is thus that of the subordination of the process of 'political accumulation' – warfare and state-building – which emerged within feudal relations of production to the competitive accumulation of capital, a transformation which has involved the increasing interpenetration of the state and capital. [Callinicos 1987, p. 170]

1) Both Mann and Callinicos stress the growth of military expenditure, but they give very different reasons for this occurrence. Explain the differences. (Hint: In talking about the nation-state and its need for arms, one emphasizes an 'internal' reason and the other an 'external' reason.)
2) How do these views on the military apparatus relate to more general Marxist and Weberian approaches to explaining political change and revolution?

The Eastern European revolutions of 1989

For many years political sociologists devoted much of their time to exploring the contrast between capitalism and communism. The version of communism analysed was that operative in Eastern Europe (and China and Cuba), and the debate took place in a climate affected by the Cold War.

How might the Cold War have affected this debate?

The thrust of much pluralist writing was to argue that the communist regimes were similar to that of Nazi Germany on the basis of their totalitarianism. The fall of the Stalinist regimes in Eastern Europe was thus hailed by pluralist thinkers as a vindication of the superiority of the liberal democratic model. The more radical pluralists have also seen in the events of 1989 models of how to build movements for mass participation in the political process. These ideas are being developed both by social-democratic pluralists and by ex-Marxists who are interested in developing a new radical analysis of democracy.

An alternative reaction to the fall of the Eastern European regimes based on New Right thinking has been to emphasize the superiority of free market capitalism. The most notable exponent of this type of analysis is Fukuyama (1989, 1992), who has argued that the Eastern European revolutions represent the end of history, meaning that they expose the idea of progress beyond capitalism as historically bankrupt.

One problem with this type of analysis has been the rising unpopularity of the free market policies that have dominated Eastern European politics since 1989. In some cases this resentment has led to the re-emergence of the former Communists as a large electoral force; for example in Hungary the Socialist Party, successor to the former Communist Party, were returned to power in May 1994.

Use newspaper cuttings or CD-ROM to investigate the revolutions in Eastern Europe in 1989. In particular, look at the contrasting experiences of Czechoslovakia and Romania. Write a short report of about 300 words outlining how these examples can be used to develop our knowledge of revolutionary change.

Marxism and the revolutions of 1989

The theoretical tradition that has been most affected by the revolutions of Eastern Europe is of course Marxism. The official ideology of the Stalinist states was Marxism, and it has therefore been argued that the failure of those regimes and their overthrow in 1989 shows that Marxism as a social theory is also bankrupt.

Indeed, a number of thinkers who were aligned with Marxism now declare themselves to be post-Marxists, partly as a result of these changes and partly because they have been impressed by the growth of new social movements that stress other bases of political action than social class. For instance Laclau and Mouffe (1985) and Mouffe (1992) now argue for a form of radical democracy, and virtually all the remaining ex-Althusserian Marxists now offer a mixture of neo-pluralism and neo-corporatism (see for example Hirst 1990; Hindess 1987; Pearce 1989). Another example of a move away from Marxism is the school associated with the *New Times* project (Hall and Jacques 1989), closely associated with the Communist Party journal, *Marxism Today*, which has now ceased to exist.

According to Miliband (1991), social democracy will in future be the main alternative to the right; socialists will be marginalized and reduced to a sort of pressure group. He argues that autocratic regimes arose out of the anti-capitalist revolutions in Eastern Europe partly as a consequence of the Leninist concept of the vanguard. He concludes that while socialists need to be critical of the limitations of *capitalist* democracy, they must be the staunchest defenders of the idea of democracy, and this means developing it in radical directions by fostering many centres of power outside the state, and developing autonomous associations.

There are continuing Marxist traditions. Some writers have always denied that the Stalinist states of Eastern Europe were genuine embodiments of Marxism. There are broadly two traditions that uphold such views.

The first, prominent in academic sociological circles, is that of analytical Marxism. One of the leading members of this trend is Erik Olin Wright, who explains his continuing adherence to Marxism by reference to its usefulness as a social theory:

> In both the popular press and the scholarly media the collapse of regimes ruled by communist parties is often equated with the collapse of Marxism as a social theory. However, while there is an unquestionably an historical link between Marxism and capital-C Communism, they are not interchangeable. Marxism is a tradition of social theory, albeit a tradition that has been deeply embedded in efforts to change the world. [Wright 1994, p. 234]

He believes that the events of 1989 require a reformulation of Marxism, but he nonetheless argues that a reformulated Marxism is preferable to the post-modernist radical visions which are the main alternative. He maintains that class analysis will remain central to sociological analysis in the future.

 How convincing do you find Wright's defence of Marxism? Do you feel it has any future as a sociological perspective after the events of 1989?

A second tradition is based on the writings of Leon Trotsky, a leader of the Russian Revolution who denounced the regime established by Stalin as a betrayal of communism. One important current here is associated with the journal *New Left Review*. One of its editors, Robin Blackburn, has edited a collection by socialist and Marxist writers reflecting on the events of 1989 entitled *After The Fall*. Blackburn himself argues that there is a need for a more complex understanding of society than Marxists have traditionally advanced, but it is still necessary to expose the many problems involved in capitalist society and to defend the idea of the socialized market against the free market ideas of the New Right.

The notion that the market can in any way be useful for socialists is rejected by other Marxists such as Harman (1989). Along with others (see especially Cliff 1974) he has argued that the Soviet Union and the states of Eastern Europe were not communist but state capitalist. This means that a ruling class did exist in these states, and lived off the proceeds of the exploitation of others. These states were in competition with the West through military competition, and this was the underlying dynamic that forced the ruling classes in those societies to exploit others.

Conclusion

Revolutions have played an important role in political and social change, and the classical sociologists all reflected on the effects of the revolutions of their time.

The revolutions that spread across Eastern Europe in 1989 are having a similar effect on contemporary social thinkers. In particular they have prompted a re-evaluation of the meaning of Marxism, a debate which will have wide-raging implications for the future of social theory and indeed political action, and generated renewed interest in neo-pluralist theory with its emphasis on liberal democracy as the system that offers the best hope for the future. The radical ex-Marxists effectively offer a vision of a more participatory form of democracy which largely rejects the Marxist emphasis on the need for a revolution to overthrow capitalism.

Essay Questions

1) 'The passing of state power from one class to another is the first, the main, the basic principle of revolution, both in the strictly scientific and in the practical political meaning of that term' (Lenin, *State and Revolution*).

'Questions of state power have been basic in social-revolutionary transformations, but state power cannot be understood only as an instrument of class domination, nor can changes in state structures be explained primarily in terms of class conflicts' (Skocpol, *States and Social Revolutions*).

Explain and evaluate these contrasting theories of revolution.

2) Giddens (1985) remarks that revolutions are distinctly modern affairs since they are aimed at the nation-state, an invention of modernity. Some would argue that we now live in a post-modern era in which the nation-state is losing its importance, and as a consequence notions of revolution may now be outmoded. How far does sociological evidence support this suggestion?

Coursework suggestions

1) The 'revolutions' that took place in Eastern Europe in 1989 constituted an important set of tests for sociological theories. Consider whether these events were really revolutions in the traditional sense of the term. Which 'classic' revolution did the events of 1989 most resemble? Another comparison you might like to draw is with the Sandinista revolution in Nicaragua.

Undoubtedly the best book detailing

sociological theories of revolution is Kimmel (1990). Numerous books have appeared on the transformations in Eastern Europe from a variety of perspectives; consult the Bibliography for sources.

2) A second question to consider is the causes of these revolutions. Apply the analyses outlined in this chapter, and consider which theory is best supported by the evidence.

Bibliography

Anderson, P. (1974) *Lineages of the Absolutist State,* London: Verso

Blackburn, R. (ed.) (1991) *After The Fall: The Failure of Communism and the Future of Socialism*, London: Verso

Brenner, R. (1986) 'The social basis of economic development', in J. Roemer (ed.) *Analytical Marxism*, Cambridge: Cambridge University Press

Callinicos, A. (1991) T*he Revenge of History,* Cambridge: Polity

Callinicos, A. (1987) *Making History*, Cambridge: Polity

Cliff, T. (1974) *State Capitalism in Russia*, London: Pluto

—— (1976) *Lenin: All Power to the Soviets,* London: Pluto

Durkheim, E. (1947) *The Division of Labour in Society,* New York: Free Press

Fukuyama, F. (1989) 'The end of history?', *The National Interest*, Vol. 16, Summer

—— (1992) *The End of History and the Last Man,* London: Hamish Hamilton

Gerth, H.H. and Mills, C.W. (eds) (1948) *From Max Weber: Essays in Sociology,* London: Routledge

Giddens, A. (1985) *The Nation-State and Violence*, Cambridge: Polity Press

Hall, S. and Jacques, M. (eds) (1989) *New Times,* London: Lawrence & Wishart

Harman, C. (1989) 'The myth of market socialism', *International Socialism Journal*, Spring

Hindess, B. (1987) *Politics and Class Analysis,* Oxford: Blackwell

Hirst, P. (1990) *Representative Democracy and Its Limits,* Cambridge: Polity

Huntingdon, S. (1968) *Political Order in Changing Societies*, New Haven: Yale University Press

Johnson, C. (1964) *Revolution and the Social System*, Stanford, CA: Hoover

Kimmel, M.S. (1990) *Revolution: A Sociological Interpretation*, Cambridge: Polity

Laclau, E. and Mouffe, C. (1985) *Hegemony and Socialist Strategy*, London: Verso

Le Bon, G. (1913) *The Psychology of Revolution*, New York: Putnams

—— (1960) *The Crowd*, New York: Viking

Lenin, V.I. (1902) 'What is to be done?', reprinted in *Collected Works*, Moscow: Progress, 1981

—— (1917) *The State and Revolution*, reprinted in *Collected Works*, Moscow: Progress, 1981

Lukes, S. (1973) *Emile Durkheim: His Life and Work,* London: Allen Lane

Mann, M. (1986) *The Sources of Social Power,* Vol. 1, Cambridge: Cambridge University Press

—— (1988) *States, War and Capitalism*, Oxford: Blackwell

—— (1993) *The Sources of Social Power,* Vol. 2, Cambridge: Cambridge University Press

Marx, K. (1867) *Das Kapital [Capital],* 1976 edn, Harmondsworth: Penguin

Marx, K. and Engels, F. (1848) *Manifesto of the Communist Party*, reprinted in *Selected Works*, Moscow: Progress, 1968

Miliband, R. (1991) 'Reflections on the crisis of Communist regimes', in R. Blackburn (ed.) *After the Fall*, London: Verso

Moore, B. (1966) The *Social Origins of Dictatorship and Democracy*, Harmondsworth: Penguin

Mouffe, C. (1992) *Dimensions of Radical Democracy: Pluralism and Citizenship*, London: Verso

Nietzsche, F. (1969) *Thus Spake Zarathustra*, Harmondsworth: Penguin

Pearce, F. (1989) *The Radical Durkheim,* London: Unwin Hyman

Poggi, G. (1978) *The Development of the Modern State,* London: Hutchinson

Skocpol, T. (1979) *States and Social Revolutions*, Cambridge: Cambridge University Press

Sukhanov, N.N. (1955) *The Russian Revolution 1917: A Personal Record,* London: Oxford University Press

Wallerstein, I. (1974) *The Modern World-System*, London: Academic Press

Wolfenstein, E.V. (1971) *The Revolutionary Personality: Lenin, Trotsky, Gandhi*, Princeton, NJ: Princeton University Press

Worsley, P. (1982) *Marx and Marxism,* London: Tavistock

Wright, E.O. (1994) *Interrogating Inequality*, London: Verso

7 Theories of the state

Working in groups, draw up a table to identify the key differences between the perspectives outlined in this chapter, namely: pluralism, elite theory, Marxism, the New Right, and feminism. One possible way is for each group to take one main perspective.

Read the information on each perspective in this chapter, and consult other sociological textbooks in the library.

Draw up a short summary of each perspective under the following headings:
- What is the basis of power in society?
- How is power distributed in society?
- How democratic is the existing political system?
- What are the main causes of change in the political system?
- The main thinkers
- Varieties of the perspective
- Details of any empirical evidence that broadly supports the perspective

Present a summary of the findings of each group to the whole class. Collate the findings together to produce a comprehensive table. Write this out on large sheets to produce a wall-chart or on smaller paper to produce a summary for your notes.

Pluralist theories

Pluralism centres upon the contention that there is a diversity of groups and beliefs in society, resulting from the increasingly differentiated and fragmented nature of modern life. Pluralists argue that there are now a number of possible bases for identity such as class, gender, ethnicity and age among others.

In relation to politics, these multiple divisions will leave people with multiple allegiances, often potentially cross-cutting. Individuals may find themselves opposing people on one issue with whom they are allied on another.

Crucially, pluralists also believe that these divisions are evident in leadership groups in society. This leads them to reject theories that posit a united leadership able to manipulate and/or exploit the mass of the population. The government, according to pluralists, is composed of a range of separate organizations (Parliament, the civil service, the courts and so on), and for this reason they refuse to endorse the concept of a unitary 'state'.

This view is still pluralist in that it believes reforms to the system can create the kind of democracy alluded to in classical pluralist thinking.

Neo-pluralists still basically work within a pluralist framework as they see liberal representative government as the best possible system, but they now recognize some of the problems. Government is seen as responsive to electoral pressure and the activities of interest groups, but it is also recognized that government is responsive to economic pressures from business. These two pressures might pull the government in opposite directions. This position has been described by Dahl (1971, 1982) as a 'deformed polyarchy': choices are limited to those that will maintain the capitalist economic system, and any attempt to move beyond this will be resisted by the power of business.

Nonetheless, neo-pluralists stress that a wide variety of alternative political and social choices is compatible with the continuation of capitalism. The availability of choice stressed by classical pluralist writers is therefore still acknowledged in neo-pluralism, albeit modified by the recognition of the power of business.

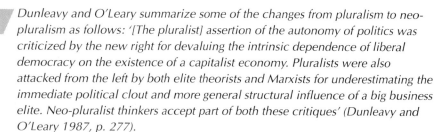

Dunleavy and O'Leary summarize some of the changes from pluralism to neo-pluralism as follows: '[The pluralist] assertion of the autonomy of politics was criticized by the new right for devaluing the intrinsic dependence of liberal democracy on the existence of a capitalist economy. Pluralists were also attacked from the left by both elite theorists and Marxists for underestimating the immediate political clout and more general structural influence of a big business elite. Neo-pluralist thinkers accept part of both these critiques' (Dunleavy and O'Leary 1987, p. 277).

1) What do you understand by the phrase 'the autonomy of politics'?
2) What is meant by the 'structural influence' of big business?

Corporatism

The key ideas in the theory of corporatism derive from the political sociology of Emile Durkheim. He was concerned with how an emphasis on individualism and economic contracts could be reconciled with the continuation of society. He attempted to analyse how society held together in the face of the increasing division of labour characteristic of modern society.

His answer was that societies have moved from a state of mechanical solidarity to one based on organic solidarity. He envisaged a society held together by a moral consensus in which the rights and liberties of individuals are guaranteed by the expansion of the state, contrary to the New Right's assertion that the state is a negative entity in society. He argued that the law evolved from a highly repressive form to a more restitutive form to reflect the changing nature of the collective conscience (the moral consensus that held society together).

The significance of the change from mechanical to organic solidarity evolved throughout Durkheim's work, and later he developed the idea that a forced division of labour could result in 'anomie' – a condition that occurs when individuals are insufficiently integrated into society. Anomie is the source of a number of social problems such as crime, suicide and industrial and political conflict.

Although this concept implies that conflict is abnormal, Durkheim did recognize it would arise from time to time and set about outlining societal reforms that could minimize the problems associated with it. This led him away from a faith in automatic evolution towards active support for societal reform. He advocated the abolition of inherited wealth and the development of a meritocratic society. Crucially, he came to believe that there is a need for intermediary organizations between the state and society to act as effective moral regulators of the economy. His models for this role were the medieval guilds which regulated the work of craftsmen and merchants. He argued that professional associations could play a similar role in modern times, allowing society to be based on self-regulation and thus held together by a genuine consensus rather than observance of values imposed from the top.

1) *Describe in greater detail the sort of reforms you would expect to be supported by a Durkheimian.*
2) *What do you understand as the key difference between pluralism and corporatism?*

Elite theory

Classical elite theory

'In all societies – from societies that are very meagrely developed and have barely attained the dawnings of civilization, down to the most advanced and powerful societies – two classes of people appear – a class that rules and a class that is ruled.'

Mosca (1939), p. 50

'. . . whether universal suffrage prevails or not, always it is an oligarchy that governs.'

Pareto (1966), p. 52

Classical elite theorists not only believed that all societies were run by an elite, but that this should be the case. The rise of democracy was seen as a potential threat to this idea.

Elite theorists believed that those arguing for democracy were promoting a myth, as they argued that the people could never really rule. In this respect elite theorists shared with Marxists a belief that rule by the people was impossible in liberal democracies. However, elite theory differs from Marxism in a number of important respects, and the elite theorists themselves were strongly anti-Marxist.

First, they rejected the idea that it was possible to analyse who the elites were simply on the basis of class, and instead argued that there were many bases for elite rule. Pareto argued that elites possessed superior personal qualities, while the work of Robert Michels and Gaetano Mosca focuses much more on their superior organizational skills.

Second, they strongly disagreed with the Marxist view that following a proletarian revolution and the establishment of a socialist classless society the state would wither away. They believed that a division between an elite and the mass is a feature of all societies. One of the key reasons they believed this was their negative assessment of the capacities of the mass of the population, whom Pareto referred to in these terms: 'the masses by themselves could do nothing unless they were led by elements from the governing class' (Pareto, 1935, p. 1807).

The inevitability of elite rule was endorsed by the other two key writers of the classical elite tradition, Michels and Mosca. However, in explaining this Michels (1949) focused on the growth of bureaucracy in society: according to his Iron Law of Oligarchy, the growth of bureaucratization meant that even formally democratic organizations were in fact run by an oligarchy, a group of leaders who were able to displace the goals set by the members of the organization and instead run it in their own interests.

Mosca (1939) attributed the superior skills of the elite to their intellectual superiority deriving from their different social background. Rule by such an elite was required because society must be planned and organized to ensure the maintenance of stability.

Criticisms of classical elite theory

Pareto's theories leaned heavily on a set of psychological assumptions that were never really explained. Moreover he argued that human nature is unchanging, yet he wrote of a circulation of elites, which implies that the quality of an elite can decline.

Michels can be criticized for overgeneralizing with his 'Iron Law'. In a study of internal democracy inside the International Typographical Union, Lipset, Trow and Coleman (1956) argued that they had found an exception. Once an exception is found an 'Iron Law' collapses.

Democratic elitism

Ultimately Mosca's ideas reconciled support for representative democracy with elite theory (somewhat reversing the negative view of democracy he held earlier in his life) by arguing that elections could serve as a mechanism for the circulation of elites. Thus he opened up a new direction for elite theory that was later developed by Max Weber (1968).

At the heart of Weber's theories is the notion that the rise of bureaucracy was a key element in the development of modern society. He also disagreed with the Marxist claim that the state in capitalist society is dominated by the bourgeoisie. He argued that the political arena has a large degree of autonomy from the economic – a contention reflected in his argument that there are three distinct bases of domination: class, status and party.

For Weber the development of the bureaucratic rational state is not an effect of the rise of capitalism but precedes its emergence and helps to promote its development. Politics is a system of power parallel but not identical to the economic power system. Modern government is inevitably bureaucratic, with state administration in the hands of educated, expert salaried officials. The positive side of this, according to Weber, is that bureaucrats are technically efficient. However, the negative side is that the growth of bureaucracy threatens individual freedom.

Weber therefore feared that the growth of bureaucracy would develop into an 'iron cage' threatening the future development of society. He argued there was a need to reassert political control to check the growing importance of economic considerations as determinants of people's behaviour. For Weber the political process can and should counteract bureaucracy.

Critics of democratic elitism

Hungarian Marxist Georg Lukács argued that the views developed by Weber were the result of specific conditions in Germany and Italy and that their findings cannot be generalized: 'It was . . . not by chance that the leader problem was raised precisely by sociologists of those countries where there was no really advanced bourgeois democracy (Max Weber in Germany, Pareto in Italy)' (Lukács 1980, p. 628).

The democratic elitists' idea of democracy seems to be limited to electing leaders. The rejection of more active political participation by the people reflects a characteristic elite theory belief in the lack of ability of the mass of the population.

 How democratic do you think democratic elitism is?

Neo-Weberian elite theory: bringing the state back in

In contrast to theories that depict a state dominated by societal elites, some neo-Weberian thinkers have emphasized the extent to which the state apparatus and the personnel within it are immune from pressures arising from society. This leads them to reject what they call 'society-centred' views of the state which assume such pressure is the major force behind state actions, whether that force be organized by a capitalist class as in Marxist formulations, by an elite as in radical elite theory or by the people as in pluralist models.

Instead they argue that the autonomy of the state must be considered as a real factor and therefore advocate 'state-centred' theories of the state. The key writers in this tradition are Nordlinger and Skocpol, but recent work by Michael Mann also falls broadly within this category.

What all these writers share is a belief that in the modern world the state is the most extensive and powerful organization in society and that it must be considered as an active agent and not merely as a mirror of society: 'Questions of state power have been basic in social-revolutionary transformations, but state power cannot be understood only as an instrument of class domination, nor can changes in state structures be explained primarily in terms of class conflicts' (Skocpol 1979, p. 284).

The key elements of such a theory of the state are therefore struggles within the state apparatus and also, since states in the modern world are effectively nation-states, struggles between nations and the arguments within state elites about preparations for such struggles, meaning effectively war and preparation for war.

The work of Michael Mann (1986, 1988) provides an important contemporary example of this argument. His view is that the autonomy of the state flows from its unique nature, namely that it is the only organization capable of power in a territorially centralized form. State elites are different from economic classes, military elites and ideological movements because of this unique organizational factor. Mann points out that the economic power of General Motors does not extend to rule of the territory around Detroit, and economic power is therefore more diffuse. The same is true of ideologies, which only cover segments of a society's population.

Mann does admit that there is a large degree of overlap between military power and state power in this sense, but he stresses that military power is not always able to penetrate all areas of society, and military networks often extend beyond state boundaries.

None of the alternative forms of power therefore possesses the ability to penetrate and coordinate society, a power Mann calls infrastructural power. The fact that societies are relatively territorially delineated is both a reflection and a further source of the state's power.

The neo-Weberian approach has provided an alternative framework for considering the state and its relationship to society. The influence of its state-centred approach can also be detected in the work of neo-Marxist and post-Marxist writers.

 Marxism has often been accused of being a form of 'technological determinism'. How might an emphasis on war invite the same accusation?

Radical elite theory

The forms of elitism discussed so far have had one thing in common: a concern with the quality of political leadership. When elite theory crossed the Atlantic to America, however, it was given a very different meaning. Classical elite theorists believed that society would and should be run by elites and were concerned that the rise of democracy would threaten such rule; radical elite theorists agreed that an elite ruled society but were concerned that its power was undermining democracy. Thus while classical elite theory was associated with a conservative critique of democracy, radical elite theory represented a critique of classical pluralism from the left. The key difference that separated the radical elitists from Marxism was their belief that elite rule was not based purely on economic factors.

 Oliver Stone's film JFK *offers a common-sense version of what might pass for radical elite theory to explain the assassination of President John F. Kennedy. It questions the accepted view that Lee Harvey Oswald, acting alone, was responsible for the murder, and it gives an insight into the atmosphere surrounding the US government at the time.*
The film is now available on video. Watch it and see how convincing you find its thesis.

C. Wright Mills (1956) argued that American society was controlled by a number of interlinked, unelected elites – a view that contrasted sharply with the democratic elitists' concentration on elected elites. According to Mills, in the twentieth century power has become centralized so that there are three key institutions whose leaders monopolize effective power: the major business corporations, the military and the government. He saw these elites coordinating their actions and becoming ever more interconnected through a shared social background.

The key reasons for the increasing centralization of power were the massive growth in the size of the armed forces and the domination of a small number of large corporations in the economic sphere. At the time Mills was writing it was clear that there were links between the elites he identified since the involvement of the USA in the Korean and later the Vietnam War involved all three of the institutions he identified. Governments declare war, the military fights wars and the large companies provide the hardware to enable them to do so.

A fundamental difference between Mills and Marxists lay in his use of the term 'power elite' as a conscious rejection of the Marxist term 'ruling class'. Mills explained his position as follows:

> The phrase 'ruling class' is a badly loaded phrase. 'Class' is an economic term; 'rule' a political one. . . . specifically the phrase 'ruling class' in its common political connotations does not allow enough autonomy to the political order and its agents, and it says nothing about the military as such . . . We hold that such a simple view of 'economic determinism' must be elaborated by 'political determinism' and 'military determinism'; that the higher agents of each of these three domains now often have a noticeable degree of autonomy. [Mills 1956, p. 277]

'the bureaucratic triumvirate of Professor Mills would appear to have a high potential for control. . . . but a potential for control is not . . . equivalent to actual control. If the military leaders of this country and their subordinates agreed that it was desirable, they could most assuredly establish a military dictatorship of the most overt sort; nor would they need the aid of leaders of business corporations or the executive branch of our government. But they have not set up such a dictatorship. For what is lacking are . . . agreement on a key political alternative and some set of specific implementing actions. That is to say, a group may have a high potential for control and a low potential for unity' (Dahl [1958] 1973, p. 285). How far do you think this is a valid criticism of Mills' theory?

Radical elite theory developed in debate with pluralist writers. One of the key early studies in the radical elite tradition was Floyd Hunter's study of decision making in Atlanta, Georgia (1953). On the basis of this study Hunter claimed that there existed a local elite, and that within this elite business interests were dominant. This conclusion was clearly challenged by Dahl's findings from his New Haven study (see page 126), which were in their turn contested by Newton (1969), who offered his own defence of radical elite theory.

The debate between Dahl and Newton has been summarized in a table by Stewart Clegg (1989). Reassemble the table by sorting the following statements into those that summarize Dahl's pluralist position and those that describe Newton's radical elite critique. (There are seven of each.)
* *Many people do not vote.*
* *Modern American pluralism is not inclusive of all groups.*
* *Modern America is an inclusive pluralist system.*
* *A workable democracy is the outcome of compromises between competitive groups that produce some general distribution of satisfaction.*
* *Some groups are denied access to the decision-making process.*
* *Most people exercise power through voting.*
* *Resources are not equally distributed, but neither are the inequalities cumulative in the structure of the system.*
* *Resources are inequitably distributed and political inequalities are cumulative.*

- *The political system does not distribute power at all equally; the system does not deliver general satisfaction, but heavily favours some groups or sections against others.*
- *The major actors in the political system are the leaders of a wide variety of interest groups that have political resources available to them.*
- *The system of leaders and decision makers is a relatively open process.*
- *A set of competing oligarchies does not make a pluralist system.*
- *Some groups do not gain representation, and some groups are politically weaker than others.*
- *While each interest group may be oligarchical, the end result is pluralist because they are competitive.*

In relation to the UK, Scott (1991) has developed an analysis of political rule which draws upon both Marxism and radical elitism. He argues that the work of Ralph Miliband in developing an empirical investigation of the political elite is useful, but that his concepts are not fully developed. According to Scott, it is necessary to analyse the form of rule in the UK in terms of the concepts of the power elite and the power bloc.

The key mechanism Scott identifies for recruitment to the political elite is the public school system. He makes the point that between 1951 and 1964 virtually all cabinet ministers had a public school background, and while by 1983 this had fallen to 75 per cent, an Oxbridge education remained a crucial unifying force. He notes the predominance of one school – Eton. In 1959 there were six old Etonians in the Cabinet and by 1979 this had increased to seven. Figure 7.1 illustrates the composition of the two main parliamentary parties from 1918 to 1955, and Table 7.1 summarizes the position in 1985.

Figure 7.1

The British political elite, 1918–55

Source: Guttsman (1963), p. 96

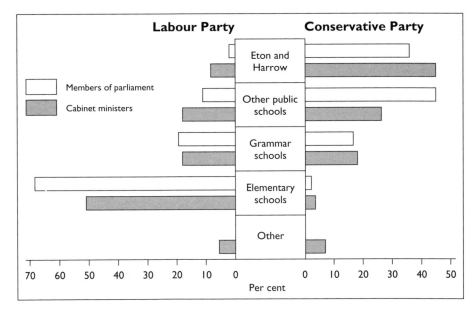

Harold Macmillan (Conservative Prime Minister in the 1950s) once said about the previous Labour government and its Prime Minister, Clement Attlee: 'Mr Attlee had three Old Etonians in his cabinet. I have six. Things are twice as good under the Conservatives' (quoted in Scott 1991, p. 133).

1) *How far do you agree that this statistic is an indicator of good government?*
2) *Find out how many (a) Old Etonians, (b) ex-public school pupils, (c) Oxbridge graduates there are in (a) the present cabinet, (b) the shadow cabinet. Use* Who's Who, Dod's Parliamentary Companion *or* The Times Guide to the House of Commons *for this exercise. These should be available in your local reference library.*

Table 7.1 A Cabinet's privilege

Fifteen out of the twenty-two Cabinet members went to public school.
Fifteen out of twenty-two went to Oxbridge.

Public school (1985 fees per year before extras)	
Eton (£5,310)	Paul Channon, Lord Hailsham, Douglas Hurd, Nicholas Ridley
Winchester (£5,760)	Sir Geoffrey Howe, Nigel Lawson, George Younger, Viscount Whitelaw
Latymer (£2,295)	Peter Walker
Westminster (£5,625)	Nicholas Edwards
Rugby (£5,535)	Tom King
St Pauls (£4,878)	Kenneth Baker
Nottingham High School (£6,180)	Kenneth Clarke
Marchiston Castle School (Edinburgh) (£4,800)	John MacGregor
George Watson's College (£1,860)	Malcolm Rifkind
Cambridge	
Emmanuel College	Tom King
Gonville & Caius	Kenneth Clarke
Jesus College	John Biffen
Trinity College	Nicholas Edwards, Norman Fowler, Douglas Hurd, Viscount Whitelaw
Trinity Hall	Sir Geoffrey Howe
Oxford	
Balliol	Nicholas Ridley
Christ Church	Paul Channon, Lord Hailsham, Nigel Lawson
Magdalen	Kenneth Baker
New College	George Younger
Somerville College	Margaret Thatcher

Source: Labour Research Department (1987), p. 19

Scott argues that the dominance of the public school/Oxbridge system is constant throughout all spheres of the state. However, while this shows a consistent bias in terms of the social background of the state elite, which allows us to assert the existence of a power elite, attendance at a public school and Oxbridge is not exclusive to the capitalist class. Members of the service class and the petite bourgeoisie attend these institutions as well. Scott argues that the dominance of the capitalist class is maintained by a 'power bloc' based on this common background that is wider than the capitalist class itself.

Figure 7.2 summarizes the various models of the state offered by elite theories. Use the accounts of the varieties of elite theory given above to place the following writers into the categories provided:
Floyd Hunter, C. Wright Mills, Max Weber, John Scott, Michael Mann, Theda Skocpol.

Figure 7.2

The main sub-types of elite theory models of the state

Source: Dunleavy and O'Leary (1987), p. 187

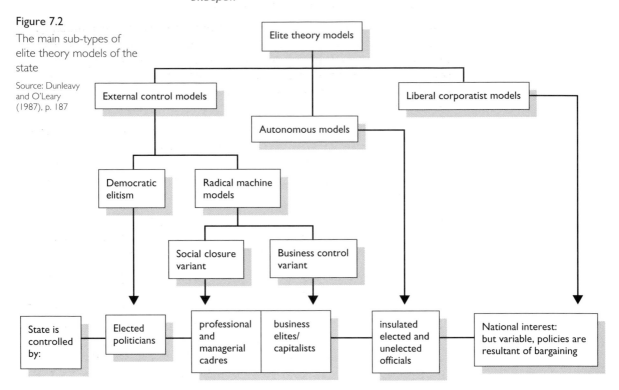

Marxist theories of the state

> 'When, in the course of development, class distinctions have disappeared . . . the public power will lose its political character. Political power . . . is merely the organized power of one class for oppressing another.'

> *Marx and Engels (1848), p. 53*

> 'The State . . . is a product of society at a certain stage of development; it is the admission that this society has become entangled in an insoluble contradiction with itself, that it has split into irreconcilable antagonisms which it is powerless to disperse.'

> *Engels (1884), p. 576*

Miliband versus Poulantzas

The most famous debate among Marxists about the nature of the state took place between Ralph Miliband and Nicos Poulantzas. Miliband argued that the state in Britain could be characterized as a capitalist state on the basis of the links between the personnel who actually held positions in that state:

> In an epoch when so much is made of democracy, equality, social mobility, classlessness and the rest, it has remained a basic fact of life in advanced capitalist countries that the vast majority of men and women in these countries has been governed, represented, administered, judged, and commanded in war by people drawn from other, economically and socially superior and relatively distant classes. [Miliband 1973, p. 62]

He provided empirical evidence to undermine the pluralist notion that no one group dominates the state, by showing that most of the dominant state positions are occupied by members of the dominant class. He concluded that the state in all essentials will act to defend the interests of the dominant class. This has been termed an 'instrumentalist' theory of the state.

Some Marxists questioned whether this approach was very fruitful. An emphasis on the people who occupy positions in the state might lead to the conclusion that a change of personnel could alter the state's fundamental character.

The main proponent of this line of criticism was Poulantzas (1973). He argued that it is the institutional structures which ensure that the state operates in the interests of capitalism, whether or not the actual people holding state positions are members of the capitalist class. This system is effective because it masks the continued defence of capitalist interests. By appearing open to anyone, the state appears class-neutral and therefore legitimate. A second benefit, according to Poulantzas, is that divisions between different parts of the capitalist class can be overcome and the state can act in the common interests of the capitalist class as a whole.

Poulantzas therefore argues that, in order to protect the long-term interests of capitalism, the state must have a degree of relative autonomy from direct control by the bourgeoisie. However, the state remains capitalist since it is ultimately shaped by the structures of society, notably the economic relations prevailing at any time.

Poulantzas' view has become known as a 'structuralist' one. The key functions of the state in the overall capitalist structure are to reproduce the conditions of production and to promote social cohesion.

You can find extracts from the work of Miliband and Poulantzas in Urry and Wakeford (1973). If you can locate this book, use it to make more detailed notes on the argument between these two Marxist writers. List the criticisms each makes of the other. Whose case do you think is the stronger?

Neo-Marxist theories

Neo-Marxist writers reject any automatic correspondence between the form of the economy and the form of the state, a notion that they regard as 'economistic'. Instead they emphasize the 'relative autonomy' of the state from capitalism and capitalists.

One very influential starting point for recent neo-Marxist theories is the work of

Antonio Gramsci. Gramsci rejected the rather crude form of 'economic determinism' characteristic of Stalinism and instead sought to explain the role of the state with reference to the way capitalism in Western Europe is maintained with the consent of the people. He argued that the state is composed not merely of the directly 'political' elements of society – the army, police and the legal system – but also includes elements of what he called 'civil society' – the mass media, the church, trade unions and political parties.

He argued that capitalism maintains its rule by securing the consent of the people through the operation of all these elements. This situation he described as 'hegemony'. He did not ignore the economic structures of society, nor indeed the repressive apparatus of the state (being imprisoned for many years by Mussolini would have reminded him of that), but his elaboration of the notion of consent through ideological hegemony has been his most lasting legacy.

Taking their lead from Gramsci, the Eurocommunists laid great stress on ideological and cultural struggle. The best representatives of this trend in Britain were the journal *Marxism Today* and the writings of Stuart Hall and Martin Jacques. This emphasis on culture and ideology at the expense of the economic struggle and class conflict led Dunleavy and O'Leary (1987, p. 256) to comment: 'post-Althusserian and post-Gramscian Marxism is indistinguishable from pluralism except in its vocabulary'.

An alternative neo-Marxist strand of writing is based on the work of the Frankfurt School. Key contemporary representatives of this strand of Marxist thinking are Jürgen Habermas and Claus Offe. Early writers in this tradition, notably Herbert Marcuse (1964), argued that capitalism had successfully bought off the workers with a supply of material goods and trivial entertainment through the development of a mass culture. This view is broadly taken over by Habermas (1976), who emphasizes that crisis in the capitalist state will not necessarily take a directly economic form but will centre around a loss of legitimacy.

Offe (1984) provides a detailed picture of the institutional constraints of states in capitalist society. He argues that a number of mechanisms produce a systematic class bias in the operation of the state. In particular he emphasizes the mechanism by which the state raises revenue to fund expenditure. The major sources of revenue are taxation based on private production and borrowing from private financial institutions. In order to increase its revenue the state is therefore forced to act in ways which promote the continued financial health of private capitalist accumulation.

Offe criticizes the notion that the welfare state can overcome the inequalities that arise from capitalism: 'the welfare state, rather than being a separate and autonomous source of well-being which provides incomes and services as a citizen's right, is itself highly dependent upon the prosperity and continued profitability of the economy' (Offe 1984, p. 148). The welfare state faces contradictory pressures to provide services for people but also not to threaten the continuation of capitalism since it is dependent on the tax revenue a thriving economy will provide.

However, this still leaves open the question of the exact balance between services and taxation. State administrators try to avoid open class warfare or conflict, but there will be divisions between sections of the capitalist class about the balance, allowing the state some degree of autonomy. The state defends the collective interests of the capitalist class as a whole, but this may bring it into conflict with certain sections of that class from time to time. However, crises may sometimes occur when the state is unable to manage these contradictions or when its interventions generate unintentionally negative consequences for capitalism.

Another significant trend in neo-Marxist analysis is that of analytical Marxism. One of the most influential contemporary Marxist writers, Erik Olin Wright, is a prominent exponent of this school of thought.

Wright has for some time been considering the problem of bureaucracy for the Marxist theory of the state. As is well known, after the Russian Revolution the state did not wither away. According to Wright (1994), the erosion of party competition and democracy after the revolution were important political factors that accelerated the growth of bureaucracy. He argues that the control of the bureaucracy is a crucial question for Marxists, and that the crucial agent for such control is the working class. Marxists must therefore develop strong democratic forms of organization based on the direct participation of workers in order to defend proletarian democracy in socialist societies. He also feels that elements of the bureaucracy might be won to support such policies due to their 'contradictory class locations', by which he means that state officials (among others) in contemporary society are not unambiguously either bourgeois or proletarian.

A working-class movement consciously seeking to democratize the whole of society might therefore achieve a degree of state power through elections; it could then use this power to introduce large-scale reform. However, Wright points out that such a government in a pre-figurative socialist position would still face two key problems. First, the state would remain capitalist overall because of its structural dependence on capitalism for tax revenue; and second, such a government would undoubtedly face opposition, including military repression. The example Wright seems to be thinking of here is the government of Salvador Allende in Chile, which was overthrown by a military coup.

It is his realism about the potential use of military force by capitalists and his emphasis on the class struggle as a key element in the dynamic models he draws that distinguish Wright from neo-pluralism. The key defence against such force would be the ability of the government to mobilize the population to act, and this could only be achieved by a socialist government dedicated to democratization, giving people real power. This requires a socialism very different from the highly bureaucratic regimes that have passed as Marxist in the past.

Criticisms of Marxist theories

These theories have been subject to a number of criticisms, most of which concern whether a ruling class exists and the extent to which the state is independent of relations in the economic sphere. It is often argued, for instance, that the actual running of the state has in large part not been undertaken by members of the ruling class – in fact, a whole number of groups have gained access to the state.

The key problem for neo-Marxist theories is that once the idea that the state can be relatively autonomous of the economy is accepted, the question then becomes how relative is relative. Much neo-Marxist writing comes close to the neo-Weberian position that the economic and the political are autonomous but linked spheres of society.

The New Right and the state

'A minimal state, limited to the narrow functions of protection against force, theft, enforcement of contracts and so on, is justified, and that any more extensive state will violate person's rights not to be forced to do certain things, and is unjustified.'

Nozick (1974), p. ix

'My personal preference is for a liberal dictator and not for a democratic government lacking in liberalism.'

Hayek (1960), quoted in New Internationalist, *November 1993, p. 24*

'The market sector is more genuinely democratic than the public sector, involving the decisions of far more individuals and at much more frequent intervals.'

Adam Smith Institute (1983), p. 13

One of the central features of New Right thinking is the belief that the best way to organize society is to maximize the degree of choice and liberty for individuals. This has been expressed through a renewed enthusiasm for the notion of the free market, which is presented as a key alternative to societies based on planning by the state. This renewed emphasis on the market has been labelled neo-liberalism, and it is characterized by negative views on the state and a consequent wish to minimize its impact.

There are various strands to the New Right. Use your library resources to research the various components of this perspective. Try to locate the following: Levitas (1986), Hall and Jacques (1983), Kavanagh (1987) and Benyon (1989).

Examine the different views of Milton Friedman and Friedrich Hayek. Write a short report of about 400 words on their views, showing where they agree and where they differ. The articles by Andrew Gamble and David Edgar in Levitas (1986) provide useful starting points for this exercise.

Milton Friedman (1962) argues that the free market is an inherently superior form of organizing society than one based on active state intervention, and also that increased state expenditure undermines the private sector. Borrowing by governments to finance expenditure pushes up interest rates and increases the costs for private business. Government borrowing is said to progressively 'crowd out' the private sector, leading to a greater share of the economy falling into state control. The solution is privatization of state enterprises and the reduction or elimination of government borrowing through tight control of the money supply.

An alternative strand of New Right thinking which also provides a very negative view of the state is that of Friedrich Hayek. He is perhaps most famous for arguing that there is no middle way between capitalism and socialism. In *The Constitution of Liberty* (1960) he argued that modern societies are too complex to be run on the basis of planning by the state and instead advocates a society based on the free market. In *The Road to Serfdom* (1944) he claimed that any expansion of the state leads down the path to totalitarian socialism. Any intervention with the operation of the capitalist economy leads straight to socialism. This is as true of the welfare state as of any other expansion of the state. Intervention by the state, usually based on some notion of social justice (which Hayek rejected), inevitably restricts the liberty of others since increased state expenditure leads to higher taxes.

According to Hayek, the protection of liberty requires that the law and constitution be framed to provide areas of society where individuals are guaranteed freedom from state interference. The most important thing is to defend liberty, and if necessary this may include placing constraints on the operation of democracy. Hayek proposed limiting the right to vote and requiring majorities greater than 50 per cent plus 1 before important changes are implemented.

New Right thinkers therefore share with classical elite theorists an ambivalent attitude to democracy. They also argue that the expansion of the state leads to its becoming involved in areas where it has no expertise, and this entails increasing policy failures. This is known as the 'government overload' thesis. This is also held to occur because governments need to retain popularity and increase spending in order to do so. The political process therefore undermines rational economic calculations and makes state provision less rational than the market. This process is seen to be inflamed by pressure group activity, so the New Right disagrees with the classical pluralists on the positive benefits of pressure group activity for society.

Criticisms of the New Right argument

- The emphasis on personal liberty is contradicted by the neo-conservatives' emphasis on authority and hierarchy. It can therefore be argued that the ideas of the New Right are internally contradictory, implying greater regulation in some areas of life and less in others.

- The key problem with liberty is its effects on others. As Isaiah Berlin put it: 'The liberty of the wolf interferes with the liberty of the sheep.'

- Some have argued that it is difficult to see how the creation of the welfare state inherently leads to a totalitarian society, as Hayek argues.

- There is a very ambiguous attitude towards democracy among New Right thinkers, and it often appears to be something that they would like to see minimized. The centralization of power in the UK during the 1980s, with the undermining of local democracy and the rise of unelected quangos running important services in education and health, appears to be a practical expression of this ambivalence.

The cartoon reproduced in Figure 7.3 was published by the Labour Party. How accurate do you think it is as a portrayal of New Right approaches to the state?

Figure 7.3

Thatcher rolls up the welfare state

Source: Manwaring and Pitkin (1984)

Feminist theories of the state

> *'The sexual-reproductive organization of society always furnishes the real basis, starting from which we can alone work out the ultimate explanation of the whole superstructure of economic, juridical and political institutions as well as of the religious, philosophical and other ideas of a given historical period.'*
>
> *Firestone (1971), p. 21*

> *'"patriarchy" then is the sexual politics whereby men establish their power and maintain control. All societies and all social groups within these are "sexist" in the sense that . . . the entire organization, at every level, is predicated on the domination of one sex by the other. Specific variations are less significant than the general truth.'*
>
> *Mitchell (1971), p. 65*

One of the key assertions made by feminists has been that all social relationships are political in that they all involve the unequal distribution of power. They explain gender inequalities by reference to the idea of patriarchy – the systematic domination of women by men. This is conceived as a universal system underpinning all other forms of domination. Feminists have been concerned to show how the state operates to create and maintain a particular role for women and how this operates to perpetuate gender inequalities.

The gendered construction of democracy

In her book *The Sexual Contract* (1988) Carole Pateman outlines a theory of the origins of the modern state. She argues that the very definition of politics underpinning the legitimacy of the state rests upon the exclusion of women.

The key to this idea is that the creation of the modern liberal-democratic state ('the contract') laid down a series of powerful conventions that distinguish sharply between public and private spheres of life. Democracy is clearly identified with the public sphere and effectively excludes the private sphere. Thus democracy is conceived to be operative in institutions and activities associated with men.

There was a missing half to the contract, covering conduct in the private sphere. Questions of behaviour inside the private home were excluded from the process of democratization seen to be operating elsewhere. The effect of this was to ensure that men continued to dominate women in the private sphere (outside the process of democratization evident in the public sphere). This inequality was most evident inside family structures, where patriarchal relations remained and were consolidated and perpetuated over time.

The division between private and public spheres has consequences for women in both spheres of life. Patriarchal ideas were incorporated into assumptions about the respective roles of men and women in public life, for example, at work. Pateman argues that contracts of employment embody these patriarchal assumptions: 'the construction of the "worker" presupposes that he is a man who has a woman, a (house)wife to take care of his daily needs' (p. 131).

1) What do you understand by the terms 'public sphere' and 'private sphere'?
2) In what ways have men maintained their power over women in the private sphere?
3) How does this affect women in the public sphere?
4) Trowler (1991) includes a section on 'Women and social policy' in Chapter 5. Read this and make a list of laws which enshrined a patriarchal ideology within them. How do your findings fit in with Pateman's notion of the 'sexual contract'?

Patriarchy – from the private sphere to the public

Sylvia Walby (1990) also considers the relationship between patriarchy and the state. She argues that patriarchy is a system of oppressive social relations that operates deep in the structures of society. She lists six distinct but interrelated patriarchal structures: paid employment, household production, culture, sexuality, violence and the state. All of these are areas of society where patriarchy operates to oppress women in various ways.

1) Provide a concrete example of the way each of these six social structures is oppressive to women.
2) To what extent do you think all women are equally affected by these forms of oppression?

Walby argues, however, that while all of these areas are characterized by patriarchy, its nature throughout history is not constant. As a result of the struggles of early feminists, for instance, the emphasis in the UK has shifted from a predominantly private system of patriarchy based on unequal power relations inside the private household to a predominantly public system in which the oppression of women is perpetuated in more impersonal ways through the state and the job market.

The state, the law and the freedom to exploit women

Catherine MacKinnon (1989) explains the way in which the state and its actions have contributed to the oppression of women. She argues that the primary form of oppression in society is that of women by men and that this is a universal feature of all human societies based on the division of labour. MacKinnon then goes on to look at the way in which the state has become involved in women's lives and the effect this has had.

The central aspect of concern in the book is the way in which the state and the laws it passes enshrine the oppression of women. A key example is pornography. MacKinnon has argued that pornography is one of the most important ways in which oppressive relations between men and women are perpetuated, but that the production of such material is protected by an emphasis on freedom and liberty, which she sees as a mask for the freedom to oppress women:

> male forms of power are affirmatively embodied as individual rights in law . . . freedom of speech, which gives pimps rights to torture, exploit, use, and sell women to men through pictures and words, and gives consumers rights to buy them; the law of privacy, which defines the home and sex as presumptively consensual and protects the use of pornography in the home . . . Real sex equality under law would qualify or eliminate these powers of men, hence men's current 'rights' to use, access, possess, and traffic women and children. [MacKinnon 1989, p. 244]

She maintains that the production of pornography is linked to attacks on women, and therefore pornographers should be made legally responsible for the damage inflicted by their products.

 The Times Higher Education Supplement of 10 December 1993 published contributions by writers for and against laws to restrict pornography. Find a copy of this feature in the library, or on CD-ROM, and make a detailed list of the arguments for and against MacKinnon's proposals.
Which arguments do you think are stronger?
What problems might be involved in using the state to pass laws to protect women from the effects of pornography?

Conclusion

This chapter has outlined both classical and more contemporary theories of the state within a framework which will hopefully by now be reasonably familiar.

It is of course quite important to be aware of the ways in which these theories differ, but it is sometimes forgotten that there are areas of overlap and similarity, which it is equally important to acknowledge.

 Figure 7.4 suggests various areas where the perspectives on the state outlined above partly overlap. There are six areas of overlap in total. Two of these are identified in Table 7.2. Your task is to correctly identify which numbered areas on

the diagram correspond to the other four by considering which two perspectives outlined above share these views. Two of the three occurrences in which the overlap involves pluralism have also been identified to give you a start.

Copy out the figure and the table and complete the missing details in the table. Re-reading the sections on the various theories outlined above should help with this exercise.

Figure 7.4

Overlap between theories of the state

Source: Dunleavy and O'Leary (1987), p. 323

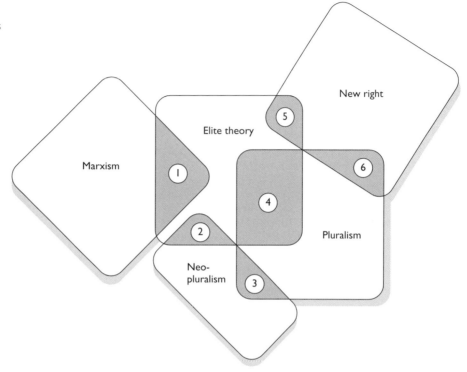

Table 7.2   Overlap between theories of the state

Area of Overlap	Between which perspectives	Identifed on diagram as number
State is seen as an instrument dominated by those from a business background		
State is seen as increasingly professionalized	Elite Theory/Neo-pluralism	2
State is seen as a deformed polyarchy	Pluralism	
State is seen as being run in the interests of a 'new class' of state employees	Elite Theory/New Right	5
State is best characterized as Democratic Elitist	Pluralism	
State is seen as suffering from 'government overload'		

Source: Adapted from Dunleavy and O'Leary (1987), p. 323

Essay Questions

1) How relevant is the concept of a 'political elite' to the study of British politics? (Oxford, June 1985)

2) Examine the similarities and differences between pluralist and elitist theories of the nature and distribution of political power. (AEB, June 1988)

3) Compare and contrast Marxist and elite theories of the nature and distribution of political power. (AEB, June 1987)

4) Critically examine the usefulness of pluralist theories to an understanding of the relationship between power and the state in modern societies. (AEB, June 1994)

Coursework suggestions

Much of the detailed information on the British political elite is now quite dated. This provides an opportunity for an updating of the contours of the elite.

In order to study the political elite you will first need to decide exactly which groups are to be included in it. You will need to consult the work of writers such as John Scott and Anthony Giddens. Once you have decided exactly who comprises the elite, decide what characteristics about them you wish to investigate. Draw up a list of characteristics.

You will then need to locate biographical information on as many members of the elite as you can find. There are a number of possible sources of this information but you will no doubt be spending a lot of time in the local reference library.

Compare your findings with those of other recent accounts of the political elite and consider whether your findings suggest there is any need to modify existing theories of the political elite.

Bibliography

Adam Smith Institute (1983) *The Omega File: Local Government, Planning and Housing,* London: Adam Smith Institute

Banfield, E. (1966) *Political Influence,* New York: Free Press

Beetham, D. (1974) *Max Weber and the Theory of Modern Politics,* London: George Allen & Unwin

Benyon, J. (1989) 'Ten Years of Thatcherism', *Social Studies Review,* May

Clegg, S. (1989) *Frameworks of Power,* London: Sage

Dahl, R.A. (1956) *A Preface to Democratic Theory,* Chicago, IL: University of Chicago Press

—— (1958) 'A critique of the Ruling Elite Model', *American Political Science Review,* Vol. 52, No. 2, reprinted in Urry and Wakeford (1973)

—— (1961) *Who Governs?,* New Haven, CT: Yale University Press

—— (1971) *Polyarchy,* New Haven, CT: Yale University Press

—— (1982) *Dilemmas of Pluralist Democracy,* New Haven, CT: Yale University Press

—— (1989) *Democracy and Its Critics,* New Haven, CT: Yale University Press

Domhoff, W.G. (1978) *Who Really Rules?,* Santa Monica, CA: Goodyear

Dunleavy, P. and O'Leary, B. (1987) *Theories of the State,* London: Macmillan

Engels, F. (1884) *The Origin of the Family, Private Property and the State,* reprinted in Marx, K. and Engels, F. *Selected Works,* Moscow: Progress Publishers (1968)

Firestone, S. (1971) *The Dialectic of Sex,* London: Paladin

Friedman, M. (1962) *Capitalism and Freedom,* Chicago, IL: University of Chicago Press

Galbraith, J.K. (1969) *The New Industrial State,* Harmondsworth: Penguin

Gramcsi, A. (1971) *Selections from Prison Notebooks,* London: Lawrence & Wishart

Guttsman, W.G. (1963) *The British Political Elite,* London: MacGibbon & Kee

Habermas, J. (1976) *Legitimation Crisis,* London: Heinemann

Hall, S. and Jacques, M. (eds) (1983) *The Politics of Thatcherism,* London: Lawrence & Wishart

Hayek, F. (1944) *The Road to Serfdom,* London: Routledge

—— (1960) *The Constitution of Liberty,* London: Routledge

Hunter, F. (1953) *Community Power Structure,* Chapel Hill, NC: University of North Carolina Press

Kavanagh, D. (1987) 'The Rise of Thatcherism', *Social Studies Review,* November

Labour Research Department (1987) *The Widening Gap,* London: LRD

Levitas, R. (ed.) (1986) *The Ideology of the New Right,* Cambridge: Polity

Lindblom, C. (1977) *Politics and Markets,* New York: Basic Books

Lipset, S.M., Trow, M. and Coleman, J. (1956) *Union Democracy,* Glencoe, IL: Free Press

Lukács, G. (1980) *The Destruction of Reason,* London: Merlin

MacKinnon, C. (1989) *Towards a Feminist Theory of the State,* Cambridge, MA: Harvard University Press

Mann, M. (1986, 1993) *The Sources of Social Power,* Vols 1 and 2, Cambridge: Cambridge University Press

—— (1988) *States, War and Capitalism,* Oxford: Blackwell

Manwaring, T. and Pitkin, J. (eds) (1984) *Thatcher's Britain 1984,* London: Labour Party and *New Socialist*

Marcuse, H. (1964) *One-Dimensional Man,* London: Sphere

Marx, K. (1867, 1885) *Das Kapital,* republished as *Capital,* Harmondsworth: Penguin (1976)

—— and Engels, F. (1848) *The Communist Manifesto,* reprinted in *Selected Works,* Moscow: Progress Publishers (1968)

McGrew, A. (1992) 'The state in advanced capitalist society', in J. Allen, P. Braham and P. Lewis (eds) *Political and Economic Forms of Modernity,* Cambridge: Polity Press

Michels, R. (1949) *Political Parties,* New York: Free Press

Miliband, R. (1973) *The State in Capitalist Society,* London: Quartet

Mills, C.W. (1956) *The Power Elite,* Oxford: Oxford University Press

Mitchell, J. (1971) *Women's Estate,* Harmondsworth: Penguin

Mosca, G. (1939) *The Ruling Class,* New York: McGraw-Hill

Newton, K. (1969) 'A critique of the pluralist model', *Acta Sociologica,* Vol. 12

Nordlinger, E. (1981) *The Autonomy of the Democratic State,* Cambridge, MA: Harvard University Press

Nozick, R. (1974) *Anarchy, State and Utopia,* Oxford: Blackwell

Offe, C. (1984) *The Contradictions of the Welfare State,* London: Hutchinson

Pareto, V. (1935) *The Mind and Society,* London: Cape

—— (1966) *Sociological Writings,* edited by S.E. Finer, London: Pall Mall

Pateman, C. (1988) *The Sexual Contract,* Cambridge: Polity

Pearce, F. (1989) *The Radical Durkheim,* London: Unwin Hyman

Polsby, N. (1963) *Community Power and Political Theory,* New Haven, CT: Yale University Press

Poulantzas, N. (1973) *Political Power and Social Classes,* London: Verso

Richardson, J.J. and Jordan, A.G. (1979) *Working Under Pressure,* Oxford: Martin Robertson

Scott, J. (1991) *Who Rules Britain?,* Cambridge: Polity

Skocpol, T. (1979) *States and Social Revolutions,* Cambridge: Cambridge University Press

Trowler, P. (1991) *Investigating Health, Welfare and Poverty* London: Collins Educational

Urry, J. and Wakeford, J. (eds) (1973) *Power in Britain,* London: Heinemann

Walby, S. (1990) *Theorizing Patriarchy,* Oxford: Blackwell

Weber, M. (1968) *Economy and Society,* Berkeley, CA: University of California Press

Wright, E.O. (1978) *Class, Crisis and the State,* London: Verso

—— (1994) *Interrogating Inequality: Essays on Class Analysis, Socialism and Marxism,* London: Verso

8

Democracy, citizenship and rights

The concept of democracy is at the heart of debates about the nature of political organization in society. The basic principle underlying democracy is revealed in the meaning of the Greek words from which it originates: *demos* means people, and *kratos* means rule. So democracy is rule by the people. But whether democracy is possible or desirable, and how it can best be established, have been hotly debated from ancient times to the present day.

Democracy and classical sociology

'The pre-eminent themes of political sociology in its formative period during the first half of the nineteenth century were the social consequences of the emergence of democracy as a form of government and the political significance of the development of social classes on the basis of industrial capitalism.'

Bottomore (1993), p. 12

As Bottomore points out, differences about the meaning of democracy and its implications for society lay at the heart of debates between the classical sociologists over their conceptions of society.

Classical pluralists and elite theorists agreed that any idea of the people directly exercising power was unrealistic. The classical pluralists argued that society would be governed by a small group of leaders, but these people would be responsive to the wishes of all groups in society, crucially through elections and pressure group activity. Classical elite writers, in contrast, held very negative views about democracy. Both Pareto and Michels were supporters of the Italian Fascist leader, Benito Mussolini. Mosca, however, moved towards the end of his life to a belief that democracy was not incompatible with elite rule.

Democratic elite theorists accepted that elections might be a useful mechanism for securing the circulation of elites, but in no sense did they believe they would or should be responsive to pressure from the mass of the population in between elections, as suggested by pluralist thinkers. The limited role of the mass of the population in their conception is shown in the following account of a conversation between Max Weber and the Germany militarist Erich Ludendorff, who had criticized the former for his part in bringing democracy to Germany:

Weber: In democracy the people elect a leader in whom they have confidence. Then the elected leader says: 'Now shut up and obey me.' People and parties may no longer meddle in what he does.

Ludendorff: I should like that kind of democracy.

Weber: Afterwards the people can sit in judgement. If the leader has made mistakes – to the gallows with him. [Quoted in Beetham 1974, p. 236]

Weber seems here to be reversing his earlier support for parliamentary democracy and pressing instead for a strong leader. Wolfgang Mommsen (1984) has drawn attention to this strand in Weber's thinking and argues that there appears to be a connection between this view of a strong leader and the later rise of Adolf Hitler, who seemed to embody such notions. While it is not suggested that Weber would have supported Hitler, the nationalist and elitist strands in his thinking perhaps failed to provide sufficient safeguards against the emergence of National Socialism. Hitler was elected to the Chancellorship, but then he used emergency powers in the Constitution, designed to ensure strong leadership, to create a dictatorship.

 Write a short critique of about 200 words on Max Weber's views on democracy.

Both radical elite theorists and Marxists reject the analysis presented by pluralist writers. They stress that unelected groups have much greater influence in society than the pluralists acknowledge.

They differ about the basis of this power. Marxists argue that although in representative democracies everyone has an equal right to vote, this formal equality is undermined by the unequal distribution of economic power, which allows the bourgeoisie to rule society. A new form of democracy is needed, based on participation from below. The classic models for Marxists are the Paris Commune of 1870 and the Soviets formed by workers during the Russian Revolution.

Radical elite theorists argue that it is not only on the basis of economic power that elites rule society. Durkheim also argued that revolutions were more disruptive than productive. He advocated greater participation by the mass of the population through a network of intermediary organizations. This idea is often seen as the origin of corporatism.

Citizenship and rights

Political sociologists have been concerned to understand the relationship between the emergence of new political systems and the types of citizenship and citizenship rights provided by such systems.

If democracy means rule by the people (either directly or indirectly) then one important question concerns exactly who is to comprise the people, and exactly what citizenship entails.

Marshall's theory of citizenship

One of the most influential modern writers on the subject of citizenship rights has been T.H. Marshall. Marshall (1963) argues that there have been three stages to the struggle for and attainment of citizenship. These are the civil, political and social spheres of citizenship.

By civil citizenship Marshall means the rights necessary for individual freedom, notably freedom of speech, the freedom of thought and belief, the right to own property and the right to justice as well as the liberty of the person. The crucial institutions defending these rights are the rule of law and the law courts. He argues that these rights emerged in the eighteenth century.

By political citizenship Marshall means the right to participate in political decision making, either directly or by virtue of having the right to vote in elections. These rights were gained as large working-class movements emerged, leading to the extension of the right to vote and the establishment of political parties. These rights emerged in the nineteenth century.

By social citizenship Marshall means the right to economic welfare and security and therefore the right to live the life of a civilized being according to the standards prevailing in society at the time. This vision clearly goes beyond the right to freedom and the right to vote since it is concerned with the economic and social spheres of society and leads to much more extensive conception of rights, including the right to an education, the right to work and the right to health care and a healthy life.

Marshall argues that this third aspect of citizenship has developed through the twentieth century, crucially with the emergence of the idea of the welfare state. He saw this as a step towards mitigating the contradiction between political equality and social and economic inequality which he believed to be the crucial weakness in the liberal view of citizenship, which is simply concerned with citizenship in the civil and political senses.

1) *Obtain a copy of the Student's Charter (it is your right to have a copy), and make a list of the rights it contains.*
2) *The National Union of Students has compiled an alternative charter aimed at students in further education. Obtain a copy of this and compare and contrast the two documents.*
3) *How do each compare with the notions of citizenship contained in Marshall's writings?*

Mann's model

Michael Mann (1987) argues that the crucial defect in Marshall's theory of citizenship is that it is entirely about Great Britain and as such cannot be considered as a general theory about how citizenship rights developed. He argues that there are five distinct ways in which citizenship rights have developed in advanced industrial countries. The factors that determine which of the different routes to citizenship is taken are the cohesion of the ruling class and the position of the country in the world political system, or 'geo-politics' as Mann calls it. He rejects the evolutionary schema in Marshall's model, according to which citizenship appears to evolve from one form to another in an almost automatic way.

The five routes Mann identifies are the liberal, reformist, authoritarian monarchist, fascist and authoritarian socialist strategies. He cites as key examples of these routes the USA (liberal), Great Britain (reformist), Germany, Austria, Russia and Japan (authoritarian monarchist), Nazi Germany (fascist) and the Soviet Union (authoritarian socialist).

He also argues that there is nothing inherently superior about the social democratic version of citizenship outlined by Marshall that has ensured its existence today. This is due to geo-political factors, notably war, which 'assassinated' the authoritarian and fascist models of citizenship.

Citizenship from below, and human rights

Bryan Turner (1986, 1990) argues that Mann's criticisms of Marshall are problematic on two counts. First, Mann concentrates on the actions of the ruling class in 'handing down' the form of citizenship that emerged in various countries. This concentration on citizenship from above leads to an underestimation of the impact of social struggles, which have won forms of citizenship from below.

Second, Turner argues that Mann's approach uses an implicit Marxist model since it is based on relationships between classes. This limits its usefulness in examining the role of the new social movements in the struggle for the expansion of citizenship rights, since many of these movements are not based on class. Turner cites the peace movement, feminism, Solidarity in Poland, the Green movement, animal liberation and movements for children's rights.

Turner (1993) has also suggested that the idea of citizenship is centrally linked to the nation-state. This is certainly true of Marshall's model. His point is that, with the rise of the global economy, the nation-state is not as central at it once was. As a result national identity as the basis of citizenship may appear outdated, and theories of citizenship have to assume a global character. Sociologists therefore need to develop a theory of rights to complement the earlier theories of citizenship. Human rights are not confined to a particular nation-state, and therefore may be more appropriate to a world context.

'. . . to justify human rights sociologically suggests that animals must be protected, because a threat to the existence of animals is indirectly but ultimately a threat to the continuity and survival of the human species' (Turner 1993, p. 505).
Turner himself believes there are problems with the idea of animal rights. Make a list of the arguments for and against the idea.

There are problems in devising a theory of rights that is applicable across different cultures. Turner notes that the UN Universal Declaration on Human Rights is often seen as overly individualistic and based on Western ideas of liberty and freedom, which are not necessarily shared by other cultures. However, drawing on Foucault's ideas (see pages 192–3), he suggests that a sociological theory of human rights could overcome these problems by starting from the common frailty of the human body.

Listed below is a selection of the rights contained in the United Nations Universal Declaration of Human Rights (1948):

- *Everyone has the right to work, to free choice of employment.*
- *Everyone has the right to own property.*
- *Everyone has the right of life, liberty and security of person.*

- *Everyone has the right to take part in the government of his [sic] country, directly or through freely chosen representatives.*
- *Everyone has the right to social security.*
- *Everyone has the right to education.*
- *All are equal before the law and are entitled without any discrimination to equal protection of the law.*
- *Everyone has the right to freedom of peaceful assembly and association.*

1) *Judging from this selection, how valid is the criticism of the Declaration noted by Turner?*
2) *Which of Marshall's levels of citizenship does each of these rights belong to?*
3) *How many of these rights are upheld in contemporary Britain?*

Marxist views on citizenship

The Marxist approach to the notion of citizenship takes as its starting point Marx's criticisms of the Declaration of the Rights of Man, proclaimed during the French Revolution. Marx (1843) argued that these were merely rights of the *individual,* and since they did not abolish private property and therefore economic inequality, they enshrined the equal right to create inequality. They created a sphere of society free from state intervention and therefore free from the control of democracy. They did not offer full equality and therefore conferred only partial citizenship. As long as capitalism was maintained, it would be impossible to achieve full and equal citizenship rights for all.

This exposes the central question at the heart of this debate, namely whether it is possible to remove the inequalities produced by capitalism by means of the extension of citizenship rights. Social-democratic thinkers from Marshall onwards have broadly argued that it is possible, but Marxists broadly argue that it is not and that there is a need for the revolutionary overthrow of capitalism if real citizenship rights are to be established.

Figure 8.1

An anarchist conception of rights

Source: Rooum (1985)

Anarchist writers have also been critical of the notion of rights because they take a negative view of the state, the guarantor of rights according to supporters of theories of rights. An anarchist view of rights is portrayed in Figure 8.1.

 Yuri Andropov, at the time General Secretary of the Communist Party of the Soviet Union, responded to Western criticism of Soviet violations of human and civil rights by saying: 'Surely one cannot speak of real civil rights for the broad

popular masses in the capitalist countries, where people live in constant fear of losing their jobs and consequently their wages . . . Really, these millions of unfortunates [the unemployed] and their families do not feel better because they are allowed to go up to the gates of the White House or Hyde Park's Speaker's Corner and express themselves on particular questions there' (quoted in Heater 1990, p. 315).

1) To what extent do you consider this to be a valid argument?

2) How does Andropov's statement fit into general Marxist views on citizenship and rights?

Working in three groups, write reports of about 500 words on the three imaginary societies outlined below. Each group can be responsible for one report, which it can present to the whole class.
What objections to each society might arise, and from whom? How would government operate? On what basis would it legitimate itself? What might such a political system be called? Do examples of such a society exist today?

1) Imagine a society based on civil citizenship alone. This means that everyone has the right to own property, to be free from persecution and to be equal before the law.

2) Imagine a society based on civil and political citizenship. Everyone has the right to own property, to be free from persecution and to be equal before the law, and everyone also enjoys political equality – fundamentally the right to vote.

3) Imagine a society based on civil, political and social citizenship. Everyone has the right to own property, to be free from persecution and to be equal before the law, and everyone also enjoys political equality. In addition, there are no areas of life free from the collective will of society and there is therefore no private sphere of civil society.

Contemporary debates about citizenship in the UK

Neo-pluralist views

Many writers in the neo-pluralist tradition have pointed out that citizens lack real power over the actions of government and the state. Most now recognize the validity of the criticisms that were made of classical pluralism. Neo-pluralists remain within the pluralist tradition, however, in their belief that liberal representative democracy is the best achievable form of governmental system, and their proposals are designed to modify rather than reject it wholesale.

Perhaps the best example of the neo-pluralist approach is Charter 88. It was founded in 1988 (hence 88), and was modelled on a human rights group formed in Czechoslovakia in 1977, Charter 77. Charter 88 calls for a 'constitutional revolution', introducing a Bill of Rights to guarantee a number of key rights that citizens should enjoy but presently lack in the United Kingdom.

One of the key arguments for a Bill of Rights is that governments, once elected, act like dictators. Paul Hirst expressed this idea as follows:

> Mrs Thatcher's government ... is using the great authority given by democratic elections for what are often highly unpopular and divisive policies ... Mrs Thatcher has set out to use her majority, a form of minority rule with 43% of the popular vote, to dictate by constitutionally unchallengeable state authority and unlimited legislative sovereignty how others shall live. [Hirst 1993, p. 6]

Marxist critics of Charter 88 argue that institutional change, such as a written constitution, does not guarantee a more democratic society since it does not fundamentally alter the economic inequalities in society. They point to the USA, which possesses a written constitution but decision making remains in the hands of the rich.

Citizenship and the New Right

One of the key ideas promoted by John Major's government has been the Citizen's Charter. This specifies standards that public services are supposed to meet, and in certain circumstances allows the citizen to obtain financial redress for services that fail to meet these standards. This is a market-based, non-political version of citizenship based on a sort of commercial contract.

The principal rights the Citizen's Charter confers are concerned with receiving information and being able to complain. There is nothing substantial in the way of new political or social rights. Thus it appears to be confined to the realm of what Marshall called civil citizenship, and some have argued that it misuses the word 'citizen'. However Dawn Oliver (1993) points out that this criticism reflects an old-style fixation upon rights provided by the state, whereas today the idea of citizenship also extends to rights *against* the state, such as the rights of consumers of public services to complain.

The development of democracy and citizenship rights in the UK

At the heart of the idea of democracy lies the belief that all people are equal. For some people to be granted citizenship rights while others are excluded runs somewhat counter to the democratic ideal. Yet in reality even political equality in the UK has been a long time coming, as Figure 8.2 illustrates.

During the struggle for the universal franchise two key movements of contemporary significance came into being. The first was the Labour movement, whose first mass organization in this country was the Chartists, named after a charter presented to Parliament (see Figure 8.3).

1) *How many of these demands are met by the present British system of democracy?*
2) *Which of these demands do you think would be written differently today?*

The second key movement was the Suffragettes, who campaigned for women's right to vote. As shown in Figure 8.2, this right was eventually granted in 1918 and 1928.

The UK was not abnormal in taking its time to recognize universal suffrage. For instance, in the USA there were voting restrictions in place until the mid-1960s that effectively excluded the black population from the vote; and in Switzerland women

Figure 8.2

The long march to a universal franchise in the UK

Source: Gleeson (1990), p. 38

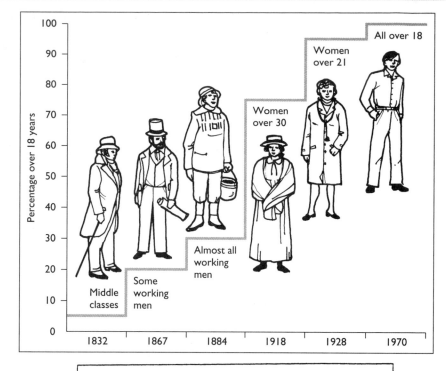

Figure 8.3

The People's Charter, 1838

Source: Reproduced in Lane (1972)

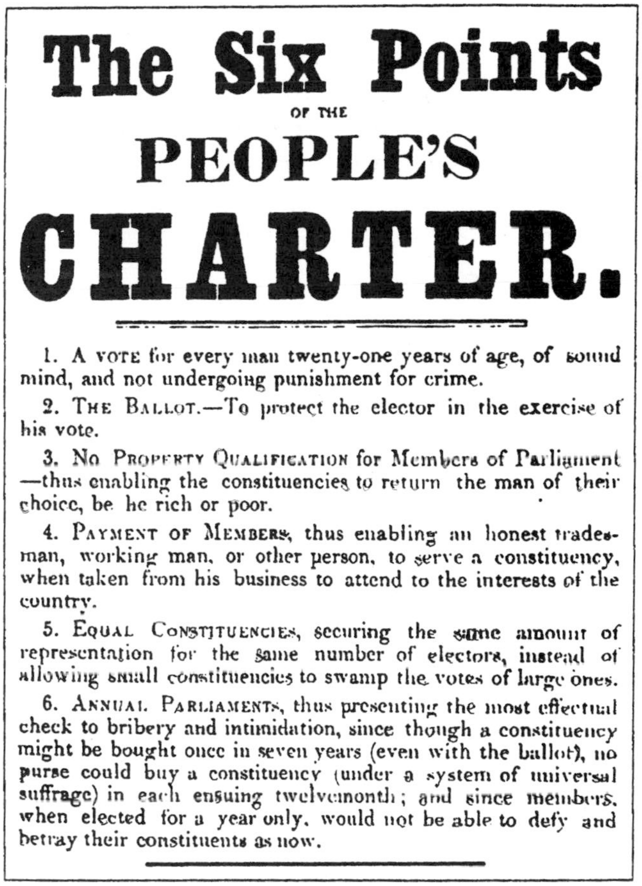

The Six Points
OF THE
PEOPLE'S
CHARTER.

1. A VOTE for every man twenty-one years of age, of sound mind, and not undergoing punishment for crime.

2. THE BALLOT.—To protect the elector in the exercise of his vote.

3. No PROPERTY QUALIFICATION for Members of Parliament —thus enabling the constituencies to return the man of their choice, be he rich or poor.

4. PAYMENT OF MEMBERS, thus enabling an honest trades-man, working man, or other person, to serve a constituency, when taken from his business to attend to the interests of the country.

5. EQUAL CONSTITUENCIES, securing the same amount of representation for the same number of electors, instead of allowing small constituencies to swamp the votes of large ones.

6. ANNUAL PARLIAMENTS, thus presenting the most effectual check to bribery and intimidation, since though a constituency might be bought once in seven years (even with the ballot), no purse could buy a constituency (under a system of universal suffrage) in each ensuing twelvemonth; and since members, when elected for a year only, would not be able to defy and betray their constituents as now.

could not vote until 1971. Table 8.1 illustrates how recently most liberal democracies were established.

Table 8.1 The universal franchise – a recent arrival

Country	First attainment of democracy
Australia	1903
Austria	1918
Belgium	1948
Canada	1920
Denmark	1915
Finland	1919
France	1946
Germany	1919
Italy	1946
Japan	1952
Netherlands	1919
New Zealand	1907
Norway	1915
Sweden	1918
Switzerland	1971
UK	1928
USA	1970

Source: Therborn (1977), p. 11

 Even today certain groups are excluded from the right to vote in the UK: the insane, peers of the realm, the monarch, those serving a prison sentence, those under the age of 18.

1) *Why are these groups denied voting rights? How far do you agree these are valid exclusions?*
2) *Consider whether the list needs extending in any way.*
3) *Write a short report on a proposal to reduce the age of eligibility to vote to 16.*

The extent of democracy today

Throughout nearly all of human history the idea that decisions should be reached by considering everyone's views is missing. Moreover, anything resembling a democratic form of government is still the preserve of a minority of the world's population.

In a survey conducted for the Channel 4 series *Bite the Ballot* (Smyth, Jones and Platt 1994) researchers found that only forty of the world's 192 states were highly democratic, and fifty-four were undemocratic, with the rest (including the United Kingdom) in between. Roughly 788.6 million people live in highly democratic countries, whereas those living in undemocratic countries total 1,779 million, a third of the world's population. For every person enjoying highly democratic rights, 2.25 people around the world were living a life marked by the absence of such rights.

 Table 8.2 provides extracts from statistics compiled by Smyth, Jones and Platt (1994). High numbers in column 1 indicate relatively high levels of democracy.

Table 8.2   The democracy rating for a selection of countries

The columns show: 1 Democracy rating; 2 Population; 3 Life expectancy; 4 Adult literacy (%); 5 Annual Income per capita (US$)

CENTRAL/EASTERN EUROPE	1	2	3	4	5
Bosnia	16	4.4m	71	86	3,000
Bulgaria	51	9.02m	73	93	1,840
Croatia	30	4.85m	71	96	5,600
Czech Republic	82	10.42m	73	99	2,450
Hungary	82	10.56m	72	99	2,590
Macedonia	45	2.2m	70	89	3,100
Poland	75	38.5m	72	99	1,830
Romania	37	23.2m	72	96	1,340
Serbia/Montenegro	16	10.5m	71	89	4,500
Slovakia	72	5.34m	73	99	2,450
NORTHERN EUROPE					
Denmark	85	5.18m	76	99	23,660
Finland	90	5.02m	76	99	24,400
Greenland (Denmark)	85	58,000	66	n/a	6,000
Iceland	89	270,000	78	99	22,580
Norway	85	4.3m	78	99	24,160
Sweden	85	8.7m	78	99	25,490
WESTERN EUROPE					
Austria	89	7.9m	75	99	20,380
Belgium	84	10.05m	76	99	19,300
France	87	57.6m	77	99	20,600
Germany	87	80.8m	75	99	23,650
Greece	88	10.3m	77	93	6,230
Ireland	86	3.6m	76	99	10,780
Italy	79	58.1m	77	97	18,580
Luxembourg	86	396,000	76	100	31,080
Malta	86	380,000	74	84	6,850
Netherlands	84	15.2m	78	99	18,560
Portugal	89	10.45m	75	98	5,620
Spain	84	39.2m	77	95	12,460
Switzerland	87	7m	78	99	33,510
United Kingdom	75	58m	76	99	16,750
WEST AFRICA					
Benin	77	5.16m	48	23	380
Burkina Faso	27	9.81m	50	18	350
Cameroon	24	12.8m	56	54	940
Cape Verde	74	390,000	68	53	750
Equatorial Guinea	4	390,000	48	50	330
The Gambia	74	920,000	45	27	360
Ghana	70	16.7m	56	60	400
Guinea	32	7.7m	45	24	450
Guinea-Bissau	22	1.05m	44	37	190
Ivory Coast	41	13.5m	55	54	690
Liberia	7	2.7m	56	40	600
Mali	64	8.75m	44	32	280
Niger	72	8.5m	47	28	300

Continued over page

Senegal	39	7.9m	49	38	720
Sierra Leone	7	4.4m	43	21	210
Togo	18	4.1m	55	43	410

Source: Smyth, Jones and Platt (1994)

1) Is there any relationship between the level of democracy and the level of economic production shown in this table?

2) Identify the most and least democratic countries in Europe.

3) Look at the criteria the compilers of this table used to define democracy. How far do you agree that these are key criteria for democracy? Are there any other factors you feel should be added or any that should not be included?

4) The researchers concluded on the basis of their criteria that the United Kingdom was only partly democratic. What reasons might there be for such a conclusion? How far do you agree with their assessment?

5) Make a list of those countries considered more democratic than the UK.

The changing face of British democracy since 1979

'We are well on the way to making Britain a country safe from socialism.'

Margaret Thatcher, Sunday Express, 17 May 1987

'There is a crisis at the heart of British democracy. Freedom and the right to dissent have been curtailed.'

Blunkett and Jackson (1987), p. 1

Margaret Thatcher and the New Right came to power with a very negative view of the activities of the state. A key political as well as economic objective of the new government was to curb public expenditure. Another of Mrs Thatcher's earliest declared aims was to prune the number of quasi-autonomous non-governmental organizations (quangos), which she saw as a key indicator of the damaging tendency of the state to continually expand its sphere of operations. These two objectives have come into conflict, with far-reaching and unexpected consequences for British democracy.

In its attempts to control public expenditure, central government soon ran up against the wishes of Labour-controlled councils to expand their services and therefore their expenditure. Its solution was to abolish a whole layer of elected local government in the metropolitan areas and severely curtail the power of other local councils to act in accordance with the manifestos on which they had been elected. Stringent (and complex) new controls were imposed on the ability of local authorities to raise revenue and to spend what money they had. Table 8.3 lists some of the powers removed from local authority control since the Thatcher government took office.

Suspicion arose that decisions about the funding of local government were being made in such a way as to favour Conservative local authorities. For example, a

Table 8.3   Major functions lost by local governments since 1979

EDUCATION

Local education authorities: Have lost control of sixth-form and further education colleges. Now managed by their own independent boards and funded by the Further Education Funding Council.

Polytechnics: Now funded by the Higher Education Funding Council.

Grant-maintained schools: 'Opted-out' of LEA control, funded by the Department for Education, managed by independent boards.

Training and Enterprise Councils: Have taken over many training functions and 'appropriate' funding has been switched to them.

City Technology Colleges: Set up with government funding and run by their own boards of governors. City Colleges for the Technology of the Arts are being created.

Funding agency for schools: To be established, taking over planning responsibilities from LEAs. Will have powers to close schools in areas where more than three-quarters of primary or secondary schools are grant-maintained.

HOUSING

Housing Action Trusts: Council tenants can form these, taking over management of estates.

Housing associations: Now own and manage low-cost housing, though councils may retain nomination rights.

Right-to-buy legislation: Council houses sold to private buyers.

HEALTH

NHS trusts: Self-managing hospitals previously run by district and health authorities.

Regional health authorities: Direct local council representation removed.

OTHERS

Compulsory competitive tendering: Private contractors provide a variety of services, such as staff selection, previously controlled by councils.

Police authorities: Government proposals would cut local council representation from two-thirds to half. chairmen and other key positions would be appointed by the Home Secretary.

Urban development corporations: Have taken over some planning and economic development functions.

National Environmental Protection Agency: Will take over functions such as waste management.

Source: *Observer*, 4 July 1993

comparison has been made between Conservative-controlled Westminster and Labour-controlled Liverpool councils (*New Statesman and Society*, 15 April 1994). The Band D council tax in Westminster for 1994–5 was £245, whereas Liverpool's was £867; yet Westminster's budgeted expenditure per head of population was £1,047 against Liverpool's £969. Westminster's greater expenditure with a lower local tax rate was made possible because it received a far more favourable level of grant from central government.

Westminster council was embroiled in further controversy when a report by the District Auditor accused the ruling Conservatives of gerrymandering. The accusation arose from their policy of selling council houses. Such sales were concentrated in marginal wards. The idea seemed to be to reduce the number of council tenants and to increase the number of home-owners in these wards, in the hope of retaining a Conservative majority on the council. The auditor argued that this policy had lost the council an estimated £21.25 million, and Conservative Westminster councillors from that period may face potential surcharge to make this loss good. However, the Conservative councillors have rejected this interpretation of events and the report will no doubt be the subject of an appeal.

As for abolishing quangos, the early Thatcher administration did close down a number of such organizations, but these were often replaced by others that differed from their predecessors mainly in being more tightly controlled by central government. In addition, many of the functions previously carried out by local councils, and therefore subject to some degree of democratic control via local elections, have been hived off to various unelected agencies, so that an unelected elite is now responsible for large amounts of public expenditure.

According to Weir and Hall (1994), in May 1994 there were 5,521 executive agencies responsible for total expenditure of £46.6 billion – nearly a third of all public expenditure. These quangos, whose governing bodies are appointed by ministers and central government, were staffed by over 70,000 people. This compares with a total of 25,000 elected councillors. These bodies are often virtually unaccountable since only 1 per cent of quangos are subject to investigation by any ombudsman, only a third are subject to public audit and more than 90 per cent are under no obligation to hold an annual public meeting.

Some suspect that the appointments to these bodies are influenced by party-political considerations. An *Observer* survey found that the 'bosses of 40 per cent of the largest quangos had direct links with the Tories' (McGhie and Lewis 1993, p. 11). The growth of quangos has been particularly spectacular in Wales, and it has been suggested that one reason for this is that the Conservatives are unable to win elections there. After the local elections in May 1995 Wales has no Conservative-controlled councils and only 42 Conservative councillors out of a total of 1,273.

William Waldegrave, the Minster for Open Government, has argued that quangos are accountable to Parliament via ministerial accountability, so they are still subject to democratic control; he has also claimed that they improve local services to the community by depoliticizing the provision of services and improving the service to the consumer, and that they therefore result in a democratic gain.

This line of reasoning reflects the wider argument over the form of democracy and the rights attached to it. The New Right is principally concerned with people as consumers of services, and for this reason the Citizen's Charter is invoked as a key means of making local services more answerable to the people; on the other hand, more radical versions of citizenship such as that supported by Charter 88 maintain that democracy is the best form of accountability.

Conclusion

The rise of the quangocracy has led to renewed divisions over democracy and accountability, and has highlighted the differences in the notions of citizenship held by the proponents of differing perspectives.

Democracy may be something we all take for granted in the UK, but this chapter has illustrated some of the arguments about this notion that were central to the rise of political sociology and remain important today. Democracy, although probably universally supported in this country, is far from being universally applied.

Essay Question

Stopping the rot within the British state will not be easy. A spoils system of government has become firmly established. . . . The *Independent*'s two-day investigation has revealed discreet but widespread connections between business and the ruling party that mean decisions are made with little reference to Parliament or voters.

MPs look impotent and irrelevant besides the biggest quangocrats, who hold multiple unelected posts and are responsible for spending millions of taxpayers' pounds. [Editorial in *Independent,* 17 March 1994]

To what extent does sociological evidence support this view of the state and democracy in Britain?

Coursework suggestions

In this project you will be investigating which vision of citizenship, if any, people in this country support.

Study the detailed summary of T.H. Marshall's work in Turner (1986). Next you should operationalize the various rights involved in each of Marshall's concepts of citizenship, and on this basis construct a questionnaire with a list of potential rights.

Use your questionnaire to test the attitudes of a sample of people in your locality. You will need to pay particular attention to the make-up of your sample.

Use your results to consider whether there are any social differences in your respondents' views on citizenship rights in terms of their class, gender, age, party affiliation and so on.

Use your knowledge of sociological debates about citizenship to consider explanations of these differences. You will find the references in the bibliography helpful; they should all be available in a local higher education library.

Bibliography

Beetham, D. (1974) *Max Weber and the Theory of Modern Politics,* London: Allen & Unwin

Blunkett, D. and Jackson, K. (1987) *Democracy in Crisis,* London: Chatto & Windus

Bottomore, T. (1993) *Political Sociology,* 2nd edn, London: Pluto Press

Gleeson, D. (1990) *Sociology: A Modern Approach,* Oxford: Oxford Universitry Press

Heater, D. (1990) *Citizenship,* London: Longman

Hirst, P. (1993) *The Pluralist Theory of the State,* London: Routledge

Lane, P. (1972) *Political Parties,* London: Batsford

Mann, M. (1987) 'Ruling class strategies and citizenship', *Sociology,* Vol. 21, No. 3

Marshall, T.H. (1963) 'Citizenship and social class', in Marshall, T.H. *Sociology at the Crossroads,* London: Heinemann

Marx, K. (1843) *On the Jewish Question,* reprinted in Colletti, L. (ed.) *Early Writings,* Harmondsworth: Penguin (1975)

McGhie, J and Lewis, P. (1993) 'Tories put friends in high places', *Observer,* 4 July

Mommsen, W. (1984) *Max Weber and German Politics, 1890–1920,* Chicago: Chicago University Press.

Oliver, D. (1993) 'Citizenship in the 1990s', *Politics Review,* September

Rooum, D. (1985) *Wildcat Anarchist Comics,* London: Freedom Press

Smyth, G., Jones, D. and Platt, S. (eds) (1994) *Bite the Ballot: 2,500 Years of Democracy,* London: Channel 4/New Statesman and Society

Therborn, G. (1977) 'Capital and the rise of democracy', *New Left Review,* May

Turner, B.S. (1986) *Citizenship and Capitalism,* London: Allen & Unwin

—— (1990) 'Outline of a theory of citizenship', *Sociology,* Vol. 24, No. 2

—— (1993) 'Outline of a theory of human rights', *Sociology,* Vol. 27, No. 3

Weir, S. and Hall, W. (eds) (1994) *Ego Trip: Extra-governmental Organizations in the UK and Their Accountability,* London: Democratic Audit/Charter 88 Trust

9

Globalization, the nation-state and nationalism

'The internationalization of production, finance and other economic resources is unquestionably eroding the capacity of the state to control its own economic future.'

Held (1989), p. 194

'Despite the trends towards the internationalization of capital, the nation-state retains considerable power to affect the rate and distribution of capital accumulation within its borders.'

Callinicos (1989), p. 140

One of the most far-reaching debates of present times, in terms of its implications for the whole of sociology and beyond, is the debate surrounding the notion of globalization. It is particularly relevant to political sociology since it concerns the role and importance of the state in modern societies.

At its simplest the notion of globalization stresses that economic, social and political change now occurs on a global level as a result of processes that operate on a global level and have global effects. We now live in a world that is enormously more integrated than it was even a generation ago.

One way to illustrate this is to consider what you eat for breakfast:

> For people in London the corn that has gone into the breakfast cornflakes was harvested in Tennessee or Brazil. The wood for the table was cut in Malaysia. The sugar, the tea or coffee, the Formica table top – each detail concludes such an enormous and complex world division of labour that no single person can comprehend it.
> The world economy is not some external phenomenon, it is present in each kitchen. [Harris 1983, p. 9]

> *Make a study of the extent to which the world economy is manifest in your own kitchen.*

In a world of nation-states, the borders between them serve to limit the powers of the state, but also to delineate identities, even when they encompass different nationalities. This is of course true of Great Britain or the United Kingdom.

However, if most of the processes that affect our lives today do not occur within the limited territory we inhabit, they may be said to be beyond the power of the individual state to regulate. The key implication of globalization is therefore that the most powerful political institution of modern times, the nation-state, has been substantially and perhaps fatally weakened.

The rise of the global economy

The increasing importance of the global economy is associated with changes in the role of the state and a renewed emphasis on free-market economics. After the Second World War there was a consensus in social thinking that stressed the active involvement and central position of the state in society. This reflected a rejection of previous ideas on how to run a society that had been based on the free market and minimal state involvement. Lash and Urry (1987) characterize this change as leading to what they call 'organized capitalism', a system which shows the following features:

- the concentration of industry in large companies

- the development of mergers and cartels, reducing economic competition

- regulation of the economy by the state in a corporatist accord with big business and the organized labour movement

- state provision of welfare through the welfare state

- the growth of a professional 'service class', often in state jobs.

This form of social organization went into crisis in the early 1970s. Economic difficulties led to problems in funding the welfare state, and there was talk of cuts in that area for the first time.

The New Right argued that state involvement in the economy was the key cause of economic crises, and they therefore proposed to reduce the amount of state expenditure and at the same time promote free-market economic policies to build up the private sector.

In response to the economic crisis and the fall-off in profitability in the advanced industrial economies, capitalist corporations began to seek profitable returns in new areas. This led to a growth in foreign investment and the idea of global production. The process was further advanced by the large profits accrued by oil companies (after the 1973 price rise) and the deregulation of financial markets by New Right governments in the 1980s. Large amounts of money looking for profitable investment could now be moved around the world much more easily, a trend that continued to accelerate in the 1990s. For example, Lash and Urry (1994, p. 289) have reported that $600 billion worth of foreign exchange transactions take place in London every day. At the heart of these processes are a number of companies, known as multinational or transnational corporations, which operate on a world scale.

A good example is the 'British' car industry. Both Ford and Vauxhall are ultimately owned by US car companies; Rover is owned by BMW, a German company; Ford also owns Jaguar; and the largest exporter of cars from Britain is Nissan, a Japanese company. Figure 9.1 illustrates some of the complexity of the multinational manufacturing process today.

Figure 9.1

Global manufacturing: the component network for the European model of the Ford Escort

Source: Dicken (1986), p. 304

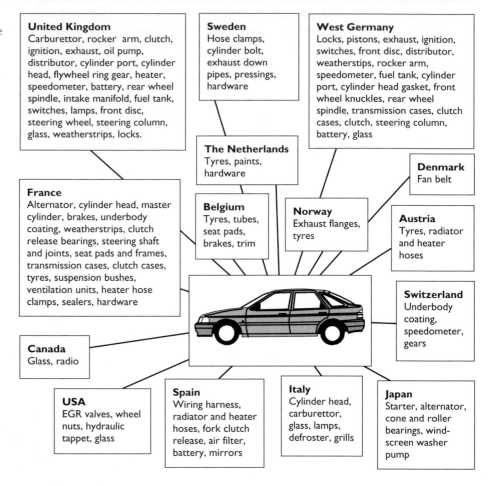

United Kingdom
Carburettor, rocker arm, clutch, ignition, exhaust, oil pump, distributor, cylinder port, cylinder head, flywheel ring gear, heater, speedometer, battery, rear wheel spindle, intake manifold, fuel tank, switches, lamps, front disc, steering wheel, steering column, glass, weatherstrips, locks.

Sweden
Hose clamps, cylinder bolt, exhaust down pipes, pressings, hardware

West Germany
Locks, pistons, exhaust, ignition, switches, front disc, distributor, weatherstrips, rocker arm, speedometer, fuel tank, cylinder port, cylinder head gasket, front wheel knuckles, rear wheel spindle, transmission cases, clutch cases, clutch, steering column, battery, glass

The Netherlands
Tyres, paints, hardware

Denmark
Fan belt

France
Alternator, cylinder head, master cylinder, brakes, underbody coating, weatherstrips, clutch release bearings, steering shaft and joints, seat pads and frames, transmission cases, clutch cases, tyres, suspension bushes, ventilation units, heater hose clamps, sealers, hardware

Belgium
Tyres, tubes, seat pads, brakes, trim

Norway
Exhaust flanges, tyres

Austria
Tyres, radiator and heater hoses

Switzerland
Underbody coating, speedometer, gears

Canada
Glass, radio

USA
EGR valves, wheel nuts, hydraulic tappet, glass

Spain
Wiring harness, radiator and heater hoses, fork clutch release, air filter, battery, mirrors

Italy
Cylinder head, carburettor, glass, lamps, defroster, grills

Japan
Starter, alternator, cone and roller bearings, wind-screen washer pump

Investigate the extent to which production is now global in two industries of your choice. Write a short report of 100–200 words and present your findings to the rest of the class.

The political implications of globalization

Many sociologists now argue that the globalization of world production has important political and social implications. Since the largest companies in the world now operate in more than one country they can shop around to find the most attractive political climate in which to conduct their business; they will seek countries where tax levels are low and other legislation designed to control the activities of companies, such as health and safety legislation, is lenient or non-existent.

The ability of the state to provide a system of regulation and welfare benefits depends on its ability to obtain tax revenue to fund this expenditure. It is argued that this is seriously threatened in the era of global capitalism, since it is not in the interests of companies to locate in countries where the tax burden is high. Since wages are lower in Third World countries, there will be a haemorrhage of investment to those countries unless wage costs in the industrialized world can be kept down.

According to this argument, the kind of policies pursued in the 1950s and 1960s are no longer viable because firms will refuse to pay the necessary taxation, and will merely relocate their operations elsewhere. The ability of individual governments to regulate economic and social life and therefore to carry out policies based on their political manifestos is gone. It is said that the growth of international capital has reached such heights that we now need to talk of 'transnational corporations' whose operations are in no way tied to particular countries.

Lash and Urry (1987) claim that we have now entered a new period which they entitle 'disorganized capitalism'. It has the following features:

- The power of transnational companies undermines the economic power of nation-states.

- The growth of investment in the Third World contributes to the decline of manufacturing industry in the advanced Western countries.

- This leads to a decline in the size of the working class and therefore the decline of class-based politics.

Political decisions can no longer really be taken within individual nation-states. The ideal that each state is sovereign over its own territory is eroded and therefore the old political strategies of effecting change through control of or influence on individual nation-states is no longer possible. A new politics must develop, focused either upon the development of international political agencies or alternatively away from the state, in civil society.

Table 9.1 The growth of international organizations

Date	Intergovernmental organizations	International non-governmental organizations
1905	37	176
1951	123	832
1972	280	2173
1984	365	4615

Source: Held (1989), p. 196

Held (1989) has charted the growth in international political associations (see Table 9.1). He argues that this process fundamentally undermines any attempt to bring about social change through the nation-state and that this threatens the kind of policies traditionally pursued by the Labour Party. A Labour government could no longer raise tax revenue to fund social expenditure as companies would move elsewhere, causing unemployment to rise; in any case, as a result of the internationalization of production the working class – the traditional base for support for the Labour Party – is in decline, threatening it with electoral oblivion. Insofar as the type of policies pursued by the Labour Party in the 1950s and 1960s, marked by a large degree of state involvement in the economy and a welfare state financed out of taxation, are considered to be the embodiment of socialism, then Held argues that globalization has killed off the prospect of socialism.

Leslie Sklair (1991) has argued that we need to develop a sociology of the global system in order to be able to comprehend these developments. Throughout the world key economic control is in the hands of the transnational corporations and key political control is wielded by the global capitalist class. Socialists, according to Sklair, need a democratic internationalist vision, so he rejects all varieties of socialism based on gaining control of the nation-state. He argues instead that the global capitalist system uses the myth of the nation-state, sometimes in the form of reactionary nationalist ideologies, to divert people away from the reality of the global nature of capitalist production in the contemporary world.

 Consult Sklair (1993) and make detailed notes on the three competing models of globalization that he identifies. Draw up a table to summarize the three models. Evaluate the relative merits of each model in a report about 700 words long.

Is the nation-state doomed?

No one seriously questions the internationalization of the world economy, but the political implications that flow from this phenomenon are matters for debate. The notion of globalization has often seemed to conjure up doomsday-like visions in the minds of socialists whose policies are focused on the state. According to David Gordon (1988), these visions have 'helped foster . . . a spreading political fatalism in the advanced countries'. Gordon and another Marxist social theorist, Alex Callinicos, present an alternative view of the operation of globalization along the following lines:

- The growth of the international economy is not in dispute.

- However, the scale of the phenomenon is sometimes exaggerated.

- Transnational companies do not in reality flit around the globe at will.

- Transnational companies still require the protection of states.

- Therefore the process of globalization will not lead to oblivion for the nation-state.

- The process is only seen as fatal to socialism because of the incorrect identification of socialism with state control of society.

The starting point of this perspective is to stress that the global economy is largely limited to the advanced industrial West, which is far from encompassing the whole world. The vast majority of investment undertaken by transnational companies is in the West. Approximately 70 per cent of all corporate foreign investment went to France, Japan, the USA, the UK and Germany, and 90 per cent of the headquarters of multinational companies are located in the industrial world (see Figure 9.2).

Gordon denies that there is a major threat of transnational companies relocating to low-wage economies in the Third World; the key factor for companies making investment decisions is not low wages but rather a stable social and political structure, which is crucially influenced by the state.

The idea that these companies are willing to flit about the globe at will is also undermined by the difficulty of any real transnational corporations – that is, genuinely stateless companies. *Business Week* (14 May 1990) identified forty-seven companies that it regarded as stateless, but all of these had a majority of their shares owned in a 'home' country and only fourteen had most of their assets outside that country. Paul

Figure 9.2

The destination of
multinational investment

Source: *New Internationalist,*
August 1993

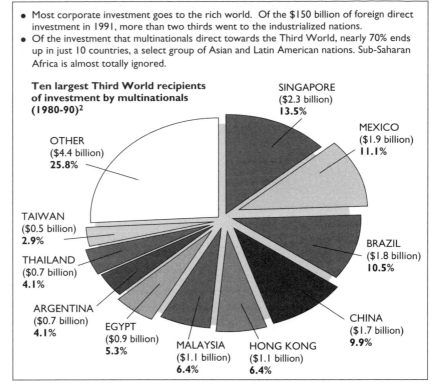

- Most corporate investment goes to the rich world. Of the $150 billion of foreign direct investment in 1991, more than two thirds went to the industrialized nations.
- Of the investment that multinationals direct towards the Third World, nearly 70% ends up in just 10 countries, a select group of Asian and Latin American nations. Sub-Saharan Africa is almost totally ignored.

Ten largest Third World recipients of investment by multinationals (1980-90)[2]

SINGAPORE
($2.3 billion)
13.5%

MEXICO
($1.9 billion)
11.1%

OTHER
($4.4 billion)
25.8%

BRAZIL
($1.8 billion)
10.5%

TAIWAN
($0.5 billion)
2.9%

THAILAND
($0.7 billion)
4.1%

CHINA
($1.7 billion)
9.9%

ARGENTINA
($0.7 billion)
4.1%

EGYPT
($0.9 billion)
5.3%

MALAYSIA
($1.1 billion)
6.4%

HONG KONG
($1.1 billion)
6.4%

What implications does Figure 9.2 have for the globalization thesis?
The whole issue of New Internationalist from which this figure was taken is concerned with the 'New Globalism'. Obtain a copy and make notes on the articles in it.

Hirst (1993) has commented that 'we are nowhere near a fully globalized economy, and are unlikely to get there'.

There have been important examples of state intervention in the economy in the 1980s and 1990s. For instance:

- The US government pumped money into the economy to deal with the banking crises that occurred in the early 1980s as a result of bad debts incurred by lending too lavishly to newly industrializing countries, notably Mexico and Brazil.

- The US government again pumped money into the economy after the 1987 stock exchange crash.

- Ronald Reagan reinforced the importance of the state by engaging in vast expenditure on military hardware, most notably 'Star Wars'.

Callinicos (1989) maintains that no state was able to achieve complete economic independence from the world economy during the post-war 'managed capitalism' era, not even Soviet Russia. The stability of this era cannot be explained on the basis of the interventionist Keynesian economic policies. 'The long boom reflected not so much successful state intervention as the effect of very high levels of peacetime arms expenditure in offsetting what Marx called the tendency of the rate of profit to decline.' The crises of the 1970s resulted from the decline of this 'permanent arms economy', which ran into difficulties because arms expenditure was supplanting more productive uses of capital, and countries not burdened with such expenditure (notably Germany and Japan) were becoming serious economic competitors to the USA.

Despite this decline, arms expenditure remains at significant levels. In 1992/93 British government expenditure on defence stood at £24.18 billion, representing 10.6 per cent of total public expenditure. This is important since military power is still organized by nation-states. Multinational companies have not spawned private armies to fight their wars, so they are still ultimately dependent on the military power of nation-states to protect their worldwide activities. This was obvious in the Gulf War, when various state armies joined together to protect oil interests in the Middle East. In many ways the boom of the 1980s can also be explained by the growth of military expenditure during the Reagan administration, notably on the ill-fated 'Star Wars' project. This form of expenditure is crucially directed through the state.

It could, of course, be argued that military activities are now organized internationally, notably through NATO, and therefore military action is now beyond the scope of individual states. However, member states maintain a degree of independence even within NATO. France, for example, has kept independent control of its nuclear forces, despite being a member of NATO, as indeed has Britain (see Figure 9.3).

Figure 9.3

Global nuclear power

Source: *The Times,* 16 November 1993

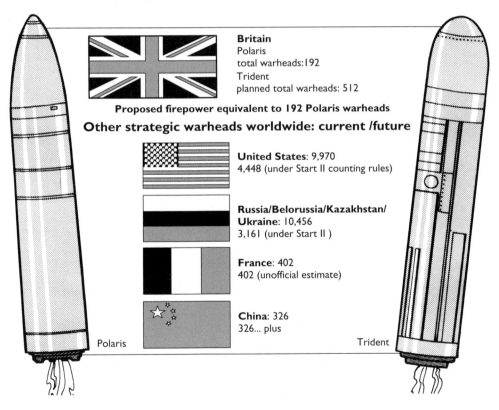

Britain
Polaris
total warheads: 192
Trident
planned total warheads: 512

Proposed firepower equivalent to 192 Polaris warheads

Other strategic warheads worldwide: current /future

United States: 9,970
4,448 (under Start II counting rules)

Russia/Belorussia/Kazakhstan/Ukraine: 10,456
3,161 (under Start II)

France: 402
402 (unofficial estimate)

China: 326
326... plus

Polaris

Trident

One contemporary example of the tension between the internationalizing of military operations and the continuing attempts of individual nation-states to retain some control is given by the problems the United Nations faces in collecting finance to support its operations in Bosnia in former Yugoslavia.

The UN Protection Force in Bosnia (Unprofor) is financed by member states of the UN. However, the Secretary General of the UN, Boutros Boutros-Ghali, has warned that its operations are threatened by the reluctance of member states to pay the bill. The biggest culprit, as on previous occasions, was the USA, which owed almost $115 million on its Unprofor assessment, more than $46 million on its Somalia assessment and $39 million on the successful Cambodian operation. It was also in arrears on most of the UN's twelve other peace-keeping operations. Among the other significant defaulters are the Russian Federation and Ukraine.

The implications of globalization: a summary

It is quite clear that on an economic level there have been immense changes in the internationalization of production. Whether we are justified in calling this a global economy is very much a matter of debate. Most of the money for investment and the investment itself seems confined to a group of advanced industrial nations comprising the USA, Japan and Western Europe. Obviously this does not constitute the whole globe. However, the activities of investors in these countries affect the lives of people throughout the world. It therefore seems to matter whether we are describing the location of this economy or its effects.

The political debate centres around whether the internationalization of production has led to the eclipse of the nation-state. One issue is the transfer of power from largely democratically elected governments to unelected multinational entities. According to Noam Chomsky (1994), there is now an unelected world government and therefore globalization has undermined democracy. He argues that for the rich and powerful 'This has the very useful property that it removes power from parliamentary institutions, which are considered dangerous, naturally, because they might fall, at least partially, under the influence of the rabble.'

Nationalism

It may seem paradoxical to link discussion of nationalism with globalization, since one is based on identity with a particular nation-state and the other is arguably undermining any basis for such an identity as a viable political strategy. However, there is an important link, as Tom Nairn makes clear: 'Nationalism has always been a response to globalization – the particular brought to life both by and against the universal' (Nairn 1994, p. xxxvi).

There are a number of possible explanations for why the internationalizing process of globalization might foster a seemingly opposite process of the growth of nationalism. For instance:

- The development of international agencies might undermine the nation-state, but it does not necessarily undermine attachments to that nation-state. This might cause the intervention of international agencies to be viewed as a new form of 'imperialism'.

- The very fact that globalization may undermine existing nation-states might provide the political space for the growth of alternative nationalisms, previously submerged within a united all powerful nation-state. This could help explain the development, for example, of Scottish and Welsh nationalism.

In the European Union the power of the elected European Parliament remains limited and the real power lies with the unelected Council of Ministers. The level of democratic control over the actions of the European Union is therefore weak, creating what has been called the 'democratic deficit'. This may stimulate attempts to reassert some control, fighting the influence of these supranational entities by appealing to quasi-nationalist sentiment.

The rise of nationalism

For the reasons outlined above, and no doubt for other reasons too, recent years have seen a marked rise in movements based on nationalism. For instance, Figure 9.4 shows the large number of areas around the world where nationalist movements are seeking statehood.

Figure 9.4

Movements seeking statehood

Source: *Guardian*, 23 February 1993

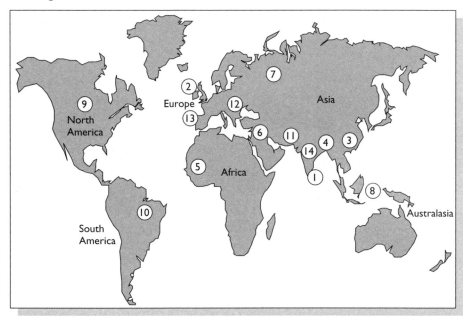

1. SRI LANKA
An uprising by mostly Tamils in the north and east has been carried out against the government, which is dominated by the mostly Buddhist Sinhalese. Since 1983, an estimated 28,000 people have been killed in the Tamil rebellion.
2. N.IRELAND
Some favour continued union with Britain while others want to join with the rest of Ireland. More than 3,000 people have been killed in fighting between British troops, Protestant paramilitary groups and the Irish Republican Army since 1969.
3. CHINA
Tibetans rebelled against Chinese rule in 1959, with an estimated 87,000 Tibetans killed. After an easing of Chinese rule, China cracked down in 1987. In Xinjang, China suppressed a rebellion among Muslims of Turloc descent in 1990 in which an estimated 50 people died.
4. BHUTAN
A revolt by ethnic Nepalese against the government and reprisals by government forces have led to thousands of Nepalese fleeing the country in the last two years.

5. MALI

A demand for sovereignty by ethnic Tuaregs, a nomadic people living in both Mali and neighbouring Niger, has led to fighting in both Mali and Niger.

6. ISRAEL

The *Infada*, an uprising of Palestinians against Israeli occupation of the Gaza Strip and the West Bank of the Jordan River, began in 1987. About 1,000 Palestinians have been killed by Israeli soldiers. 500 have been killed by fellow Palestinians, and about 100 have been killed in Palestinian attacks.

7. RUSSIA

Chechenya and Ingushetia have broken apart and want greater self-rule within Russia. Ingushetia and Northern Ossetia are fighting over territory in clashes that have killed more than 300 people.

8. INDONESIA

A civil war broke out in East Timor in 1975 after Portugal withdrew its rule. Indonesia crushed the pro-independence rebellion. Human-rights organizations believe 100,000 to 200,000 of the 600,000 mostly Roman Catholic East Timorese have died. A separatist movement also exists in northern Sumatra.

9. CANADA

Some people in the Canadian province of Quebec would like to become a separate country.

10. BRAZIL

Native tribes in the Amazon region are pressing the government in Brasilia to recognize their traditional homelands. In the northern Amazon state of Roraima, the federal government is campaigning to expel gold miners from the lands of the Yanomami tribes.

11. AFGHANISTAN

After the withdrawal of Soviet troops and the overthrow of the Soviet-installed leader, President Najibullah, the country has collapsed into civil war. The Hazars control central and western areas near Iran, the Pathans are largely in control in the east and the Tajiks in the north. Thousands are estimated to have been killed.

12. BOSNIA-HERZEGOVNIA

Serbian forces have captured about 70 per cent of the country and carried out an 'ethnic cleansing' campaign in which they have expelled and killed Muslims and Croats.

Tens of thousands of people have been estimated as killed and 15 million uprooted from their homes.

13. SPAIN

Nationalists claiming to represent three million Basques seek an independent state on the border of Spain and France. Since 1968, 717 people have been killed in Spain and 49 in France over the issue.

14. INDIA

Tensions between Hindus and Muslims exploded into riots and killings in December when Hindu militants razed a mosque in the northern state of Utar Pradesh in Kashmir. 5,000 militants, civilians and Indian troops have been killed since a rebellion by the largely Muslim population began in 1990. An estimated 120,000 people, mostly Hindus, have fled Kashmir for other parts of India. In Punjab about 20,000 Hindus and Sikhs are estimated to have been killed since a rebellion by Sikh militants began in 1982.

Sociologists are interested in identifying the basis of nationalism in modern societies as this is clearly an important form of political mobilization in the late twentieth century. Nationalism as a set of ideas was unknown much before the eighteenth century since the concept of the nation originates with the transformations of society which took place at that time, ushering in the modern era. The nations we know today are thus very modern phenomena. Derbyshire and Derbyshire (1989) point out that if we consider the 165 states which exist in the world today, 123 were created in the twentieth century, and of these seventy-four were created after 1959. In the Middle East and Africa only three of today's sixty-five states were in existence before 1910, and even in Europe only forty per cent of today's states were in existence before 1910.

There is a great deal of debate about the actual origins of nations. This debate is important since most nationalists claim as the basis of their legitimacy a link with a particular race or culture enshrined in the idea of a particular nation. If they are right, nations are older than the ideology of nationalism, and nationalism is based on something real. If, however, nations were effectively created by nationalism, the traditions on which nationalists today base their claims to legitimacy may be considered inventions of the modern mind.

Nations as 'natural units' of human society

The idea that nations are in some way 'natural' is held by many functionalist thinkers. Edward Shils (1957) considered the nation to be a natural unit of society on the basis that human beings have always formed bonds based on similarities (and therefore also on differences) of language, religion, race, ethnicity and territory. Nations are merely a large-scale example of such a tendency, and thus have a long history.

This has been characterized as a primordialist view of nations. In contrast, most sociologists today argue that nations are not a natural unit that humans have always adopted; on the contrary, they are characteristic of modern times. Not unsurprisingly, this is known as the modernist view of the rise of nations.

A third position is advocated by Anthony Smith (1986). He too rejects the idea that

Figure 9.5

Ethnic kingdoms and migrations in Western Europe, c. AD 400–1000

Source: Smith (1986), p. xvi

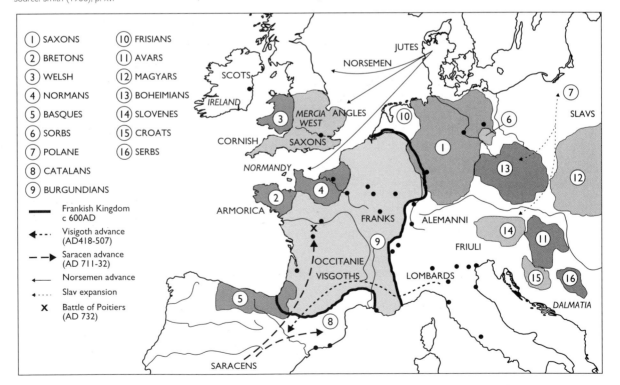

nations are natural, pointing to such examples as Nigeria, India and Indonesia, which do not have a shared identity, as evidence that this idea is wrong. However, he does argue that nations may have roots in pre-existing ethnic communities and in particular the myths and symbols developed to foster identity in these communities. Thus he suggests that the idea of a nation was present before nationalist ideologies were fully developed.

Which modern-day nationalities can be identified from the ethnic map shown in Figure 9.5? How far do you think this provides an adequate explanation of contemporary nationalisms?

America is a geographical entity, and we can point to it on the map, but the USA does not seem to be characterized by any overall shared identity as writers who see nations as outgrowths of earlier identities would suggest. Its official language is English (not 'American') – though Spanish may become the predominant language in use there in the future. In Brazil they speak Portuguese, and in Switzerland they speak three languages (French, German and Italian) in different parts.

Critics of the view that nations are natural point to the problem of delineating nations as they actually exist on the basis of shared characteristics; they are not the homogeneous entities that this type of theory would predict. Consider the United Kingdom: Is it possible to identify any shared identity underpinning the existence of the UK that would qualify it as a 'natural' nation?

While those who see the nation as a modern invention can all be categorized as modernists, there are divisions within this view. The key division is between those writing in the Marxist tradition, who see the rise of nations as linked to the rise of capitalism, and those working in an essentially Durkheimian perspective who see them as the result of industrialization.

Ernest Gellner and the Durkheimian perspective

Durkheim argued that the key mechanism for social change in the modern world was the developing division of labour. The new society required a standardized form of education to allow for continued economic growth and to enable workers to move from job to job by providing them with certain common skills. In his analysis of how societies retained a sense of solidarity in the age of individualism, Durkheim pointed to the common value system developed by a common education and also to the role of religion in allowing us to worship society.

Gellner applies this analysis explicitly to the rise of nations and nationalism. He explains the connection as follows: 'Durkheim taught that in religious worship society adores its own camouflaged image. In a nationalist age, societies worship themselves brazenly and openly, spurning the camouflage' (Gellner 1983, p. 56).

He totally rejects the idea that pre-industrial society had any conception of the nation since the elite was always separated from the mass of the population in terms of style of living and culture. This lack of common identity makes it impossible for people to be united around the idea of a nation, which is essentially the basis of nationalism.

In the development of industrial society old traditional cultures are destroyed, and the emergence of a common culture leads to the establishment of nations.

Nationalism as a doctrine is linked to this creation of nations and both are caused by the transformations of the Industrial Revolution and the advent of modern society.

In relation to contemporary society, the spread of industrialization around the world leads to a continual overturning of traditional cultures, and if those affected are not assimilated into the new dominant culture, one possible response is the rise of nationalism based around this group. This may or may not lead to the creation of a new nation.

Marxist perspectives

Eric Hobsbawm

Hobsbawm (1992) agrees that the nation is a modern invention. He also argues that it is impossible to produce a satisfactory definition of what constitutes a 'nation' either on an objective basis (meaning some root in language or ethnicity) or on a subjective basis (meaning pre-existing identities). In relation to the former, he proves they in fact serve more often to divide than unite; and in relation to the latter he argues that not all the people or movements who have claimed nation status (and therefore possess a pre-existing identity) have actually become nations. Something else must therefore be needed. For Hobsbawm this something is association with a state. The key to the rise of nations is the rise of the state: 'Nations are more often the consequence of setting up a state than they are its foundations' (p. 78). Nationalism is therefore linked to the arguments over citizenship rights within a state-formed nation.

The origins of the nation lie with the concept of citizenship that arose with the French Revolution. According to Hobsbawm, the original citizen-nation concept was not based on any common identity. In order to become a French citizen at that time, you did not even have to speak French, you merely had to exhibit a willingness to learn. As a result, anyone could choose their nationality, a position strongly at odds with the present situation.

Hobsbawm argues that the need to get the population to fight in wars and therefore to secure their loyalty to the state was the key reason that nationalism became transformed from a notion linked to citizenship into one based on ideas of patriotism, stressing ancient loyalties and differences. This process was taken further with the rise of pseudo-scientific theories of racial difference, which attempted to provide some objective justification for the ideas of nation and race. In this way nationalism became linked to the idea of difference between people based on ethnicity. It became a movement of the political right whereas previously it had been associated with democracy and citizenship.

In Hobsbawm's view the most successful nationalist movements drew upon the democratic historical legacy by promoting social reform, since on this basis they could attract working-class support. However, he believes nationalism now has no future because nations are more heterogeneous than ever (he cites the example of Papua New Guinea, where a population of 2.5 million speak over 700 languages) and nationalism has no positive programme to offer: 'Nationalism . . . is simply no longer the historical force it was in the era between the French Revolution and the end of the imperialist colonialism after World War Two' (1992, p. 169).

In recent times the former Yugoslavia has given the world a new phrase, 'ethnic cleansing'. The brutality evident there may seem to endorse Hobsbawm's argument about the destructive nature of modern nationalism, but the fact that it is happening also raises the question whether his prediction of its decline is accurate.

The neo-Marxist approach

Benedict Anderson

Probably the most influential neo-Marxist account of nationalism is to be found in the work of Benedict Anderson. While he retains a characteristic Marxist concern with the material basis of the growth of nationalism, he has been concerned to include as a key element the role of culture.

In his book *Imagined Communities* (1991) Anderson argues that the origin of nationalism lies in the ability to imagine communities which gave people something to identify with in the face of the decline of the Catholic religion and the Latin language it used. The rise of Protestantism combined with the rise of print-capitalism created the basis for unified language communities, so in Anderson's account nations were a product of the rise of a particular form of technology – printing:

> In pre-print Europe ... the diversity of spoken languages ... was immense; so immense, indeed, that had print-capitalism sought to exploit each potential oral vernacular market, it would have remained a capitalism of petty proportions. But these varied idiolects were capable of being assembled, within definite limits, into print-languages far fewer in number ... speakers of the huge variety of Frenches, Englishes, or Spanishes, who might find it difficult or even impossible to understand one another in conversation, became capable of comprehending one another via print and paper. In the process they gradually became aware of the hundreds of thousands, even millions, of people in their particular language-field, and at the same time that only those hundreds of thousands, or millions, so belonged. These fellow-readers, to whom they were connected through print, formed ... the embryo of the nationally imagined community. [Anderson 1991, pp. 38–44]

This imagination is not a form of falsehood contrasted with some true form of community, as Gellner tends to argue, since Anderson believes that all communities larger than those that allow face-to-face contact with all their members are imagined. If we see ourselves as British we imagine an affinity with some 56 million other British people even though it is clear we will never meet more than a tiny fraction of these people in our lives. Anderson points out:

> the Soviet Union shares with the United Kingdom of Great Britain and Northern Ireland the rare distinction of refusing nationality in its naming ... Anyone who has doubts about the UK's claims to such parity with the USSR should ask himself what nationality its name denotes: Great Brito-Irish? [Anderson 1991, p. 2]

> *Do you agree with Anderson about this? What name would you give to the United Kingdom if you wanted it to signify a nationality?*

For Anderson there is nothing natural about nations, and they are thus inventions or, to use his phrase, imaginings. He cites the 'tombs of the Unknown Soldier', whose nationality is often unstated since it is obviously the nationality of the nation in which the tomb is located, and he also points to the complete absence of 'a tomb of the Unknown Marxist or a cenotaph for fallen Liberals'; the reason, he argues, is that nationalism is centrally concerned with the emotions surrounding death while the other ideologies are not. The continuing mortality of humans therefore explains the attachment to nationalism today. This tends to suggest that, unlike classical Marxists, Anderson views nationalism as unlikely to die out.

Nationalism in the UK today

It is interesting to note the relative political unimportance of English nationalism. An English nationalism exists, but Tom Nairn (1977) has argued that it is linked to traditional symbols of authority, notably the monarchy, and as such it is encompassed by British nationalism and has not been politically significant. British nationalism, however, could not be based on ethnic identity since its central institution, the royal family, was originally Hanoverian (part of Germany).

According to Nairn, the popularity of the monarchy is one of the cornerstones of English nationalism, and this has affected the social and industrial development of the UK, leading to a form of backwardness. In the most recent edition of his book, however, he points out that the popularity of the monarchy is no longer so evident. For instance, 80 per cent of people surveyed in a newspaper poll in December 1993 felt the Royal Family should get no support from public money.

 Professor Steven Hassler, Chairman of Republic, wrote the following to the London Evening Standard (17 June 1994), commenting on the D-Day celebrations: 'it was fitting that the American and French elected heads of state should represent their countries, whereas poor old Britain could only offer – on this, one of democracy's great days – an anachronistic hereditary family to represent its people. (And it was also ironic and somewhat sad, in view of the banning of Herr Kohl from the proceedings, that the only Germans on the beaches that morning were our Royals.) . . . The reality is that the world out there . . . no longer finds the monarchy of any relevance at all.'
Explain and evaluate this point of view.

Scotland

The Scottish National Party (SNP) was founded in 1933, but it did not come to prominence until the 1970s, winning its first seat in a general election in 1970 and going on to win eleven seats in the October 1974 election. Its aim of independence for Scotland was enhanced with the discovery of North Sea oil, which some saw as rightfully belonging to Scotland. A referendum held in March 1979 showed that 51.6 per cent of those voting favoured an assembly for Scotland, but a low turn-out meant this was only 32.5 per cent of the electorate, below the level of 40 per cent required for the constitutional change to be enacted.

Support for the SNP declined in the late 1970s and early 1980s but revived again in 1987, when its vote rose by 2.3 percentage points to 14.0 per cent and it gained three MPs. One of the key reasons for the upturn in the SNP's fortunes was the feeling that, although support for the Conservative Party was very low in Scotland (only 24.2 per cent in 1987), Scotland would be ruled from Westminster by a Conservative government pursuing Conservative policies, including the proposed Poll Tax which was to be tried out in Scotland first.

A tradition of Scottish nationalism goes back to the period of the union between Scotland and England in 1707; there were revolts by Highlanders against the English and the lowland Scots in 1714 and 1746. It is to that period, and accounts of an even earlier Scottish identity, that proponents of a distinct Scottish culture return. However, a study of this period by Hugh Trevor-Roper (1992) suggests that the notion of an indigenous culture in Scotland based on the Caledonians is misleading; in fact artefacts such as the kilt and the bagpipes were later inventions. The kilt, for instance, was invented in the late 1720s by an Englishman, Thomas Rawlinson, and the differentiated clan tartans were an even later invention first used to differentiate Highland regiments in the British Army.

Wales

The nationalist movement in Wales has, if anything, been even more culturally based than Scotland's. There is no equivalent of North Sea oil in Wales, but there is a more clearly defined cultural difference in the strength of Welsh-speaking communities, especially in the north-west of Wales.

Prys Morgan (1992) has argued that Welsh nationalism was a reaction to the destruction of the traditional Welsh lifestyle consequent upon the incorporation of Wales into the UK in 1536. Welsh nationalism was in fact developed by Welsh people resident in London. The Eisteddfod, for instance, was a feature of ancient Welsh life, first held in 1176, but by the latter part of the sixteenth century it had begun to die out and was only really revived in 1780 when it became linked to the Welsh Society, mainly located in London.

As with Scotland, our attention is being drawn to the invention of tradition in an attempt to provide national cultural continuity. There are several other examples of such inventions. The use of the leek on St David's Day only became widespread in 1714, before which time it was much more common to use the three plumes insignia which to this day is used as a motif of the Welsh Rugby team. The Red Dragon was also absent in these days and really only came to prominence in the twentieth century. The Welsh national anthem 'Hen Wlad Fy Nhadau' ('Land of My Fathers') was composed in 1856.

Because of the lack of any real economic alternative programme until the 1980s, and the lack of a separate legal system and consequent separate institutions, Welsh nationalism has therefore been much more cultural than its Scottish counterparts. At the centre of the cultural movement is the Welsh Language Society.

The Welsh nationalist party, Plaid Cymru, has existed since 1925. One of its problems was that by the 1920s only a minority of Welsh people actually spoke Welsh, and in the south in particular the Welsh working class was drawn towards involvement in the Labour movement. Plaid Cymru has remained strongest in North Wales, and the support it enjoys in South Wales comes mostly from the middle class. A referendum on a Welsh assembly in March 1979 was quite heavily defeated, but this overtly political type of demand was never quite as important for Plaid Cymru as it was for the SNP, and the greater cultural emphasis was assuaged somewhat by the creation of the Welsh-language television channel S4C.

There remains a strong current of nationalism in North Wales, directed against the purchase of houses by the English, which has had the effect of increasing prices beyond the reach of many Welsh people. But this support remains restricted largely to the Welsh-speaking part of Wales, whereas in the south it is limited by strong support for the Labour Party.

The National Library of Wales List of July 1981 showed the following number of Welsh-language publications for counties in Wales and also for Cardiff and Liverpool:

- *Gwynedd*   *17*
- *Dyfed*   *14*
- *Clwyd*   *5*
- *Powys*   *4*
- *West Glamorgan*   *2*
- *South Glamorgan*   *1*
- *Cardiff*   *1*
- *Liverpool*   *1*

This provides some indication of the relative numbers of Welsh speakers in each part of Wales. Look up the latest election results for Wales and consider whether there is any relationship between the figures quoted above and the relative strength of support for Plaid Cymru.

Northern Ireland

In Northern Ireland divisions between two sections of the population have led to the intervention of the British Army, and for twenty-five years paramilitary organizations, most prominently the Irish Republican Army (IRA) and the Ulster Freedom Fighters (UFF), have pursued their political objectives through the use of force. With the minor exception of a group intermittently operating in Wales, this recourse to arms is unique in the UK. A summary of the recent period of political and military unrest in Northern Ireland is provided in Figure 9.6.

Figure 9.6

Source: *Guardian*, 12 August 1994

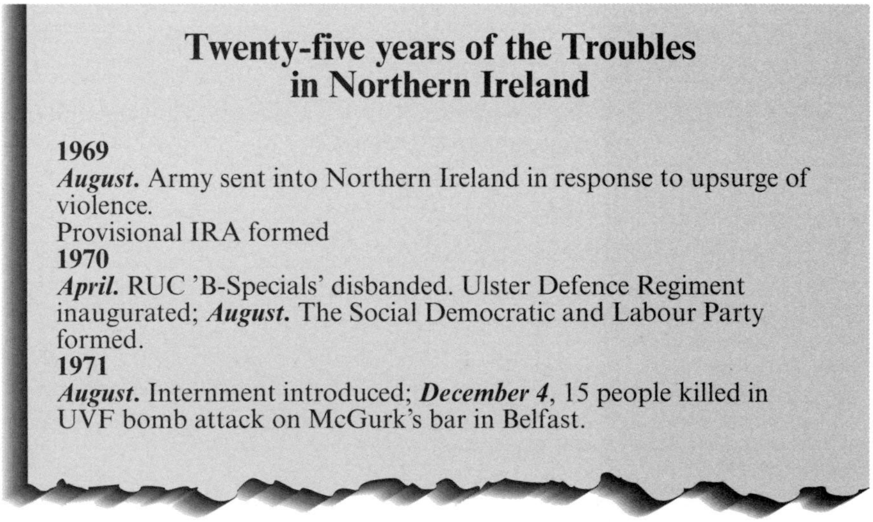

Twenty-five years of the Troubles in Northern Ireland

1969
August. Army sent into Northern Ireland in response to upsurge of violence.
Provisional IRA formed
1970
April. RUC 'B-Specials' disbanded. Ulster Defence Regiment inaugurated; *August.* The Social Democratic and Labour Party formed.
1971
August. Internment introduced; *December 4*, 15 people killed in UVF bomb attack on McGurk's bar in Belfast.

1972

January 30. Bloody Sunday. 1st battalion Parachute Regiment shot dead 13 people taking part in a banned civil rights march in Londonderry; *February 22.* Aldershot bombing. Seven killed and 15 hurt when a bomb exploded at the Parachute Brigade HQ, marking the start in earnest of the IRA's mainland campaign; *March.* Direct rule from London imposed, Stormont Parliament prorogued; *July 21.* Bloody Friday. 11 killed and 130 injured when IRA set off 26 bombs in Belfast; *July.* Ulster Secretary William Whitelaw meets IRA leaders for secret talks in London. Operation Motorman. Army break down 'no go' areas in west Belfast and Londonderry.

1973

December. Sunningdale Constitutional Conference.

1974

January. Power-sharing executive takes up office; *February 4.* M62 coach bomb. 12 people died when a bomb exploded on a coach packed with soldiers on the M62 near Leeds; *May.* Ulster Workers strike. Executive resigns, direct rule reimposed; *November 21.* Birmingham pub bombs. 21 people killed in IRA bombing of two pubs in the city.

1975

May. constitutional Convention set up; *December.* Internment ended.

1976

January 5. Kingsmills massacre. Ten Protestant workers shot dead when their works minibus was ambushed at a bogus road block in South Armagh; *March.* Convention dissolved; *August.* Peace People established with huge rally against death of three children.

1977

May. Second Ulster Workers strike.

1978

February 17. La Mon House massacre. 12 Protestants killed when IRA fireball bomb exploded at restaurant near Comber, Co Down.

1979

March 3. Airey Neave murdered; Conservative shadow Northern Ireland secretary, killed by INLA bomb attached to his car in the Commons car park; *August 27.* Warrenpoint massacre. 18 soldiers killed on Bank holiday Monday by double IRA bombing in the Co Down coastal resort. Hours earlier Lord Mountbatten was killed by an IRA bomb which blew apart his boat off the Co Sligo coast in the Irish Republic.

1980

January. Constitutional Conference starts at Stormont.

1981

May. Bobby Sands dies on hunger strike in Maze Prison, the first of 10 IRA and INLA prisoners to starve to death.

1982
July 20. 11 soldiers killed and 50 people injured in attacks on Household Cavalry in Rotten Row and at the band stand in Regent's Par; *October.* Assembly elections; *December 6.* Ballykelly bombing. INLA bomb destroyed the Droppin' Well Bar, killing 17 people, 11 of them soldiers from a nearby army base.
1983
December 17. Harrods bomb. Six killed, three of them police, and 90 injured in IRA bombing.
1984
October. Five people killed and 30 injured when the IRA planted a bomb at the Grand Hotel during the Conservative Party conference. The main target, Lady Thatcher, escaped uninjured.
1985
February 28. Newry mortar attack. Nine RUC officers killed when the IRA mortar-bombed the border town's police station; *November.* Anglo-Irish Agreement signed.
1986
June. Assembly dissolved.
1987
May 8. Loughall shooting. Eight-man IRA unit shot dead in SAS ambush as they mounted a bomb attack on a RUC station. A civilian caught in the cross-fire also died; *November 11.* Poppy day massacre. 11 killed when the IRA bombed the Remembrance Day service in Enniskillen.
1988
March 6. Gibraltar shooting. Three IRA members shot dead by the SAS in Gibraltar. Nine days later at their Belfast funeral, loyalist Michael Stone killed three mourners. Four days later two soldiers who drove into the funeral of IRA man killed by Stone were lynched and shot dead; *June 15.* fun run bombing. Six soldiers blown up in their van after taking part in a charity fun run at Lisburn, Co Antrim; *August 30.* Ballygawley bombing. Eight

soldiers killed and 27 injured when the IRA blew up the bus taking them back to base in Co Tyrone after returning from leave.
1989
September 22. Deal barracks bombing. eleven Army bandsmen killed after bomb explosion at the Royal Marines School of Music, Kent.
1990
January. Northern Ireland Secretary Peter Brooke offers Unionists 'new arrangements'; *July 30.* Ian Gow murder. Conservative MP, killed by IRA bomb under his car outside his home in East Sussex. October 24. Man strapped into bomb-laden van by IRA and forced to drive to Buncrana border crossing where bomb killed him and five soldiers.
1991
March. Mr Brooke announces three-strands talks process; *June.* Talks process starts at Stormont.
1992
January 17. Eight Protestants killed by IRA bomb which blew up their minibus on leaving a Co Tyrone army base; *February 5.* Five Catholics shot dead in UFF gun attack on Bookmakers in Belfast's Ormeau Road; *April 10.* Three killed when IRA bomb exploded outside the Baltic Exchange in the City of London; *September.* Ulster Unionists visit Dublin for talks; *November.* Talks suspended without agreement.
1993
March 20. Warrington bombing. Two IRA bombs kill Jonathan Ball, three, and Timothy Parry, 12; *October 23.* Ten killed by IRA bomb which exploded in a shop in west Belfast's Shankill Road; *October 30.* Seven Catholics killed in UFF shooting at the Rising Sun Bar, Greysteel, Co Londonderry; *December.* Downing Street Declaration signed by John Major and Irish Premier Albert Reynolds.
1994
June 18. Loughinisland massacre. Six Catholics shot dead in O'Toole's bar by UVF while watching TV; *July.* Sinn Fein gives its response to the Declaration, rejecting key elements. Renewed speculation that the IRA will call a long ceasefire, possibly in September.

Nairn (1977) argues that the turbulence in Northern Ireland is the result of the development of a relatively advanced industrial sector centred on the Ulster Protestant community. This links into his argument about the effects of uneven development on the rise of nationalism.

There are two distinct traditions. The 'republican/nationalist' community aspires to the eventual unification of Ireland. One of the most important grounds for seeing this as a legitimate aspiration is the all-Ireland vote in December 1918 when Sinn Fein won 73 out of the 105 seats. This community is divided today between support for the nationalist SDLP, which pursues a parliamentary path, and the republican Sinn Fein, which has supported the armed struggle of the Provisional IRA.

The other tradition in Northern Ireland is 'loyalism'. Nairn identifies this as in origin a variant of the British nationalism, based around the monarchy, that he has described;

however, it has evolved into a form of ethnic nationalism based on the Protestant community. Politically there is a split between the Ulster Unionist Party and the Democratic Unionist Party. In addition, an important phenomenon of recent years has been the rise of loyalist paramilitary groups. Particularly since the Anglo-Irish Agreement of 1985, which initiated a system of consultation between the British and Dublin governments concerning Northern Ireland, large sections of the Unionist community have felt betrayed by the British government, and some have lent their support to the paramilitaries.

In late 1993 details of a proposed peace settlement devised by Gerry Adams (President of Sinn Fein) and John Hume (Leader of the SDLP) began to emerge and led to a new round of proposals for peace talks. However, the initiative received a frosty reception from the Unionist community and the leaders of the two main Unionist political parties, James Molyneaux of the Ulster Unionist Party and Ian Paisley of the Democratic Unionist Party.

A later document endorsed by the British Prime Minister, John Major, and the Irish Premier, Albert Reynolds, initially met with a mixed reaction on both sides of the political divide in Northern Ireland, though it contributed to a process that led to a ceasefire by the main paramilitary groupings.

Using newspaper and magazine reports from late 1993 and early 1994, investigate the differences between the main principles involved in these two proposals and make notes of the attitude towards them expressed by the four main political parties in Northern Ireland.

Consider which position you think has the greatest legitimacy and explain your answer in a report of about 500 words.

> *The four main parties are:*
- *Sinn Fein ('Ourselves Alone')*
- *Social Democratic and Labour Party*
- *Ulster Unionist Party*
- *Democratic Unionist Party*

Find out how these parties have fared in the last three general elections.

Nationalism in the world today

The conflict in what was formerly Yugoslavia has intensified discussion about the potential power of nationalism as a basis for political mobilization today. In two years the war raging in Bosnia cost the lives of over 100,000 people and left 1.5 million homeless. The world is once again familiar with ethnic conflicts, and we have learned an appalling new phrase – 'ethnic cleansing'.

Perhaps the worst example of ethnic conflict in recent times has been Rwanda. It is estimated that up to 2 million people out of a total population of 8 million were killed in 1994–5. However, Marxists have pointed to the legacy of imperialism as the key cause of this conflict. The two main ethnic groups, the Hutu and the Tutsi, were apparently originally distinguished from one another on the basis of the number of cows they owned, but this distinction was formalized by the imperial authorities, who insisted that people's 'ethnic group' be specified on their identity cards. From this perspective the conflict in Rwanda is more of a class struggle than it is based on genuine ethnic differences.

The 'New World Chaos'?

Bosnia and Rwanda are two particularly unpleasant examples of contemporary life which seem to have deflated US President George Bush's prediction after the Gulf War that we would now see a 'New World Order'. The United Nations appears to be unable to cope with the shock-waves of these and other events. The optimism of New Right thinkers in declaring that history was over once the Stalinist states of eastern Europe collapsed seems hollow.

In contrast, the socialist academic Colin Leys has argued that 'what is happening in Africa is a perhaps irreversible decline towards that capitalism-produced barbarism of which Rosa Luxembourg warned, gradually engulfing most of the sub-continent' (quoted in the *Guardian*, 24 June 1994).

Essay Questions

1) 'Globalizing influences are not at all necessarily unifying. On the contrary, they often serve to fragment and divide; and they call forth a welter of conflicting responses. A renewed stress on local cultural identity, the springing up of a diversity of nationalisms from Quebec to the Basque country, can plausibly be seen precisely as an outcome of globalization' (Giddens 1989). Explain this statement and evaluate the extent to which it can be seen as an adequate explanation of the re-emergence of nationalism in the late twentieth century world.

2) 'if globalization genuinely takes effect, the nation-state will be its chief victim' (Waters 1995, p. 27). Evaluate the extent to which sociological arguments and evidence back up this assertion.

Coursework suggestions

1) Investigate the importance of nationalist politics in relation to either Scotland or Wales. Obtain detailed information on the socioeconomic make-up of the membership of the Scottish National Party or Plaid Cymru and similar information on their voters. Investigate and evaluate the claims to national status made by either of these parties and consider which of the various theories of nationalism can explain your findings about their membership and support.

If you wish to write to either party to obtain information, their addresses are as follows:

Scottish National Party, 6 North Charlotte Street, Edinburgh, EH2 4JH (Tel: 0131 226 3661).

Plaid Cymru, 51 Cathedral Road, Caerdydd, CF1 9HD (Tel: 01222 231944).

As always, if you do write, remember to enclose an SAE and ask nicely.

2) Investigate the extent to which the trends towards globalization in the economic arena have weakened the British nation-state.

Consult Lash and Urry (1987) or Held (1989) to find out in detail what the political implications of globalization are. Then interview your local MP and MEP to see how the power of Westminster has been altered by the rise of the European Community, and ask them for their opinions about how globalization might affect the nation-state. Try to contact the parliamentary and European parliamentary candidates of the other two main political parties and ask them the same question. Compare the answers you receive to see if there are any important differences between the political parties and between MPs and MEPs on this issue.

Finally, consider how far their views support the theories developed by sociologists such as Lash and Urry.

Bibliography

Anderson, B. (1991) *Imagined Communities,* 2nd edn, London: Verso

Callinicos, A. (1989) *Against Postmodernism,* Cambridge: Polity

Chomsky, N. (1994) 'Profits of doom', *New Statesman and Society,* 3 June

Derbyshire, J.D. and Derbyshire, I. (1989) *Chambers Political Systems of the World,* Edinburgh: W. & R. Chambers

Dicken, P. (1986) *Global Shift,* New York: Harper & Row

Gellner, E. (1983) *Nations and Nationalism,* Oxford: Blackwell

Giddens, A. (1989) *Sociology,* Cambridge: Polity

—— (1993) 'Dare to care, conserve and repair', *New Statesman and Society,* 29 October

Gordon, D.M. (1988) 'The global economy: new edifice or crumbling foundations', *New Left Review,* No. 168

Harris, N. (1983) *Of Bread and Guns,* Harmondsworth: Penguin

Held, D. (1989) 'The decline of the nation-state', in Hall, S. and Jacques, M. (eds) *New Times,* London: Lawrence & Wishart

Hirst, P. (1993) 'Globalization is fashionable but is it a myth?' *Guardian,* 22 March

Hobsbawm, E. (1992) *Nations and Nationalism Since 1780,* Cambridge: Cambridge University Press

Hobsbawm, E. and Ranger, T. (eds) (1992) *The Invention of Tradition,* Cambridge: Cambridge University Press

Lash, S. and Urry, J. (1987) *The End of Organised Capitalism,* Cambridge: Polity

—— (1994) *Economies of Signs and Space,* London: Sage

Morgan, P. (1992) 'From a death to a view: the hunt for the Welsh past in the Romantic period', in Hobsbawm and Ranger (1992)

Nairn, T. (1977) *The Break-up of Britain,* London: New Left Books

—— (1994) *The Enchanted Glass,* 2nd edn, London: Vintage

Shils, E. (1957) 'Primordial, personal, sacred and civil ties' *British Journal of Sociology,* Vol. 8, pp. 130–45

Sklair, L. (1991) *Sociology of the Global System,* London: Harvester Wheatsheaf

—— (1993) 'Going global: competing models of globalisation', *Sociology Review,* November

Smith, A.D. (1979) *Nationalism in the Twentieth Century,* Oxford: Martin Robertson

—— (1986) *The Ethnic Origin of Nations,* Oxford: Blackwell

Trevor-Roper, H. (1992) 'The invention of tradition: the Highland tradition of Scotland', in Hobsbawm and Ranger (1992)

Waters, M. (1995) *Globalization,* London: Routledge

10

Power and ideology

The pervasiveness of power

The concept of power lies at the heart of sociology. Power is about getting things done, so it is central to the process of constructing and maintaining society. Sociologists and political theorists have been concerned to discover who holds power in society and in what ways that power is used. The answers to these questions affect the view we hold about democracy and whether the particular country we live in is a democratic one.

Governments are clearly based on power (if you don't believe this, try to avoid paying tax). But power can be an element in any social relationship, such as between men and women inside conventional family structures or between teachers and pupils. Since sociology is about these social relationships, and since all involve power, the scope of the concept of power is very wide indeed.

Thus we need to consider a number of questions about power:

- Is power always based on force and coercion, or can it be based on agreement and consensus?

- Is power a necessary evil, or is it a good thing that allows us to achieve our aims?

- Does the exercise of power by some people reduce the amount of power available to others, or can its exercise maintain or increase the total amount of power available?

- Is power something possessed by individuals or by social structures?

- Is there a distinction to be made between power and authority?

Consider how the concept of power might be relevant to your education.

1) Who has the power to decide how long you are required to stay in education? Why do they have this power?

2) Why cannot a child of any age have the freedom to choose whether or not to go to school?

3) Is it seen as legitimate for children to be forced to go to school? If so, on what basis does this legitimacy rest?

Power is clearly exercised over you in the matter of your schooling between the ages of 5 and 16. It is a legal requirement that you attend school (unless your parents can provide equivalent education at home), and if you do not comply with this law certain sanctions can be applied against your parents. This is generally seen as acceptable since children of school age are deemed not to be mature enough to take rational decisions and therefore it is admissible for society to dictate to them.

Before you decide that this is all obvious, consider the implications if we substitute for the ability to dictate to children the ability to dictate to women or black people. Few people today would justify these uses of power, but they were considered acceptable in the past: it was widely held that women were frail and immature, so men had to make their decisions for them; and the contention that black people were inferior to whites was used as a justification for slavery. What is more, the fact that sexism and racism are generally not seen as acceptable today does not mean that they do not exist. Indeed they do, and these types of discrimination and the acts they entail are key examples of power structures in contemporary society.

Freedom versus authority

One of the classical debates about power and society concerned how to keep order and stop individuals endlessly fighting each other while at the same time maintaining a degree of personal freedom.

List any areas of life you believe people should have absolute freedom in. Should we, for instance, have absolute freedom in the following areas:
- *what we can say in public*
- *what material is shown on television*
- *sexual behaviour*
- *whether we pay taxes*
- *smoking*
- *what clothes we wear*
- *when we are children*
- *who we are allowed to kill?*

Classical liberal theorists attempted to deal with this problem by developing systems of government based on consent and devising limits to the power of government. This is the origin of the division in society between the private and the public spheres, and it is also the origin in sociology of the distinction between power and authority. Authority is seen as power that is legitimate according to some criterion.

Max Weber

Weber argued that power is 'the probability that one actor within a social relationship will be in a position to carry out his own will despite resistance' (1978, p. 926 [1921]). He distinguished between power, authority and legitimacy; his definitions of these terms have been summarized by Chris Brown (1981, p. 192) as follows:

> **Power** is force, coercion and repression; it is the gun, the fist or the fine; it is the police officer's hand on your arm or the bullet hole in your head. **Authority** exists where power is used by superiors with the consent of the subordinates; in these circumstances force will not be necessary although it will continue to exist as an ultimate sanction.

Legitimacy is the process by which power becomes authority; but whether legitimacy is freely given or whether it is actively elicited by rulers is a crucial issue.

In connection with the concept of legitimacy, there is a debate about whether a word that Weber used, *'Herrschaft'*, should be translated as 'authority' or 'domination'. Authority implies consent actively given by the people, whereas domination implies a more manipulative power of leaders over the rest of society.

This may seem like an arcane dispute about translation, but it has had important implications. The first English translation of Weber's work was undertaken by the leading functionalist, Talcott Parsons. He translated *'Herrschaft'* as 'authority'. He therefore emphasized the consensual legitimate use of power, and any notion of rulers dominating others disappears. In his more general work on power, Parsons (1963, 1967) appears to make no distinction between power and authority. All power is seen as legitimate.

This point of view was severely criticized by conflict writers. Steven Lukes (1974) has argued that the proper translation of *'Herrschaft'* is 'domination', and using this translation he argues that Weber's work emphasizes the way that rulers actively seek legitimacy from the rest of the population. This allows for the possibility that a leader can manipulate the wishes of the rest of society to gain legitimacy for his or her power. The dispute over translation is therefore in reality a dispute about whether consent is genuine and flows from the people or whether it is constructed, with the implication that it might be the result of manipulation. This issue is central to debates about power.

This is not an isolated example of the problems that can arise in translation. A similar difficulty arises with Marx's work. His term *'Klassenherrschaft'* is most frequently translated as 'ruling class'. Anthony Giddens (1971) and John Scott (1991) have argued instead that it is better translated as 'class dominance'. The significance of this dispute is whether the capitalist class rules directly or whether its dominance is maintained by the general power arrangements in society, such as the existence of a power bloc as Scott maintains. It therefore affects our understanding of both Marxist and radical elite theories of how power operates in society, with particular reference to the state.

 Write a report of about 300 words explaining the implications of the disputes over the translation of 'Herrschaft' and 'Klassenherrschaft' for theories of power in society.

Pluralist approaches

Weber's definition of power, focusing on the ability to achieve certain aims despite resistance, was taken up by Dahl, who wrote: 'A has power over B in so far as he can make B do something he would not otherwise have done' (1957, p. 204). Lukes (1974) has characterized this as the one-dimensional view of power.

Dahl claimed that the best way to test the relative capacity and therefore power of actors is to observe the overt process of decision making and consider the relationship between the decisions reached and the expressed preferences of the various actors. His most notable piece of research on this was his study of New Haven (1961) which we discussed in Chapter 7. He identified three contentious issues, namely public schooling, political nominations and urban redevelopment. He concluded that no one group dominated the decision-making process in New Haven and by extension society as a whole, and therefore that power was diffuse in modern society. He viewed society as composed of a number of competing interest groups that try to influence the decisions of governments, and no one group is inherently dominant.

Elite views

Dahl's account was criticized by Bachrach and Baratz (1962), who argued that decision making is only one aspect of power. An exclusive focus on explicit decision making may ignore an important element of the use of power, namely the ability to decide which issues will be placed on the agenda for discussion and thus to exclude certain views from the decision-making process: 'To the extent that a person or group – consciously or unconsciously – creates or reinforces barriers to the public airing of policy conflicts, that person or group has power' (pp. 7–8). These writers therefore focused on the issue of non-decision making. Clegg (1989, p. 77) points to some of the important ways in which non-decision making can operate: 'the powerful may not attend to, may not listen to, or may not "hear" demands articulated by the less powerful. If these demands do gain admission to the political agenda they may be effectively sequestrated via endless committees, enquiries, or co-optation.'

The radical view of power

Lukes (1974) has characterized Bachrach and Baratz's approach as a two-dimensional view of power. He believes it offers a better picture than the pluralist (one-dimensional) view, but that it nonetheless needs to be modified. Although it appears to go beyond the one-dimensional view, there is an important similarity. Both require that there are observable conflicts of interests which are then either decided upon (the focus of the one-dimensional model) or are stifled and not placed on the agenda (as in the two-dimensional model).

Lukes is interested in what happens when there is no observable conflict of interest. He contends that although for Bachrach and Baratz manipulation is a form of power, this would not show up on their model since no overt conflict would take place and there would therefore be no need for any attempt to exclude anybody's views from the agenda.

For Lukes the question is: In the absence of an observable conflict, how is it possible to distinguish between a genuine consensus and a manipulation of the wishes of the population? Unless it is possible to distinguish between these two situations, power in a dictatorship might be described as diffuse since there is no observable conflict (suppressed or not).

Lukes therefore argues that a theory of power must include a third dimension, which he calls the mobilization of bias. The expressed wants of people do not necessarily reflect their real interests, and it is certainly not possible to measure or view power by concentrating on overt conflicts since 'the most effective and insidious use of power is to prevent such conflict from arising in the first place'. Therefore what might appear to be a consensual society may be the result of the operation of this third face of power.

Consider how pluralist, elite and radical views on power might be applied to your choice of subjects at GCSE or A-level.

On the face of it, the process would seem to be well explained by a one-dimensional view of power. Individual students express their wishes and the school authorities then decide which subjects they will offer, depending on how popular each choice is. As a result some of the students' initial choices become unavailable but they will probably be able to take most of the subjects they originally chose.

1) How accurate is this as a description of the process of subject choice that you encountered?

2) Consider what a two-dimensional and a three-dimensional model of power would focus on in this context. Write a short description of each.

3) Finally, consider which of the three views best accounts for this situation.

Recent debates on power

Criticisms of Lukes

Since the publication of Lukes's book *Power: A Radical View* (1974) the topic of power has been widely discussed and several authors have identified what they see as problems with his analysis and his 'three-dimensional' view of power.

Ted Benton (1981) has argued that Lukes's conception needs to be drastically modified. In the 'three-dimensional' model there is a key problem with the notion of the distortion of the real interests of social groups: who is to define what the real interests of any social group are? It cannot be the people themselves, since their views are distorted by the three-dimensional element of power. But if another person or group is to be the arbiter of their true interests, we face the problem that some people are being viewed as superior to others. In extreme circumstances this could justify authoritarian rulers claiming the right to determine the real interests of their subjects.

Benton argues that Lukes needs to rid his theory of the notion of 'real interests'. This can be done with the help of Gramsci's notion of hegemony: according to Gramsci, groups have their own conceptions of the world, which manifest themselves in action in exceptional circumstances, but most of the time these conceptions are subordinated to the ideas of the dominant class.

Barry Hindess (1982) has also made criticisms of Lukes's model. He argues that capacity–outcome models are inadequate because they assume that the social group with the greater capacity for power will always prevail. He rejects the implicit assumption that the outcome of power struggles can be determined in advance. He cites the example of the defeat of the US army in Vietnam which could never have been predicted by looking at the relative capacities of the two main actors.

 Explain in your own words the problems that arise with the concept of 'real interests'. Is it possible ever to arrive at an objective notion of people's 'real interests'?

How might Lukes respond to the criticisms made of his work by Ted Benton and

Barry Hindess? Write a report of 200–300 words outlining the criticisms and how you think Lukes might respond.

Foucault and post-structuralism

One of the most important recent influences on social theory has been the work of the French social theorist, Michel Foucault. In his work on power (see Rabinow 1991) he adopted a very different approach to the prevailing theories. Rather than seeking the locus of power in the state, Foucault offered a 'capillary' model which considered power to be a part of all social relationships. His key concern was not to ask who exercises power or why, but how. This meant exploring what he called the techniques of power.

One of these techniques is the claim to truth. Foucault was concerned to show how the claims to truth that are associated with the development of the human sciences have become a new form of domination. In his studies of insanity, crime and sexuality he charted the way in which societal reaction to these issues changed from a sometimes arbitrary to a more systematic treatment.

The growth of systematic treatment explains the growth of the human sciences, which were invited to offer expertise to the legal authorities. For example, Foucault cited the increasing use of psychiatrists in determining the treatment of subjects in criminal cases. At the heart of this development was a concern to develop economic ways of controlling the lives of individuals.

Foucault thus denied that such developments were progressive. Instead he viewed psychiatry and the social sciences in general as a new, more encompassing disciplinary force. This is encapsulated in his key concept of power/knowledge. He denied that there is any everlasting and universal truth; rather, truth is a form of power. The truth is that which has the most power. The struggle for the truth is a power struggle.

What is true changes over time as the rules for determining the truth, or 'discourses' as Foucault called them, change. The implication is that the original belief of all the classical sociologists, namely that they would through investigation be able to arrive at the truth of how society works in order to make society better, is an illusion. Their 'truths' are merely new forms of domination. There is no escape from this power structure.

1) Write a short report supporting Foucault's view that the human sciences represent a new form of domination. (There is a detailed summary of Foucault's work in Sociology Review, November 1992.)
2) Now write a contrasting report arguing the case for the human sciences as tools for understanding the world in order to change it for the better.
3) On the basis of your studies in the human sciences, which view do you find more convincing?

Foucault was interested in the level of surveillance over people in modern society. Central to his discussion was Jeremy Bentham's idea of a Panopticon. This was a prison designed so that the warder could see all the prisoners simultaneously, but they were not able to see the warder. They would never know whether they were being watched, and therefore there was nowhere to hide or to establish any privacy. They had to assume at all times that they were being watched, and therefore always act obediently. Bentham thought this system would produce benefits in terms of economic social control.

Foucault argued that the development of the human sciences has meant that all major social institutions are now run on this basis: 'Is it surprising that prisons resemble factories, schools, barracks, hospitals, which all resemble prisons?' (Foucault 1977, p. 228).

Writers following Foucault, such as David Lyon (1993), have widened his argument to consider the extent to which surveillance has become a common feature of modern society, notably through the use of computers and electronic surveillance. There are now networks of computer databases, such as the ones used by the police, defence forces, tax authorities, secret services and social security, which can exchange information about individuals without their knowing anything about it. Similar methods have invaded the workplace, where computer systems now enable management to monitor in detail the performance of workers.

Lyon points out that there is an alternative account of the way people are subject to surveillance which stresses the active consent of the surveyed: people construct the means of their own surveillance by providing information about themselves, for instance on application forms for credit cards and when they use mail-order catalogues.

Giddens and structuration theory

Anthony Giddens has attempted to develop a new theory of the relationship between social structure and social action, and central to this project is a consideration of the concept of power. He argues that what the pluralists and their Marxist opponents share is a 'flight from power', meaning that both perspectives view power with suspicion. Pluralists do so because they see power as threatening to individual liberties, and Marxists do so because they see it as linked with conflicts which will disappear after the revolution.

Giddens argues that although there are problems with Parsons's model of power, notably its assumption that all power is legitimate, there are nonetheless benefits to be drawn from trying to reincorporate some of his framework into the analysis of power. 'Power is the capacity to achieve outcomes; whether or not these are connected to purely sectional interests is nor germane to its definition. Power is not, as such, an obstacle to freedom or emancipation but is their very medium – although it would be foolish, of course, to ignore its constraining properties' (Giddens 1984, p. 257).

For Giddens, power is therefore potentially both constraining and enabling. He argues that Foucault's 'structural' views are inadequate since his all-encompassing view of power means that the idea of human activity and resistance is all but wiped out. Power is seen as something which constrains, but there is no notion of it enabling action to take place. Giddens himself argues that we need to see structures as the products of human activity, of knowledgeable agents.

 Hugh Chignell (1992) has suggested that the theory of structuration, with its emphasis on the way in which we are constrained by structures external to ourselves but which nonetheless we create and recreate through our daily actions and interactions, is applicable to educational institutions such as schools and colleges. Such an institution is 'external or constraining to individuals and

yet at the same time is the product of patterned interaction between college members' (p. 25).

How useful do you think Giddens's theory of structuration is in explaining the forms of power found in this sort of institution? Do you feel enabled? Do you feel constrained? Who creates the constraints? Who creates the enabling structures?

Write a report of about 600 words applying this idea to a concrete study of the educational institution you are most familiar with. Explain how the notion of the dual nature of power and the way action and structure are linked can be applied to this institution. Consider any aspects of the institution where you feel this explanation is inadequate or could be criticized.

Michael Mann's four sources of social power

The ongoing work of Michael Mann represents one of the most ambitious attempts to construct a theory of social power which is applicable across time and across different societies. So far only the first two volumes of his work have been published, covering the period up to 1760 (Vol. 1) and 1760–1914 (Vol. 2).

Mann maintains that there are four separate sources of social power in society, namely economic, political, military and ideological, and no one type of power is always dominant. He therefore rejects the Marxist view that ultimately economic power is dominant and that political, military and ideological struggles are reflections of the economic class struggle.

In relation to modern capitalism he builds on Weber's notion of the growth of bureaucracy to suggest that the growth of the administrative power of the state promotes the growth of capitalism without actually being consciously planned by anyone.

The second volume ends with a consideration of the power relations that led up to the First World War. Here he delves into the area of military power that has been a consistent theme of his work. He argues that the war was an unforeseen consequence of the decisions of state leaders. Such consequences can arise because of the multiple and overlapping networks of power in modern nation-states.

Ideology

The notion of ideology is important to recent discussion of power because of its role as Lukes's third dimension of power – the power to shape the wishes and desires of the population.

The term 'ideology' can be used in a descriptive sense to denote any set of ideas. We can talk of the 'ideology of the New Right' if we want simply to describe the set of ideas that inspired the Thatcher governments, and similarly we can talk of the ideology of socialism or liberalism. However, as it is commonly used in sociology the term 'ideology' acquires a rather different meaning. Here ideology is contrasted to the truth. If something is described as ideological, it is being depicted as somehow false. Lukes's argument was that there was a form of power where the wishes and desires ('the ideas') of some people in society could be manipulated so that they were at odds with their true interests. A similar idea is contained in the term 'false consciousness'. In this usage ideology is seen as a falsehood, usually perpetrated by dominant groups in society with detrimental effects on subordinate groups.

István Mészáros (1989) cites the following extract from the Word Finder thesaurus attached to the best-selling *WordStar* word-processing program as an example of ideology:

Conservative: dim, inconspicuous, quiet, restrained, subdued, tasteful, unassuming, unobtrusive, canny, economical, frugal, provident, sparing, spartan, stewardly, thrifty, unwasteful, aloof, poised, reserved.

Liberal: advanced, broad, broad-minded, progressive, radical, tolerant, unbiased, bounteous, bountiful, free, generous, handsome, open-handed, unsparing, abounding, abundant, ample, copious, enough, galore, generous, overflowing, plentiful, plenty, prodigal, profuse, teeming.

Revolutionary: extreme, extremist, fanatic, fanatical, rabid, radical, ultra.

How might this extract be considered ideological?
Look at a thesaurus in your library or installed on the computers in your school or college to see if you can locate any similar examples.

There is a scene in Spike Lee's film *Malcolm X* where Malcolm is discussing with a fellow prisoner the relationship of black people to white people. They explore the way images of black and white people are constructed by looking up the meaning of 'black' and 'white' in a dictionary. The following two definitions are taken from *The University English Dictionary*:

Black, blak, *a.* Destitute of light; dark; gloomy; sullen; atrocious; wicked.—*n.* The darkest colour; a negro.—*vt.* To make black.

White, whit, *a.* Being of the colour of pure snow; pale; pallid; pure and unsullied.—*n.* The colour of snow; a white pigment; white of an egg, eye, &c.—*vt.* (whiting, whited). To make white.

How might these definitions be considered ideological? What effects might this have?
Look up the definitions of 'man', 'manly', 'woman', 'womanly', 'mankind' and other words associated with gender in a dictionary. How might these definitions be relevant to a discussion of ideology?

As a third example we can consider the way in which the media construct the world. Figure 10.1 is taken from the cover of a book by R. Wallis and S. Baran (1990). It depicts the way they feel the Western media view the world.

Compare this map with an atlas of the world, and write a short report on how the media could be said to be acting ideologically in this respect.
Incidentally, it is likely that the atlas you use to establish the 'truth' is also ideological. Most atlas maps are based on the Mercator Projection. It has been argued that this shows countries incorrectly by making the 'North' (Europe and North America) much bigger in relation to the 'South' (Asia, Africa, South America) than they actually are, and this distortion is held to be a reflection of the colonial world-view. For example, in most atlases the continent of Africa

Figure 10.1

The world according to the Western media

Source: Wallis and Baran (1990)

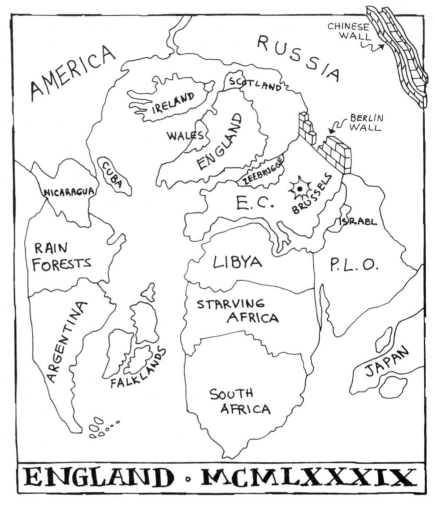

(area 30 million sq. km) is shown as smaller than North America (19 million sq. km). A new projection, called the Peters Projection, claims to accurately portray the continents according to their relative sizes. The result looks very different. You could try to obtain a copy of a Peters Projection map of the world from your reference library or a local Development Education Resource Centre.

Marxist theories of ideology

It is probably within the Marxist tradition that theories of ideology have generated most debate, at least in relation to social and political change. One important starting point is the statement Marx made in *The German Ideology*: 'The ideas of the ruling class are in every epoch the ruling ideas; i.e., the class which is the ruling material force of society, is at the same time its ruling intellectual force' (Marx and Engels 1970, p. 64).

Marx was concerned to develop a materialist theory of history, according to which practical activity rather than a system of ideas is the real foundation. He argued that ideas and ideologies flow from the material relations in society. What makes ideas into ideologies is their connection with the social conflicts involved in the labour process that lies at the heart of Marxist theory. Ideologies cover up these conflicts by obscuring the real exploitative basis of society, which alienates people from each other — a state of affairs that is presented as 'natural'. Ideologies obscure the real nature of society but are at the same time reflections of it.

Georg Lukács

Lukács (1971) developed the argument that ideology presents the economic relations prevalent under capitalism as 'natural'. Relations between people are transformed into relations between commodities, and the only link between them is the cash nexus. The social and economic organization of society subordinates the workers ideologically because it presents everything in terms of individual relations.

According to Lukács, it is only through the class struggle that they can overcome this and become both the object and the subject of history. In other words, they can develop their own ideology, a proletarian ideology which is superior to the bourgeois ideology served up under capitalism.

Antonio Gramsci

A more influential Marxist account of ideology was given by Gramsci. His theory of ideology explained how the ruling class rules not only through coercion and the use of force, but by the active consent of the population.

He argued that capitalism is sustained because its ideology, produced by intellectuals, is accepted as the common sense of society. As a result workers have a dual consciousness. On the one hand, they accept to some degree the commonsense view of society which sees capitalism as fair and inevitable; on the other hand, in their daily experience of struggling to live, for example not having enough money to pay their bills, and also in their conduct with other workers, where they stress democratic and egalitarian ideals, they partly undermine the hierarchical structure of society.

For Gramsci the task of socialist intellectuals and activists is to wage a struggle in the cultural and ideological arena, as well as the economic and political world, and in this way to wrest hegemony from the ruling class.

Western Marxism: concentration on ideology

Gramsci's views have been interpreted by some commentators, particularly those espousing what has come to be called Western Marxism, as placing greater stress on the struggle for ideas than was typical of the classical Marxist tradition, which emphasized the predominance of economic and industrial struggle, which was expected to lead to a change of ideas.

Perry Anderson (1979) has argued that Western Marxism, which embraces such figures as Louis Althusser and the Marxiant Frankfurt School of Herbert Marcuse and Max Horkheimer, overstressed the importance of ideology in inhibiting the proletariat from developing revolutionary consciousness. The Frankfurt School in particular argued that, by creating a mass culture that trivializes every aspect of life, capitalism holds back the development of serious political thought and action.

Ideology in other perspectives

Although the concept of ideology has been most important to the Marxist tradition, it also features in other traditions.

Functionalism

Durkheim (1915) argued that religion is effectively the worship of society, and thereby helps to solidify it. He also maintained that society should be seen as a social fact, and has a reality over and above that of the individuals who comprise it. Durkheim (1947) also saw the individualism propounded by the originators of what today is known as the New Right as a threat to social solidarity and the collective conscience. The resulting *anomie* might lead to a host of social problems, such as industrial unrest, crime and suicide.

Durkheim's study of the changing nature of the collective conscience led him to explore the changing nature of the law, which he saw as a measurable index of the level of solidarity in society. This work provided the starting point for Talcott Parsons's theory of normative integration, according to which society is held together by a common value system, a 'value consensus'.

Values are obviously a set of ideas, so Parsons's theory can be seen as an analysis of the key role of ideas in society. The difference with the Marxist view is that functionalists perceive a genuine consensus which reflects the consensual nature of society, whereas Marxists consider the dominant ideology to be a form of manipulation whereby the conflicting interests in society are submerged.

Critics of the 'dominant ideology' thesis

Both Marxist and functionalist accounts have been the subject of a great deal of criticism, notably by Abercrombie, Hill and Turner (1980). They point out that both schools make the assumption that a 'dominant ideology' exists, and as an illustration they quote Anthony Giddens: 'The fact that subordinate groups in society, even if they are subjected to what an outsider might appear to be extreme exploitation and degradation, accept their subordination is evident to any student of society with even a cursory knowledge of history.' Against this line of reasoning they quote Immanuel Wallerstein: 'It is doubtful if very many governments in human history have been considered "legitimate" by the majority of those exploited, oppressed and mistreated by their governments. The masses may be resigned to their fate, or sullenly restive, or amazed at their temporary good fortune, or actively insubordinate. But governments tend to be endured, not appreciated or admired or loved or even supported' (Abercrombie, Hill and Turner 1980, p. 156).

Abercrombie, Hill and Turner suggest that the 'dominant ideology' thesis is an example of an over-socialized notion of humanity, leading its proponents to exaggerate the extent to which subordinate classes are ideologically incorporated, and the extent to which societies exist as a coherent whole, with one dominant set of ideas predominating. They argue that the most important factors in maintaining the status quo have been armed coercion (more important in the past than it generally is today) and economic compulsion. Workers are forced to defer to the powerful if they are to continue to work and gain a decent income. Their only alternative is starvation, so this economic compulsion is very strong.

They concede that in late capitalism there is some evidence of the incorporation of parts of the working class, but this is only partly effective, leaving the working class with a dual consciousness. They cite a number of studies of the working class, such as Beynon's study of assembly-line workers at Ford (1973) and Willis's study of working-class school pupils (1977), which show the existence of some degree of autonomous culture. Thus even in contemporary society, when the mechanisms for transmitting dominant ideas are highly developed, they are not particularly effective in influencing ideas.

Study Table 10.1 and then write a short report of 200–300 words covering the following two questions:

Table 10.1   The power of the partisan press?

	Readers' assessment of their newspapers' party support				The party support of the newspaper's readers			
	Con	Lab	Lib/SDP	None/ Don't Know	Con	Lab	Lib/SDP	Other
Conservative papers*								
Daily Express	87	0	4	9	70	9	18	3
Daily Telegraph	85	0	3	12	80	5	10	5
Sunday Express	80	2	4	14	64	6	25	5
Daily Mail	78	2	5	15	60	13	19	8
Sunday Telegraph	78	2	2	18	78	9	9	4
Sunday Times	69	5	13	13	58	15	23	4
Mail on Sunday	68	5	8	19	61	14	20	5
Sun	63	12	7	18	41	31	19	9
The Times	61	0	33	6	56	12	27	5
News of the World	42	15	5	38	37	33	23	7
Star	23	16	7	54	28	46	18	8
Labour papers*								
Daily Mirror	2	84	8	6	20	55	21	4
Sunday Mirror	5	73	5	17	25	49	19	7
People	10	41	6	43	36	38	20	6
Guardian	13	30	43	14	22	54	19	5
Alliance Paper*								
Today	11	4	18	67	43	17	40	0
Non-partisan papers*								
Independent	12	6	20	62	34	34	27	5
Observer	13	35	31	21	28	49	18	5

* The partisanship of each newspaper is derived from its voting recommendation for the 1987 general election.

(Figures are not available for the *Financial Times* – which supported the Conservative Party.)

Source: Benyon (1987), p. 60

1) *What evidence can you find in the table for and against Abercrombie, Hill and Turner's critique of the 'dominant ideology' thesis?*
2) *What are the implications of their work for a consideration of the political role of the mass media in the UK?*

Essay Questions

1) Critically examine sociological contributions to an understanding of the nature and distribution of power in industrial societies. (AEB, June 1992)

2) Discuss the Marxist view that institutions such as the mass media maintain the political status quo by spreading the ideas of the dominant class to the rest of society. (AEB, June 1992)

3) Evaluate the claim made by some sociologists that there is a 'dominant ideology' in modern capitalist societies. (AEB, June 1995)

Coursework suggestions

1) Investigate the extent to which the development of new technology, particularly the use of computerized databases, has created a surveillance society.

   There is a growing body of literature on this issue, but the work of David Lyon (1993) is a good starting point. Gather information on a number of developments in the field of new technology, and assess whether they tend to support or undermine the notion of a surveillance society. For instance, look at the information required on forms applying for various forms of credit and consider how this information might be used in the development of surveillance.

   You should relate any information you find to the idea that such information can be used as tools of social control.

2) Analyse the impact that the mass media have on political activity in the UK. Consider the extent to which theories of ideology can be applied to the mass media, and how far the notion of a 'dominant ideology' is applicable to the successes of the Conservative Party in recent elections.

Bibliography

Abercrombie, N., Hill, S. and Turner, B. (1980) *The Dominant Ideology Thesis,* London: Allen & Unwin

Althusser, L. (1971) 'Ideology and ideological state apparatuses', in *Lenin and Philosophy,* London: New Left Books

Anderson, P. (1979) *Considerations on Western Marxism,* London: Verso

Bachrach, P. and Baratz, M.S. (1962) 'Two faces of power', *American Political Science Review,* Vol. 56

Benton, T. (1981) '"Objective" interests and the sociology of power', *Sociology,* Vol. 15, No. 2

Benyon, J. (1987) 'General Election 1987: the electoral impact of the partisan press', *Social Studies Review,* Vol. 3, No. 2, November

Beynon, H. (1973) *Working for Ford,* Harmondsworth: Penguin

Brown, C. (1981) 'Power and democracy', in McNeill, P. and Townley, C. (eds) *Fundamentals of Sociology,* Cheltenham: Thornes

Chignell, H. (1992) 'What are we going to do about Giddens?', *Social Science Teacher,* Summer*

Clegg, S. (1989) *Frameworks of Power,* London: Sage

Dahl, R.A. (1957) 'The concept of power', *Behavioural Science,* Vol. 2

—— (1961) *Who Governs?,* New Haven, CT: Yale University Press

Durkheim, E. (1915) *The Elementary Forms of Religious Life,* London: Allen & Unwin

—— (1947) *The Division of Labour in Society,* New York: Free Press

Foucault, M. (1977) *Discipline and Punish,* Harmondsworth: Penguin

Giddens, A. (1971) *Capitalism and Modern Social Theory,* Cambridge: Cambridge University Press

—— (1984) *The Constitution of Society,* Cambridge: Polity

Gramsci, A. (1971) *Selections from the Prison Notebooks,* London: Lawrence & Wishart

Hindess, B. (1982) 'Power, interests and the outcomes of struggles', *Sociology,* Vol. 16, No. 4

Lukács, G. (1971) *History and Class Consciousness,* London: Merlin

Lukes, S. (1974) *Power: A Radical View,* London: Macmillan

—— (ed.) (1986) *Power,* Oxford: Blackwell

Lyon, D. (1993) 'An electronic Panopticon? A sociological critique of surveillance theory', *Sociological Review,* Vol. 41, No. 4, November

Marx, K. and Engels, F. (1970) *The German Ideology,* London: Lawrence & Wishart; originally written in 1845

Mészáros, I. (1989) *The Power of Ideology,* London: Harvester Wheatsheaf

Parsons, T. (1963) 'On the concept of political power', *Proceedings of the American Philosophical Society,* Vol. 107

—— (1967) *Politics and Social Structure,* New York: Free Press

Rabinow, P. (1991) *The Foucault Reader,* Harmondsworth: Penguin

Scott, J. (1991) *Who Rules Britain?,* Cambridge: Polity

Wallis, R. and Baran, S. (1990) *The Known World of Broadcast News,* London, Routledge

Weber, M. (1921) *Economy and Society,* 1978 edn, Berkeley, CA: University of California Press

Willis, P. (1977) *Learning to Labour,* London: Saxon House

* *Social Science Teacher* is the journal of the Association for the Teaching of the Social Sciences. For further information, write to:
ATSS
PO Box 461
Sheffield S2 2RH

Index